MARRIAGE, SAME-SEX MARRIAGE AND THE ANGLICAN CHURCH OF AUSTRALIA

Essays from the Doctrine Commission

The Anglican Church of Australia

THE DOCTRINE COMMISSION
OF THE ANGLICAN CHURCH OF AUSTRALIA

Marriage, Same-Sex Marriage And The Anglican Church Of Australia: Essays From The Doctrine Commission

Copyright © 2019, The Anglican Church of Australia Trust Corporation.

All rights reserved. No part of this publication may be reproduced, stored in a retrieval system or transmitted, in any form or by any means electronic, photocopying, recording or otherwise, without the prior written permission of the publisher.

Broughton Publishing Pty Ltd
32 Glenvale Crescent
Mulgrave VIC 3170

First Printing, June 2019

ISBN 978-0-6482659-4-8

Contents

Foreword	*Jonathan Holland*	1

Context

The debates over the doctrine of marriage in the Anglican Communion	*Michael R Stead* 9
The doctrine of marriage of the Anglican Church of Australia	*Michael R Stead* 31
A response: An alternative reading of *BCP*	*Matthew Anstey* 49

Scripture and Hermeneutics

Scripture and moral reasoning	*Matthew Anstey* 57
Attentively reading scripture	*Mark D Thompson* 73
How does the Old Testament help us think about marriage and same-sex marriage?	*Meg Warner* 87
Belonging to God in relational wholeness	*Katherine M Smith* 105
Marriage, headship and the New Testament	*Dorothy A Lee* 123
Family ties: marriage, sex, and belonging in the New Testament	*Claire Smith* 139

History, Theology and Ecclesiology

Christian marriage: a concise history	*Muriel Porter* 155
For better or for worse: The changing shape of marriage in Christian history?	*Claire Smith* 167

Friendship and religious life in the Bible and the church | *Dorothy A Lee*	185
Friendship and the trinity | *Mark D Thompson*	201
Steps towards a theological understanding of desire | *G. J. Seach*	207
To what end? The blessing of same-sex marriage | *Rhys Bezzant*	227
Disagreement and Christian unity: re-evaluating the situation | *Stephen Pickard*	241

The Case For and Against

The case for same-sex marriage | *Matthew Anstey*	267
The case against same-sex marriage | *Michael Stead*	285

Foreword

In September 2017 members of General Synod meeting in Maroochydore, Queensland passed a motion asking Standing Committee to 'facilitate a respectful conversation in our church by means of a collection of essays on marriage and same-sex relationships that explore scriptural and theological issues relating to

    A. The doctrine of marriage expressed in the formularies of the Anglican Church of Australia

    B. Our current Australian context exploring the relationship between the state's definition of marriage and the church's doctrine of marriage

    C. Key Old Testament and New Testament texts on sex, marriage and friendship

    D. Scripture and hermeneutics

    E. A theology of blessing

    F. A theology of desire

    G. Godly disagreement on this issue

    H. The cases for and against same-sex marriage and/or the blessing of same-sex unions.'

This book is the response to that request.

Discussing issues associated with same-sex marriage is fraught with difficulties.

First, a number of those who identify with the LGBT+ community, as well as their families and friends, already feel marginalised or excluded from church life because of our current teaching and practice on marriage. They, more than many, have a personal investment in our response to the blessing of same sex unions.

Whatever path we choose to follow, how do we be sensitive to their situation?

Secondly, same-sex marriage (SSM) raises questions about the intersection between the State's definition of marriage and the Church's teaching on marriage.

Thirdly, the blessing of same-sex marriage has become a contentious and vexed issue in the Anglican Communion. Advocates for and against are equally passionate. Some Anglican Provinces have enacted canons to allow their clergy to officiate at the weddings of same sex couples. Other Provinces have responded by consecrating bishops for those who have been alienated by this action and see it as a betrayal of the gospel. As a result there has been a tear in the fabric of the Communion.

Finally, the need for the Anglican Church of Australia to express its mind on this issue became more urgent when late in 2017 the Australian Parliament amended the definition of marriage to enable same-sex marriage in Australia. This followed a national voluntary postal survey gauging support for same-sex marriage. Nearly 8 million Australians voted for the law to be changed, while 5 million voted against. How does the Anglican Church of Australia articulate its thinking to secular Australians that will carry respect?

Members of the Doctrine Commission hold differing views on same-sex marriage. Those differing views and approaches are reflected in the various chapters. Three chapters are by scholars outside the Doctrine Commission, whose contributions provide an added depth and a gender balance.

As you read a chapter—and even this foreword—it is important to understand that it represents the thinking of the author, not necessarily others on the Doctrine Commission (though each article has been much discussed by members of the Commission, and all writers are grateful for the open discussions that led to further reflection and some rewritings). Each contributor has endeavoured to set out their thinking with as much clarity and integrity and faithfulness to Christ as they can in order to aid our collective discernment. The two final chapters for and against same-sex marriage sharpen the arguments and pick up some of the key themes in earlier essays. All chapters have been written with an eye to an irenic tone in order to facilitate an honest and respectful searching after God's will in this matter. We are all trying to be faithful to God.

It is important to note what the Doctrine Commission was not asked to do. It was not asked to look at the pastoral or liturgical response of the church, nor important related matters such as intersex or transgender or covenantal relationships, nor highlight the 'lived experience' of same-sex couples. We have framed the book in accordance with the motion from General Synod. What is here therefore is a partial contribution to a much wider conversation.

It is helpful to put the SSM issue within two contexts.

The first is the incredibly large scale and pace of social and cultural change in Australia, of which same-sex marriage is the latest manifestation. Hardly an institution or cultural norm has escaped transformation in the last fifty or sixty years. Think of the changing use of Sundays, once the sole preserve of the churches; or the shape of the family as living together, re-marriage, blended families and surrogacy have gained acceptance; or the percentage of women now in the workforce; or the more liberal attitudes to drinking and gambling; or the multicultural face of Australia's cities and towns; or the revolution in communication with the advent of television, then the internet and now social media.

The Anglican Church of Australia has had to wrestle with all of these changes. Some have not affected us very much; others have had to be accommodated, whether we like them or not and still others have excited substantial debate, some feeling the Church should resist a change as incompatible with the faith, others seeking to accommodate it as consistent with what we believe. The re-marriage of divorcees in churches and the ordination of women spring to mind.

The debate then on our Church's attitude to same-sex marriage is in response to a society that has been shifting seismically in recent decades in all sorts of ways and a Church trying to work out as faithfully as it can where it should stand in relation to this latest social shift.

Secondly, behind the same-sex marriage debate lies a spiritual dilemma worth pondering. Given that we all pray to the same God, read the same Bible, recite the same Creeds and belong to the same church—given that it is the same Lord Jesus Christ who encounters each of us— then how is it that we come to such differing views on what Christ wants for us and his Church? How is it that many applaud the ordination of women as God's will for his Church, while others see it as inconsistent with the Bible and contrary to the Divine will? How is it that some believe Christ sanctions the blessing of same-sex unions, while others believe that this is contrary to the mind of Christ and the teaching of Scripture?

If we are all encountering the same Lord Jesus through Bible, prayer, sacraments and worship, then how is it that our understanding of what that encounter calls us to and demands of us can be so different?

Part of the answer must be that we are finite human beings with limited understanding. We do not always get God's will right. Although age and experience may increase our understanding and wisdom, we shall always remain finite people with a finite capacity to understand the mind of God.

More significantly, our background, experiences and conditioning distort the encounter with Christ. Sometimes we may think we are encountering Christ, when in fact we are limiting him to the scale of our biases, making him in effect someone who largely mirrors our background, experiences and cultural conditioning.

As you read this book then it might be helpful to keep in mind that:

- Firstly, our different perceptions of Christ's will for us should remind us of our need to go on repenting and learning and growing. We are all trying to be more faithful to Christ.
- Secondly, it helps to know that the problem of discerning the true Christ has been there from the beginning. The Church was wise to keep four Gospels, not just one, because no one writer could do justice to the whole Christ. There will never be entire agreement as to what it means to be like Christ or 'in Christ'. There will always be varieties of emphasis.
- Finally, we should go on sharing with others our insights about Christ's will for us and how we have encountered Christ. Jesus promised that the Spirit of truth would guide his followers into all the truth. As we share our encounters and learn from one another then we can trust that the Holy Spirit will go between us and draw us towards what is true and good.

The book is divided into five sections: how we have got to where we are; reflections from the Bible; reflections on the history of marriage; issues around blessing, desire and celibacy; and finally the cases for and against same-sex marriage.

A note of humility needs to accompany our corporate discussions. Sometimes I think the Anglican Church of Australia is a little like the blind man in Mark's Gospel, who sees by stages; or like the two on the road to Emmaus who are taught by the 'stranger' but only at the end are their eyes opened and they 'see'; or like Paul's image of seeing through a glass darkly. We are currently grappling to see issues with a common mind.

This book then is part of an ongoing conversation. Doctrine Commission members have found this as much a listening process as the articulation of ideas. They have however found in their discussions some initial 'common ground' along the following lines:

- That all people are made in the image of God, are loved by God and are welcome in the community of God's people.
- That same-sex attraction is not a sin or a mental illness or a psychological disorder.
- That same-sex attraction is not a voluntary choice. Most gay men and lesbian women would say that they have no choice in who they are attracted to and cannot—and feel no desire to—change this.
- That 'reparative therapy' to re-orient sexual attraction to heterosexual patterns is ineffective in the vast majority of cases. Individuals who have participated in such therapy based on an unrealistic hope or promise of re-orientation have experienced harm as a result.
- That some of the church's past teaching about same-sex attraction has been unhelpful and untrue to the Scriptures. Specifically, that same-sex attraction *per se* is a sin; that it is explained by 'origin stories' (bad parenting, abuse etc.); that it is fundamentally an individual's choice; and that it can be changed by any individual who is willing to change and trust God enough.
- That the church needs to find a better way to welcome and include those who experience same-sex attraction.

As you read this book you may see these signs of 'common ground' and perhaps discover some more? Whether or not that is the case, we hope that the many people who are looking for careful ethical consideration about same sex marriage will find this book helpful.

On a personal note it is a privilege to chair the Doctrine Commission. Although at times we disagree robustly, we remain brothers and sisters in Christ, who book-end our meetings with prayer and eat and drink with each other in Christian charity and unity. Perhaps when we die that will be how Christ first judges us—on our love for one another, more than whether our thinking was correct.

Bishop Jonathan Holland[1]
Chair, General Synod Doctrine Commission

---

1   Jonathan Holland is Principal of St Francis Theological College and a bishop in the Diocese of Brisbane.

CONTEXT

The Debates over the Doctrine of Marriage in the Anglican Communion

Michael R Stead[1]

The purpose of this essay is to locate the present discussion in our Church about marriage and same-sex marriage in the wider context of debates that have been happening over the past two decades in the global Anglican Communion.

Although the underlying historical events are not in dispute, there are very different lenses through which these events are understood by the participants in the debate. For the purpose of this essay, I will use the labels 'progressive' and 'conservative' to describe two of these viewpoints. It is important to stress that these labels refer only to a viewpoint on same-sex marriage. Those who are 'progressive' on this issue might be 'conservative' on other matters, and vice versa.

The prelude to Lambeth Resolution I.10

The twenty-year focus of this essay spans the period from the 1998 Lambeth Conference to the present. However, the 1998 Lambeth Conference (and, in particular, Resolution I.10 on Human Sexuality)

---

[1] The Rt Rev'd Dr Michael Stead is the Bishop of South Sydney. He gained his doctorate in Biblical Studies from the University of Gloucestershire, and is a Visiting Lecturer in Old Testament at Moore Theological College, Sydney.

needs to be understood in the context of the events several years prior to the conference.

In the United States during the 1990s, various bishops, commissions and other bodies of The Episcopal Church (TEC, previously known as ECUSA) increasingly began to affirm the acceptability of homosexual practice, therefore the need for the full inclusion of gay men and lesbian women into the life and ministry of the church. Bishop John Shelby Spong, then the Bishop of Newark, was a high-profile advocate for this. The 1994 TEC General Assembly was pivotal. Spong tabled a document entitled 'A Statement of Koinonia', signed by 68 TEC Bishops, which included the declarations that gay and lesbian persons who 'forge relationships with partners of their choice that are faithful, monogamous, committed, life giving and holy are to be honored', and that ordination should be open to 'homosexual persons who choose to live out their sexual orientation in a partnership that is marked by faithfulness and life giving holiness'.[2]

The 1994 General Assembly subsequently passed a resolution which requested a report into the 'development of rites honoring love and commitment between persons of the same sex'.[3] Spong was a member of the Theology Committee of the House of Bishops which produced the report as requested. This effect of this report was to open the door (cautiously) for rites to bless same-sex relationships (notwithstanding a strongly critical Minority Report).[4] In 1997, Spong's provocative public letter 'A Message to the Anglican Communion on the Subject of Homosexuality' sought to put the

---

2 https://www.integrityusa.org/archive/samesexblessings/a_statement_in_koinonia.htm.

3 https://episcopalarchives.org/cgi-bin/acts/acts_resolution.pl?resolution=1994-C042.

4 https://www.integrityusa.org/archive/samesexblessings/slc97.htm.

Anglican Communion's full inclusion of gay and lesbian people on the agenda for the 1998 Lambeth Conference.[5]

In response to the perceived trend in TEC towards 'the ordination of practicing homosexuals and the blessing of same-sex unions', the Anglican bishops from the Global South issued the Kuala Lumpur Statement on Human Sexuality in February 1997.[6] A motion to endorse the Kuala Statement at the 1997 TEC General Convention did not pass.

Lambeth Conference 1998

A growing concern at the progressive direction being taken by TEC (and the Anglican Church of Canada—see below) united conservative bishops from across the Anglican Communion at the Lambeth Conference in 1998. The result was that the conference passed Resolution I.10, which affirmed a theologically conservative position on human sexuality.

Resolution I.10 affirmed the 'teaching of Scripture' that the only two expressions of faithful sexuality are lifelong marriage between a man and a woman, or abstinence. The resolution called for pastoral care for those who experience homosexual orientation. At the same time, it described homosexual practice as 'incompatible with Scripture' and that the Conference 'cannot advise the legitimising or blessing of same sex unions nor ordaining those involved in same gender unions.' This resolution was passed by a substantial majority (526 to 70).

---

5 http://web.archive.org/web/19991008144148/http://andromeda.rutgers.edu/~lcrew/whitepaper.html.
6 http://www.globalsouthanglican.org/index.php/blog/comments/the_kuala_lumpur_statement_on_human_sexuality_2nd_encounter_in_the_south_10. In his letter 'A Message to the Anglican Communion', Spong described this Statement as 'ill-informed and filled with the prejudice of propaganda' and 'an embarrassing misuse of the Bible'.

Conservatives hoped that Resolution I.10 would signal to TEC that they were out of step with the majority of the Anglican Communion, and that they would step back from their progressive agenda. This proved not to be the case. The next session of the TEC General Assembly passed Resolution 2000-D039, which declared that 'the issues of human sexuality are not yet resolved'.

An irreparable rift within The Episcopal Church

The flashpoint for TEC and the wider Anglican Communion came in 2003, with the consecration of Gene Robinson, a non-celibate gay man, as Bishop of New Hampshire, despite repeated pleas not to do so from other parts of the Communion.[7] The statement of the emergency meeting of the Primates convened on the cusp of Robinson's consecration warned of the dire consequences of this action.

> If his consecration proceeds, we recognise that we have reached a crucial and critical point in the life of the Anglican Communion and we have had to conclude that the future of the Communion itself will be

---

7   The Primate's Meeting in Oporto, Portugal March 2000 stated that the 'clear and public repudiation of those sections of the Resolution [Lambeth 1.10] related to the public blessing of same-sex unions and the ordination of declared non-celibate homosexuals, and the declared intention of some dioceses to proceed with such actions, have come to threaten the unity of the communion in a profound way' — https://www.anglicancommunion.org/media/288306/primates-meeting-communique-2000.pdf.

The Primates Meeting in Kanuga, North Carolina March 2001 acknowledged 'the difficulties of those who are estranged from others because of changes in theology and practice — especially with regard to the acceptance of homosexual activity and the ordination of practicing homosexuals — that they believe to be unfaithful to the gospel of Christ'- https://www.anglicancommunion.org/media/288259/a-pastoral-letter-and-call-to-prayer-2001.pdf.

Resolution 34 of the ACC Meeting in Hong Kong in October 2002 called on dioceses and individual bishops 'not to undertake unilateral actions or adopt policies which would strain our communion with one another without reference to their provincial authorities' —

https://www.anglicancommunion.org/structures/instruments-of-communion/acc/acc-12/resolutions.aspx.

put into jeopardy. In this case, the ministry of this one bishop will not be recognised by most of the Anglican world, and many provinces are likely to consider themselves out of Communion with the Episcopal Church (USA). This will tear the fabric of our Communion at its deepest level, and may lead to further division on this and further issues as provinces have to decide in consequence whether they can remain in communion with provinces that choose not to break communion with the Episcopal Church (USA).[8]

As foreshadowed by the Primates, the consecration of Robinson had profound implications, both for TEC and the wider Anglican Communion. It created an irreparable rift within TEC between conservatives and progressives. Conservatives could not submit in good conscience to a bishop who (in their view) had rejected the clear teaching of Scripture in relation to marriage and human sexuality. This eventually led to more than 700 clergy and bishops in TEC being deposed from Holy Orders and several hundred congregations disaffiliating from the TEC. However, leaving TEC was problematic for American Anglicans for two reasons—property and episcopal oversight.

In most cases, the church buildings of the congregations wishing to leave TEC were held on trust by the diocese or denomination. What followed were years of court cases over contested property, some of which are still continuing. In the period between 2000 and 2015, in excess of US$60 million was spent on litigation between TEC and congregations and dioceses that sought to leave the denomination. Presiding Bishop Katharine Jefferts Schori wrote to the House of Bishops in 2009, instructing bishops not to sell church buildings to congregations who were leaving TEC, because

---

[8]   https://www.anglicannews.org/news/2003/10/a-statement-by-the-primates-of-the-anglican-communion-meeting-in-lambeth-palace.aspx.

'we do not make settlements that encourage religious bodies who seek to replace The Episcopal Church'.[9]

The second issue for congregations disaffiliating from TEC was that they were left without episcopal oversight. The initial solution to this problem involved African bishops who consecrated Americans as bishops of (for example) the Church of Rwanda, to exercise oversight of conservative Anglican congregations in North America. This was contentious, not least because it involved bishops from one geographical province exercising episcopal ministry in another province.

A tear in the fabric of the Communion

TEC's theological stance on human sexuality has also had profound implications for the wider Anglican Communion. During the decade between 2003 and 2013, there were repeated attempts by various instruments of the Anglican Communion to persuade TEC to return to the teaching on human sexuality articulated in Lambeth Resolution 1.10. The Windsor Report and the subsequent proposal for a Communion Covenant sought to find a way to 'mend the tear'.

The statement from the Primates' Meeting in Dar es Salaam in 2007 summarised how the Primates viewed the situation at that time.

> Since the controversial events of 2003, we have faced the reality of increased tension in the life of the Anglican Communion—tension so deep that the fabric of our common life together has been torn...

The Windsor Report identified two threats to our common life: first, certain developments in the life and ministry of the Episcopal Church and the Anglican Church of Canada which challenged the standard of teaching on human sexuality articulated in the 1998 Lambeth Resolution 1.10; and second, interventions in the life of those Provinces which arose as reactions

---

9   https://www.virtueonline.org/new-york-message-presiding-bishop-property-issues.

to the urgent pastoral needs that certain primates perceived. The Windsor Report did not see a 'moral equivalence' between these events, since the cross-boundary interventions arose from a deep concern for the welfare of Anglicans in the face of innovation. Nevertheless both innovation and intervention are central factors placing strains on our common life. The Windsor Report recognised this ... and invited the Instruments of Communion to call for a moratorium of such actions.

The Primates called for a moratorium on both 'intervention' and 'innovation', and urged TEC bishops to promise not to authorise any rite of blessing for same-sex unions in their dioceses or through General Convention, and to withhold the canonical consent for a candidate for episcopal orders who was living in a same-sex union. It became progressively clear that TEC would not do this.

In July 2009, the TEC General Convention passed a resolution calling for the development of liturgies for the blessing of same gender relationships, and encouraging bishops to offer a 'generous pastoral response' to same-sex couples in their dioceses.[10]

In July 2012, the TEC General Convention passed a resolution approving an official liturgy for blessing same-sex relationships.[11]

In July 2015, the TEC General Convention approved for trial use gender neutral marriage rites that could be used by same-sex and opposite-sex couples.[12]

In July 2018, the TEC General Convention made these marriage rites available for general use, and required a bishop who did not

---

10   https://episcopalarchives.org/cgi-bin/acts/acts_resolution.pl?resolution=2009-C056.
11   https://episcopalarchives.org/cgi-bin/acts/acts_resolution.pl?resolution=2012-A049.
12   https://episcopalarchives.org/cgi-bin/acts/acts_resolution.pl?resolution=2015-A054.

approve of same-sex marriage to allow another bishop to provide alternative episcopal oversight.[13]

There was a similar rejection of the Primates' call for a moratorium on consecrating gay bishops. Although the TEC General Convention in 2006 had passed resolution B033, which enacted a moratorium on the consecration of gay bishops, this was effectively overturned in July 2009, when the convention passed resolution D025, which allowed gay and lesbian clergy to serve openly in all offices of the Church. In May 2010, the Rev. Canon Mary Glasspool of Baltimore was consecrated as Bishop of Los Angeles, making her the second openly gay/lesbian bishop in church history.

At their meeting in Canterbury in 2016, the Primates of the Anglican Communion described TEC's change in their marriage canon as 'a fundamental departure from the faith and teaching held by the majority of our Provinces on the doctrine of marriage', and imposed the sanction that 'for a period of three years The Episcopal Church no longer represent us on ecumenical and interfaith bodies, should not be appointed or elected to an internal standing committee and that while participating in the internal bodies of the Anglican Communion, they will not take part in decision making on any issues pertaining to doctrine or polity'.[14]

Parallel developments in Canada

There have been similar developments in the Anglican Church of Canada over the same period. In 1998, the Synod of the Diocese

---

13   https://www.vbinder.net/resolutions/B012?house=hb&lang=en.

14   http://www.anglicannews.org/news/2016/01/statement-from-primates-2016.aspx. Notwithstanding the sanction imposed by the Primates, the TEC delegates attended and participated fully in ACC-16. The TEC delegates later issued a press release to refute a news report from Anglican Communion News Service (ACNS) that claimed that the TEC representatives 'did not vote on matters of doctrine or polity'. http://anglican.ink/2017/02/02/tec-rejects-aco-contention-that-its-members-did-not-participate-fully-at-acc-16-in-lusaka/.

of New Westminster passed a resolution to develop a rite for the blessing of same-sex unions. Initially, the Diocesan Bishop withheld consent, but by 2002 had agreed that he would be bound by the majority of the Synod. At the diocesan synod in 2002, the motion for same-sex blessing rites was carried by 63% of the vote. As a result, conservative ministers and parishes, representing a quarter of the Diocese, left the Diocese (and were subsequently required by the Bishop to leave their church buildings).[15]

The Canadian General Synod in 2004 considered whether the Diocese of New Westminster had unilateral power under the Constitution to authorise a rite for same-sex blessing, or whether this required the authorisation of General Synod. This question turned on whether the blessing of same-sex relationships was a matter of doctrine. This question was referred to the Primate's Theological Commission, who produced the St Michael's Report in 2005, advising that blessing of same-sex relationships was a matter of doctrine, because 'any proposed blessing of a same-sex relationship would be analogous to a marriage to such a degree as to require the church to understand it coherently in relation to the doctrine of marriage'. The implication of this was that blessing of same-sex unions required the authorisation of the Canadian General Synod.[16]

In 2007, the Canadian General Synod received the St Michael's report,[17] then passed (by a two vote margin) a resolution affirming that 'the blessing of same-sex unions is consistent with the core doctrine of The Anglican Church of Canada.'[18] Another motion to authorise

---

15   https://www.anglican.ca/news/new-westminster-synod-and-bishop-approve-same-sex-blessings/. This included Dr J. I. Packer, whom Time Magazine described in 2005 as one of the 25 most influential evangelicals in America.
16   https://www.anglican.ca/primate/tfc/ptc/smr/.
17   http://archive.anglican.ca/gs2007/rr/resolutions/a184.htm.
18   http://archive.anglican.ca/gs2007/rr/resolutions/a186.htm. This was carried in the House of Bishops 21-19.

dioceses to permit the blessing of same-sex unions was narrowly defeated (19-21) in the House of Bishops. The Synod then passed a resolution asking the Council of General Synod to consider a revision of Canon 21 (On Marriage) including a theological rationale to allow the marriage of all legally qualified persons and to report back to General Synod 2010.[19] In response to a related motion,[20] the Primate's Theological Commission produced the Galilee Report in 2009.[21]

In 2010, the Canadian General Synod issued a 'sexuality discernment statement', indicating that the Church was 'in a time of ongoing discernment'. The Synod committed itself to ongoing study in relation to human sexuality.[22]

In 2013, the Canadian General Synod resolved to vote on the issue of same sex marriage at the following Synod in 2016. The Primate appointed a Commission on the Marriage Canon, which produced a report in 2015 entitled 'This Holy Estate', including 'a biblical and theological rationale for a change in teaching on the nature of Christian marriage'.[23]

In 2016, this report was considered by the Canadian General Synod, which then voted (by a margin of one vote) to authorise a change in the Marriage Canon to include same-sex marriage. Under the ACC Constitution, this will require a second vote at the subsequent (2019) Synod in order to effect the change to the Canon. Since 2016, same-sex marriage has been permissible in the Diocese of Toronto at the pastoral discretion of the Bishop.[24]

---

19 http://archive.anglican.ca/gs2007/rr/resolutions/a189.htm.
20 http://archive.anglican.ca/gs2007/rr/resolutions/c003.pdf.
21 https://www.anglican.ca/wp-content/uploads/2010/11/galilee-report-full-with-papers.pdf.
22 http://archive.anglican.ca/gs2010/resolutions/c011/index.html.
23 https://www.anglican.ca/resources/this-holy-estate-the-report-of-the-commission-on-the-marriage-canon/.
24 https://www.toronto.anglican.ca/parish-life/same-gender-blessings/.

Also in 2016, the Diocese of Toronto elected Kevin Robertson, who is the first openly gay and partnered person to be a bishop in the Anglican Church of Canada.[25] Robertson married his partner at St James' Cathedral in Toronto in December 2018.

The Scottish Episcopal Church and the Anglican Episcopal Church in Brazil

In 2013, the College of Bishops of the Scottish Episcopal Church (SEC) gave tacit approval (but not 'official sanction') for the blessing of civil partnerships.[26]

In 2014, the SEC commenced 'A Whole Church Discussion of Same Sex Relationships'.[27] In 2015, the Doctrine Committee of the SEC produced a report on the theology of marriage.[28] In light of this, the 2015 General Synod voted to pursue a change in the SEC's canonical definition of marriage to include same-sex couples. That process commenced at the 2016 Synod, and was formally approved in the 2017 Synod. At the Primates Meeting in Oct 2017, it was confirmed that sanctions imposed in 2016 against The Episcopal Church also now applied to the Scottish Episcopal Church, as a result of their redefinition of the doctrine of marriage.[29]

In June 2018, the General Synod of the Igreja Episcopal Anglicana

---

25 http://www.toronto.anglican.ca/2016/09/17/diocese-elects-three-new-suffragan-bishops/.
26 https://www.scotland.anglican.org/wp-content/uploads/2014/02/Blessing-of-Civil-Partnerships-Nov-2013.pdf. They indicated that they expected the Diocesan Bishop to be 'consulted by clergy prior to the carrying out of any informal blessing of a civil partnership in his diocese', and that a bishop could at his or her own discretion attend the blessing.
27 https://www.scotland.anglican.org/wp-content/uploads/2014/02/Whole-Church-Discussion-Same-Sex-Relationships.pdf.
28 http://www.scotland.anglican.org/wp-content/uploads/2015/04/Doctrine-Committee-Theology-of-Marriage.pdf.
29 http://www.anglicannews.org/news/2017/10/scottish-episcopal-church-primus-briefs-primates-on-same-sex-marriage-decision.aspx.

do Brasil (IEAB)—the Anglican Episcopal Church of Brazil—approved changes to its canons to permit same-sex marriages.[30]

The emergence of Gafcon

The emergence of Gafcon (the Global Anglican Future Conference) in 2008 needs to be understood in light of these events. By 2008, it was evident that TEC and the Anglican Church in Canada (ACC) remained committed to a progressive theological stance on human sexuality. Conservatives were disappointed that the Archbishop of Canterbury had invited TEC and ACC bishops to attend Lambeth 2008, and did not invite those bishops who had been deposed from TEC, nor did he invite the new bishops appointed by the African Primates to provide episcopal oversight to disaffiliated Anglicans.

Gafcon met in Jerusalem in June 2008, prior to the Lambeth Conference, to provide fellowship and encouragement to disaffiliated and dispossessed Anglicans. In 2008, there were approximately 700 Anglican congregations (with average Sunday attendance of just under 70,000) who had left TEC and the ACC because of irreconcilable differences over doctrine and practice.[31] Their respective national Churches did not regard them as authentically Anglican. Gafcon 2008 constituted a Primates Council and authorised it to recognise Anglican churches in areas where conservative Anglicans had been deprived of their church property and deposed from Holy Orders. Gafcon recognises Anglicans on a

---

30   http://www.anglicannews.org/news/2018/06/brazils-anglican-church-changes-its-canons-to-permit-same-sex-marriage.aspx.
31   http://anglicanchurch.net/index.php/main/page/95/; https://web.archive.org/web/20090704012202/http://acnaassembly.org/media/ACNA_-_Dioceses_and_delegates_-_June_2009_-_fact_sheet.pdf. That number has grown to 1,037 congregations with an average Sunday attendance of 93,489—2017 figures. https://www.dropbox.com/sh/7stcpg36y2ou1jd/AABG02vxyvhqUkJistzf4KNea?dl=0&preview=Congregational+Report+to+Provincial+Council+2017.pdf.

confessional basis, based on assent to The Jerusalem Declaration (a statement of faith ratified by the first Gafcon Conference in 2008).

Gafcon understands itself to be a movement within the Anglican Communion, of those sharing a common doctrinal confession. A recent statement declared: 'We are not leaving the Anglican Communion; we are the majority of the Anglican Communion seeking to remain faithful to our Anglican heritage.'[32]

Since 2008, the Gafcon Primates have recognised the Anglican Church in North America (ACNA) and the Anglican Church in Brazil, and have consecrated a Missionary Bishop for Europe to provide episcopal oversight for those who are no longer recognised as Anglican by their respective national Churches. The Gafcon Primates have argued that these steps have been necessary because of the departure from 'the faith once for all delivered to the saints' by The Episcopal Church, the Anglican Church of Canada, the Episcopal Church of Brazil and the Scottish Episcopal Church. The inaugural Gafcon in 2008 has been followed by conferences in Nairobi (2013)[33] and Jerusalem (2018).[34]

Recent developments in Anglican Church in Aotearoa, New Zealand and Polynesia

New Zealand legalised civil same-sex marriage in April 2013.[35]

At the first New Zealand General Synod / Te Hīnota Whānui (hereafter GSTHW) after the legalisation enabling civil same-sex marriage (i.e., May 2014), the GSTHW passed Motion 30, which established a working group to develop a 'liturgy for blessing same-gender relationships', while at the same time making provision for

---

32   https://www.gafcon.org/news/letter-to-the-churches-gafcon-assembly-2018.
33   https://www.gafcon.org/news/nairobi-communique-and-commitment.
34   https://www.gafcon.org/news/letter-to-the-churches-gafcon-assembly-2018.
35   Same-sex civil unions have been legal in New Zealand since 2005.

those within the Church 'who believe the blessing of same-gender relationships is contrary to scripture, doctrine, tikanga or civil law'. 'A Way Forward' Working Group was formed as a result of this motion.

The report of 'A Way Forward' was considered at the next GSTHW in May 2016.[36] The report recommended changes to the canons and new formularies (i.e., official liturgies) of the Church to make provision for the blessing of all civil marriages, including same-sex marriages. The proposal to change the canons and formularies was deeply problematic for conservatives, because the Constitution of the Anglican Church in Aotearoa, New Zealand and Polynesia binds all clergy to submission to the authority of the General Synod and consent to be bound by its regulations. This would have bound conservative clergy to canonical acceptance of the change in the formularies allowing the blessing of same-sex marriages, even if they believed this to be contrary to the doctrine of Christ.

As a report later noted,

> The subsequent Synod debate was long, fraught and painful due to an inability to find a common view between the very differing theologies held by deeply spiritual Anglicans. At a critical time during the debate the late Archbishop Brown Turei proposed that space be given to have more discernment on a way forward that would not break the Three Tikanga Church. This was agreed to by the Synod and the Report, together with its recommendations, were left to lie on the table until the next General Synod in 2018.[37]

The General Synod then passed Motion 29 to establish a new working group to explore 'structural arrangements' that would allow people who hold differing convictions about same-sex relationships

---

36 http://www.anglican.org.nz/content/download/41689/210720/file/2016%20Way%20Forward%20Report%20RELEASE.docx.

37 *Final Report of the Motion 29 Working Group*, page 6.

to remain together in the Church. The Motion 29 Working Group released its report in January 2018. The Working Group did not—nor attempt to—address the question as to whether blessing same-gender relationships was consistent with the doctrine of the Church and the formularies. The working group noted:

> Our mandate was not to consider the differing theological positions or to interpret scripture on this point. Instead we had a very specific task of considering what arrangements and safeguards could be put in place to hold us together within the same ecclesial family so that no one was forced to compromise sincerely held beliefs.[38]

The report was considered by the GSTHW in May 2018, and the key proposals of the Working Group were passed as Motion 7, and enacted as via statues 747 to 751.[39]

The key proposals (as enacted) were:

- There was no alteration to the Formularies or the Church's doctrine on marriage.
- Title G, Canon XIV was changed to allow 'a non-formulary service' by which a bishop can authorise a service for the blessing of a civil marriage or civil union in his or her diocese.
- The 'Declaration of Adherence and Submission' was changed so that, instead of promising adherence to the authority of GSTHW, ministers now promise adherence to the rules and regulations of the Anglican Church in Aotearoa, New Zealand and Polynesia.
- Discipline canons were altered so that no bishop or member of the clergy can face disciplinary action either for agreeing to bless such relationships, or for refusing to do so, or for

---

38   *Final Report of the Motion 29 Working Group*, page 7.
39   http://www.anglican.org.nz/News/General-Synod-Te-Hinota-Whanui-GSTHW/Minutes-and-Statutes-of-the-63rd-General-Synod-Te-Hinota-Whanui-held-in-New-Plymouth-4-10-May-2018.

teaching that blessings are consistent (or not consistent) with Holy Scripture or the doctrine of the Church.

These changes sought to bypass the theological and constitutional questions about what may or may not be consistent with the formularies, and that what may or may not be a breach of doctrine, in two ways.

Firstly, the Canon for Authorised Services (Title G XIV) was changed. As amended at GSTHW 2018, clause 1 now reads (with the additional clause highlighted)

> Each Tikanga is authorised to approve forms of service not inconsistent with the Constitution / te Pouhere, or with the Formularies of this Church, **except for services the use of which may be authorised pursuant to clause 8**.

(Clause 8 is a new provision that allows a diocesan bishop to authorise the form of a service blessing those who are in a civil marriage or civil union recognised by the State.)

The amendment to clause 1, which exempts clause 8 services from having to be consistent with the constitution and the formularies, brackets out the question whether blessing of same-sex unions is inconsistent with the formularies.

Secondly, the changes to Title D separate doctrine and discipline. The report acknowledges the possibility that blessing same-sex marriages may be inconsistent with the Formularies but argues, even if this were inconsistent, that 'the Church is still able to regulate for itself what it does and does not discipline'. The changes to Title D provide immunity from any complaint for those who conduct (or will not conduct) services blessing couples in civil marriages or civil unions, or who wish to preach or teach that such blessings are consistent (or not consistent) with Holy Scripture or the doctrine of the Church.

The WG considers that a 'no discipline' policy is the best way to safeguard the consciences of clergy and bishops. In order for each viewpoint to safely co-exist within this Church each needs to acknowledge that the other must have freedom of conscience and action that aligns with their theological convictions and within the ministry standards of this Church.[40]

These two provisions were problematic for conservatives, because they provided General Synod authorisation for what they believe to be a 'depart[ure] from the Doctrine and Sacraments of Christ', without any possibility of this being tested or disciplined (contrary to Clause 3 of the Church of England Empowering Act 1928), and also for the authorisation of 'a service blessing those who are in any form of civil marriage' (clause 8), which (they believe) is contrary to the (unchanged) formularies that specify that marriage is only between a man and a woman.[41]

Consequences of the New Zealand decision

The Motion 29 working group stated that it sought to find a way to allow those who hold diametrically opposed theological convictions about the blessing of same-sex relationships 'to coexist peacefully in same church'. Archbishop Philip Richardson, an ex-officio member of the Motion 29 working group, is reported to have said that the group's goal was to provide 'mechanisms that will hold the integrity of different and irreconcilable positions in the same

---

40   Final Report of the Motion 29 Working Group, page 13.
41   See http://www.legislation.govt.nz/act/private/1928/0003/latest/DLM94467.html. Similar to the 'Fundamental Declarations' in the Australian Constitution, the NZ constitution begins with 'Fundamental Provisions' which make the 'doctrines and sacraments of Christ' and the formularies (*BCP*, the Ordinal and the 39 articles) an unalterable standard for the Anglican Church in Aotearoa, New Zealand and Polynesia. The General Synod is empowered by Part B to adopt new formularies (e.g., new liturgies) 'for use in the Church or any part of it', but only where these new formularies do not 'depart from the Doctrine and Sacraments of Christ as defined in the Fundamental Provisions of this Constitution.'

extended family'.[42] Conservatives participated fully in the consultation process, explaining the objections noted above and the fellowship-breaking implications for them if the General Synod were to authorise same-sex blessings, and making proposals for alternative episcopal oversight. These proposals were noted but not pursued in the working group report.

The aftermath of the Synod's decision in May 2018 was what the conservatives had foreshadowed—clergy and congregations holding a theological conviction that blessing a same-sex marriage is contrary to the doctrines of Christ announced that they had no alternative but to disaffiliate from ACANZP. The issue was particularly acute for those in a diocese where the Diocesan Bishop has declared an intention to allow same-sex blessings in that diocese.

As at December 2018, twelve clergy and five congregations (representing approximately 1000 members) have disaffiliated or are planning to disaffiliate from the ACANZP. They have indicated that they intend applying to the Gafcon Primates in April 2019 to be recognised as an extra-provincial diocese.

Recent developments in the Church of England

Civil partnerships (including same-sex partnerships) became legal in 2004, and same-sex marriage was legalised in the UK in 2013, with the first same-sex marriages taking place in 2014. The legislation enabling same-sex marriage included what was described as a 'quadruple lock' to safeguard religious organisations from being forced to conduct same sex marriages, including a provision that the legislation did not affect the canon law of the Church of England or the Church in Wales.

---

42   As reported in http://anglicantaonga.org.nz/news/common_life/29.

In 2014, the House of Bishops issued pastoral guidance on same-sex marriage,[43] which affirmed:
- The Church's doctrine of marriage is that marriage is (only) between a man and a woman. The changes of the State's definition of marriage does not change the Church's doctrine of marriage.
- Clergy are not permitted to enter same-sex marriages, because this would 'clearly be at variance with the teaching of the Church of England'. (Clergy are allowed to enter same-sex civil partnerships, but only on the understanding that the couple will remain celibate).
- As with civil partnerships, no services blessing same-sex marriages should be conducted. Clergy may at their discretion provide 'more informal kinds of prayer, at the request of the couple'. This should be 'accompanied by pastoral discussion of the Church's teaching and [the couple's] reasons for departing from it.'
- 'While the same standards of conduct [apply] to all, the Church of England should not exclude from its fellowship those lay people of gay or lesbian orientation who, in conscience, were unable to accept that a life of sexual abstinence was required of them and who, instead, chose to enter into a faithful, committed sexually active relationship… Those same sex couples who choose to marry should be welcomed into the life of the worshipping community and not be subjected to questioning about their lifestyle. Neither they nor any children they care for should be denied access to the sacraments.'

In Feb 2017, the General Synod voted 'not to take note' of a Report

---

43 https://www.churchofengland.org/more/media-centre/news/house-bishops-pastoral-guidance-same-sex-marriage.

by the House of Bishops on Marriage and Same Sex Relationships.[44] In a rare moment of unity, progressives and conservatives joined forces to vote against 'taking note' of the report—for the progressives, because the report did not go far enough, and the conservatives because it went too far.

Questions arising from two decades of debates

This brief review of the debates over the doctrine of marriage in the Anglican Communion prompts a number of questions for consideration by Australian Anglicans, as our Church begins to discuss these issues.

1. **How do we see God at work in the history of the past twenty years?**

   Both progressive and conservatives would agree with the description of the history above, but whereas progressives view this history as demonstrating God's affirmation of same-sex marriage, conservatives view it as growing departure from God's will.

2. **Can we come to a 'common mind', or have we reached 'irreconcilable differences'?**

   At the start of these debates, reports and communiques variously noted that 'we are not yet of a common mind' (or similar) and pledged to continuing dialogue and listening. More recently, the focus has shifted, to finding ways to hold 'different and irreconcilable positions in the same extended

---

44   https://www.churchofengland.org/sites/default/files/2017-11/gs-2055-marriage-and-same-sex-relationships-after-the-shared-conversations-report-from-the-house-of-bishops.pdf.

family' (to quote Abp Richardson). Is it possible for us to come to a common mind?

3. **Why has this particular issue been church-dividing in other jurisdictions, when on other contentious issues Anglicans have not divided? Is what has happened overseas likely to be repeated in the Anglican Church of Australia?**
In these debates in other jurisdictions, both sides of the debate have seen this as a 'gospel issue'. Progressives claim that it is a gospel issue, because the failure of the church to embrace what the Holy Spirit is doing today is denying the gospel to the LGBT+ community. Conservatives claim that the affirmation of same-sex intercourse is preaching a gospel without repentance and submission to the Lordship of Christ—which could result in people failing to inherit the kingdom of God. Who is right, or are neither right?

4. **Is there a *via media* (a middle way) that allows the blessing same-sex relationships instead of changing our doctrine of marriage to legitimise same-sex marriage?**
The legitimisation of the blessing of same-sex relationships has led (logically, sociologically and theologically) to the legitimisation of same-sex marriage in America, Canada (pending), Scotland and Brazil. Is that necessarily the case?

5. **What would be necessary to change our doctrine of marriage?**
In those jurisdictions that have changed (or are changing) their doctrine of marriage to include same-sex marriage, it has been recognised that this required a canon of the relevant General Synod / General Assembly. What would be necessary in our context? (The next essay will address this question.)

6. **In light of our answers to the questions above, how can our church improve its pastoral response to LGBT+ people?**

   These debates do not occur in a vacuum. We are acutely aware that both the process and the outcome of debates overseas have had a significant impact on LGBT+ Anglicans. How does our Church have conversations on these issues without further marginalising LGBT+ Christians in our midst?

7. **What is (and what should be) the relationship between the church's doctrine of marriage and the state's definition of marriage? Should Anglican clergy continue to conduct weddings under the *Marriage Act 1961*?**

   These matters raise important questions about the intersection of church and state. In Australia, this matter is further complicated by the role that religious celebrants have in solemnising marriage under the *Marriage Act 1961*.

The Doctrine of Marriage of the Anglican Church of Australia

Michael R Stead[1]

For reasons that will be explained below, the doctrine of marriage in the Anglican Church in Australia is, at present, that marriage is the voluntary union of one man and one woman arising from mutual promises of lifelong faithfulness. This understanding of our doctrine of marriage has been affirmed by a succession of General Synod resolutions, most recently in two resolutions passed in 2017.[2]

Recent legislative changes to the *Marriage Act 1961* to allow same-sex marriage have prompted some to ask whether the Church's doctrine of marriage can or should be changed, and to consider whether our current doctrine of marriage would be consistent with the Church's recognition of a civil same-sex marriage (e.g., a rite for blessing a same-sex marriage).

The peculiar situation of the Anglican Church in Australia

As noted in the prior essay, some national Anglican churches in other countries have changed their definition of marriage, following the legal recognition of same-sex marriage in those jurisdictions.

---

[1] The Rt Rev'd Dr Michael Stead is the Bishop of South Sydney. He gained his doctorate in Biblical Studies from the University of Gloucestershire, and is a Visiting Lecturer in Old Testament at Moore Theological College, Sydney.

[2] 2004: Resolutions 61–64, 2007: Resolution 52, 2010: Resolution 156, 2017: Resolution 48, Resolution 51.

However, the situation in Australia is unlike any other jurisdiction in the entire Anglican Communion. Uniquely, we have bound ourselves in our Constitution to the 1662 *Book of Common Prayer* (*BCP*) and the 39 Articles 'as the authorised standard of worship and doctrine in this Church, and no alteration in or permitted variations from the services or Articles therein contained shall contravene any principle of doctrine or worship laid down in such standard' (section 4). We are more tied to the 1662 *Book of Common Prayer* and 39 Articles than the Church of England.

The question which this essay seeks to address is whether a same-sex marriage (and/or another form of liturgical recognition of a same-sex marriage) 'contravenes' the doctrine of marriage of our Church, or whether it is—or could become—'consistent with' our doctrine of marriage, either by changing the doctrine of our Church to allow same-sex couples to be married according to Anglican rites, or by maintaining the current doctrine of our Church but creating a new form of service that would recognise/bless a civil same-sex marriage in a liturgical context.

To address these questions, we first need to consider the sources of our doctrine of marriage.

The Doctrine of the Anglican Church of Australia

The word 'doctrine' is used in this essay in the technical sense, as defined in the Constitution of the Anglican Church of Australia. Section 74(1) defines 'doctrine' to mean 'the teaching of this Church on any question of faith'.

The phrase 'any question of faith' in s.74 uses the word 'faith' with the same connotation it has elsewhere in the Constitution when used in the phrase 'faith ritual ceremonial or discipline of this Church'. As used in the Constitution, the phrase 'faith ritual ceremonial or discipline' encompasses the core beliefs and practices of our Church.[3] Clergy can be disciplined for 'breaches of faith ritual ceremonial or discipline'.[4]

The Constitution makes a distinction between 'faith' and 'ritual ceremonial or discipline'. Section 26 provides a power to make '**canons** in respect of *ritual, ceremonial and discipline* and to make **statements** as to the *faith* of this Church' (emphasis added). Section 28 provides that a 'special bill' process must be followed for canons which touch 'ritual ceremonial or discipline'.

There is no power in the Constitution to make canons in respect of the faith of this Church because matters of 'faith' are established by the Fundamental Declarations (sections 1–3) and the Ruling Principles (sections 4–6).[5]

In short, then, the 'doctrine' of our Church is that which is established by the Fundamental Declarations (sections 1–3) and the Ruling Principles (sections 4–6).

---

3 By virtue of section 4, our Church has 'plenary authority at its own discretion to make statements as to the *faith ritual ceremonial or discipline* of this Church' (emphasis added).

4 The Constitution establishes four types of tribunal with power to address 'breaches of faith ritual ceremonial or discipline'—the Diocesan Tribunal: s.54(2), the Provincial Tribunal: s.55(3), the Special Tribunal: s56(6) and the Appellate Tribunal: s59(1).

5 The Constitution makes the Appellate Tribunal the final arbiter of questions of faith, ritual, ceremonial and discipline. Section 29(4) provides two questions which may be put to the Appellate Tribunal about a (proposed) canon, rule, statement or resolution of General Synod.
   a. Is any part of the Act or Proposal identified in the reference inconsistent with the Fundamental Declarations or the Ruling Principles?
   b. Does any part of the Act or Proposal identified in the reference deal with or concern or affect the ritual ceremonial or discipline of this Church?
   Question (a) addresses the *faith* of this Church, and question (b) addresses the *ritual ceremonial or discipline* of this Church. That is, the faith of this Church is determined by the Fundamental Declarations (section 1–3) and the Ruling Principles (sections 4–6), and any act or canon must be 'consistent' with both the Fundamental Declarations or the Ruling Principles (see similarly Section 4). The Church cannot pass a canon which is inconsistent with the Fundamental Declarations (see Section 66). It can, however, pass a canon to change the Ruling Principles (see Section 67(1)(c) cf. Section 29(10)).

To differentiate between the doctrine arising from the Fundamental Declarations and the doctrine arising from the Ruling Principles, this essay will use the shorthand descriptions of level 1 and level 2 doctrine respectively.

Level 1 doctrine is that which is established by the Fundamental Declarations—that is, by the Apostles' Creed and Nicene Creed (section 1), by the 'rule and standard of faith' established by the canonical scriptures (section 2), by the 'commands' and 'doctrine' and 'discipline' of Christ (section 3) and the two sacraments and the threefold order (also section 3).

Level 2 doctrine is that which is established by the Ruling Principles. Section 4 makes the 'principles of doctrine and worship' of the formularies (i.e., the *Book of Common Prayer*, the Ordinal and the 39 Articles) the 'authorised standard of worship and doctrine in this Church'.

Section 5 gives the General Synod 'plenary authority and power to make canons, ordinances and rules for the order and good government of the Church', subject to the requirements in section 4 that any such canons, ordinances and rules must be 'consistent with' the Fundamental Declarations (i.e., level 1 doctrine) and not 'contravene any principle of doctrine or worship laid down' in the formularies (i.e., level 2 doctrine).

'Doctrine' compared with other teachings

As noted above, s.74(1) of the Constitution defines 'doctrine' to mean 'the teaching of this Church on any question of faith'. Not every 'teaching of the Church' is necessarily 'on a question of faith', and therefore a matter of doctrine. Moreover, the authoritative status of the 'doctrine and principles' of the formularies does not necessarily make every word or practice in *BCP* a matter of doctrine.

There is an important distinction between the 'principles' of *BCP* and its 'practices'. By virtue of section 4 of the Constitution, it is only the '*principles* of doctrine and worship [emphasis added]' of *BCP* which must not be contravened. There are many matters of 'practice' in *BCP* arising out of the context of Tudor England, which are no longer appropriate. For example, *BCP* states that 'yearly at Easter every Parishioner shall reckon with the Parson, Vicar, or Curate, or his or their Deputy or Deputies; and pay to them or him all Ecclesiastical Duties accustomably due, then and at that time to be paid'. This practice of *BCP* is not part of the 'doctrine' of the Anglican Church of Australia (even if some ministers or churchwardens might wish it to be so!)

The 'principles of doctrine and worship' of *BCP* are those matters which arise from a theological and/or scriptural rationale, rather than from the social circumstances of the age or practical/pragmatic arrangements of the time.

Two levels of the doctrine of baptism

The doctrine of baptism of our church provides a helpful illustration of these two levels of doctrine.

Level 1—the Fundamental Declarations commits our church to 'administer [Christ's] sacraments of Holy Baptism and Holy Communion'. Furthermore, baptism is also part of the 'commands of Christ' (s.3) and the teaching of the canonical scriptures, which are the 'ultimate rule and standard of faith' (s.2). A canon which sought to establish that baptism was not a sacrament would be *inconsistent with* the Fundamental Declarations, and therefore disallowed by section 4.

Level 2—The baptism service in the *Book of Common Prayer* and Article 25 ('Of the Sacraments') and Article 27 ('Of Baptism') inform our Church's doctrine of baptism. For example, *BCP* and Article 27 affirms the principle of infant baptism. A doctrine of baptism which repudiated infant baptism would 'contravene' a 'principle of doctrine or worship' in the formularies, and therefore be disallowed by section 4.

As noted above, section 4 safeguards the 'principles of doctrine or worship' in the formularies, and not necessarily mere practices. *BCP* assumes that baptism will be by immersion, but allows baptism by affusion (pouring) if the child is infirm. The mode of baptism (immersion or affusion) is a 'practice' of *BCP*, but not a 'principle of doctrine or worship'. The implication of this is that the baptism services in *AAPB* and *APBA*, which allow free choice between immersion and affusion, do not 'contravene' the formularies.

The doctrine of marriage

To explore the issues in relation to same-sex marriage, it is necessary to consider the doctrine of marriage established by the Fundamental Declarations and Ruling Principles.[6]

Level 1—Marriage is not mentioned explicitly in the Fundamental Declarations. The question therefore becomes—what is the doctrine of marriage arising from the 'commands', 'doctrine' and 'discipline' of Christ, and what is the 'rule and standard of faith' with respect to marriage arising from 'the canonical scriptures'? This is the key question taken up in many of the subsequent essays. Some essays argue that it is clear from the teaching of Christ and the rest of Scripture that marriage is between a man and a woman only and that same-sex intercourse is contrary to God's will, which means that same-sex marriage is contrary to 'level 1' doctrine. Others essays

---

6   There are also three canons which regulate the 'order and good government' of our church, touching on the subject matter of marriage. These canons neither allow nor prohibit a same-sex marriage.
  • *Marriage of Divorced Persons Canon 1981*
  • *Matrimony (Prohibited relationships) Canon 1981*
  • *Solemnization of Matrimony Canon 1981*

argue that the teaching of Christ and the rest of Scripture do not prohibit same-sex marriage, and therefore this is not a 'level 1' matter. In this case, it is necessary to ask what 'level 2' doctrine of marriage (if any) is established by the 'doctrine and principles' of the formularies.

Level 2 –The Form of Solemnization of Matrimony in *BCP* is the principle source for our doctrine of marriage.[7]

The doctrine of marriage according to 'The Form of Solemnization of Matrimony'

The doctrine of marriage arising from the *Book of Common Prayer* wedding service, as it bears on the question of same-sex unions, can be summarised under 6 headings.

1. **A union between a man and a woman**

   The *BCP* wedding service unites one man and one woman in marriage. The service 'join[s] together this **Man and this Woman** in holy Matrimony'. The consents and vows have a gendered reciprocity ('N wilt thou have this [**woman/man**] to thy wedded [**wife/husband**]'; 'I N. take thee N. to my [**wedded wife/wedded husband**]'). After the exchange of vows, the minister declares 'I pronounce that they be **Man and Wife together**', and later prays 'Send thy blessing upon these thy servants, this **man and this woman**'.[8]

   The man/woman principle is scripturally and theologically

---

[7] The 39 articles are largely silent on the doctrine of marriage, except Article 32, which affirms that it is lawful for bishops, priests and deacons, 'as for all other Christian men, to marry at their own discretion, as they shall judge the same to serve better to godliness.'

[8] Similarly, the *BCP* wedding service provides that, where there is no sermon 'declaring the duties of Man and Wife', the minister is required to read two sets of scriptures, which address the duties of husbands and wives respectively—Eph 5:25–32; Col 3:19; 1 Pet 3:7 addressed to the husband, and Eph 5:22–24; Col 3:18 and 1 Pet 3:1–6 addressed to the wife. These scriptural exhortations reflect differentiated and reciprocal gendered relationships.

grounded in the liturgy. The *BCP* wedding service interprets Genesis 1–2 as making the relationship between Adam and Eve normative for the institution of marriage.

- The priest declares that marriage 'joins together this Man and this Woman in holy Matrimony; which is an honourable estate, instituted of God in the time of man's innocency'. The reference to 'innocency' is a reference to Adam and Eve's pre-fall condition.
- The priest declares that God 'at the beginning did create our first parents, Adam and Eve, and did sanctify and join them together in marriage', and prays that God would similarly bless the couple being joined in marriage.
- The prayer for God's '**blessing** [on] these two persons, that they may both **be fruitful** in procreation of children' echoes Gen 1:28 ('And God **blessed** them, and God said unto them, **be fruitful**, and multiply').

Furthermore, the *BCP* wedding service also applies Genesis 1–2 in light of Jesus' words in Matthew 19, seen in the priest's declaration that God 'didst appoint, that out of man (created after thine own image and similitude) woman should take her beginning; and, knitting them together, didst teach that it should never be lawful to put asunder those whom thou by Matrimony hadst made one.' This statement reflects Jesus' interpretation of Genesis 1–2 as recorded in Matt 19:4–6.

Because *BCP* grounds the man/woman nature of marriage in theology and scripture, this is a *principle*—and not merely a practice—of The Form of Solemnization of Matrimony. As noted in the previous essay, all jurisdictions which have changed their doctrine of marriage to allow same-sex partners have had to pass a Canon to do so, recognising that this was a departure from the man/woman principle embedded in the *BCP* wedding service.

2. The purpose of marriage

BCP identifies a threefold purpose for marriage—'for the procreation of children', 'as a remedy against sin and to avoid fornication' and for 'mutual society, help, and comfort'.[9] This is further explained in Homily 18, 'Of the State of Matrimony', which states that '[Marriage] is instituted of God, to the intent that man and woman should live lawfully in a perpetual friendly fellowship, to bring forth fruit, and to avoid fornication'.

This threefold purpose of marriage is also scripturally and theologically grounded

- Marriage for the purpose of procreation derives, as already noted, from Gen 1:28 ('And God blessed them, and God said unto them, be fruitful, and multiply').
- Marriage for the purpose of 'a remedy against sin, and to avoid fornication; that such persons as have not the gift of continency might marry, and keep themselves undefiled members of Christ's body' derives from 1 Cor 7, especially 7:2 ('to avoid fornication'), 7:5–7 ('the gift of continency') and—implicitly—7:9 ('keep themselves undefiled').
- Marriage for the purpose of 'mutual society, help, and comfort' derives from Gen 2:18 ('It is not good that the man should be alone; I will make him an help meet for him [KJV].')

The procreative purpose of marriage does not mean that a marriage is **only valid** if it is procreative. Rather, according

---

[9] We should not read too much into the order of the three purposes, given that Homily 18 uses a different order.

to the *BCP* wedding service, the **only valid** context for the procreation of children is the context of a marriage between a man and woman. There are many examples in the Scriptures of couples unable to produce offspring, and there is no suggestion that their marriages were not valid. Nonetheless, marriage is the God-instituted form of relationship which is directed towards the threefold purpose of marriage, even if all three aspects are not able to be manifest in every marriage.

3. **The marriage 'covenant'—a voluntary, lifelong and exclusive union**

   The *BCP* wedding service describes marriage as a 'vow and covenant betwixt them made'. In this covenant, husband and wife each commit to love each other in a lifelong and exclusive union—'forsaking all other, keep thee only unto [her/him], so long as ye both shall live'. The lifelong nature of this promise is also highlighted in the vows, which are 'until death do us part'. The voluntary nature of these consents and vows is underscored in the marriage declaration—'Forasmuch as N. and N. have consented together in holy wedlock...'

   The exclusive monogamous nature of the marriage union reflects Jesus' teaching about adultery in Matthew 19. The lifelong nature of marriage reflects Paul's teaching in 1 Cor 7:39. Therefore, mutual promises of lifelong faithfulness are a principle of *BCP* with respect to marriage.

4. **Theologically grounded in creation, and a sign of the union between Christ and the Church**

   As noted above, the *BCP* service describes 'holy Matrimony' as being 'instituted of God' between Adam and Eve in the Garden of Eden. That is, the *BCP* wedding service understands marriage to be not merely a human or social institution, but a pattern of human relationships that was and is 'God's ordinance'. Moreover, the fact that marriage is said to be 'from the beginning', rather than commencing with the Mosaic Law, signals that marriage is God's pattern for all humanity and not merely for his covenant people.

Human marriage is also symbolic of the relationship between Christ and the Church.

> holy Matrimony ... is an honourable estate, instituted of God in the time of man's innocency, signifying unto us the mystical union that is betwixt Christ and his Church.[10]

5. Marriage is the only relationship in which couples are 'joined together by God'

The *BCP* marriage service explicitly rejects the validity of other forms of 'coupling'.

> so many as are coupled together otherwise than God's Word doth allow are not joined together by God; neither is their Matrimony lawful

It is important to note that *BCP* rejects the validity of those 'coupled together' *contrary to God's word*, not *contrary to Anglican forms*. It is not making the claim that only Anglican marriages are valid. Any marriage which conforms to

---

10 A similar idea is reflected in this prayer in the *BCP* marriage service:
O God, who by thy mighty power hast made all things of nothing; who also (after other things set in order) didst appoint, that out of man (created after thine own image and similitude) woman should take her beginning; and, knitting them together, didst teach that it should never be lawful to put asunder those whom thou by Matrimony hadst made one: O God, who hast consecrated the state of Matrimony to such an excellent mystery, that in it is signified and represented the spiritual marriage and unity betwixt Christ and his Church...

the principles outlined above—a voluntary, lifelong and exclusive union between a man and a woman reflecting God's purposes of marriage—is a marriage which is 'joined together by God'. This will include (for example) Jewish, Muslim and Buddhist weddings, and will also include civil marriages. This is the rationale for the liturgy for blessing a civil marriage, which has been released by the Liturgical Commission for trial use, as authorised locally by a Diocesan Bishop under s.4 of the Constitution.[11]

6. 'Pronouncing' and 'blessing' in God's name

The particular role of the minister in a *BCP* marriage (beyond that of officiant and witness) is to pronounce and bless in God's name. After the exchange of vows, the minister declares

> I pronounce that they be man and wife together, in the Name of the Father, and of the Son, and of the Holy Ghost.

This is followed by the following prayer:

> Send thy blessing upon these thy servants, this man and this woman, whom we bless in thy Name'

The pronouncement is a declaration that this couple has been validly joined together by God, and the blessing declares that this relationship is one which God blesses.

Implications of the *BCP* doctrine of marriage for same-sex unions

Based on the analysis above, the doctrine of marriage of the *Book of Common Prayer* is that marriage is the voluntary union of one man

---

[11] The service is available at https://www.anglican.org.au/data/Blessing_of_a_Civil_Marriage.pdf. General Synod resolution 114/10, 'welcomes the resources issued by the Liturgy Commission in 2007–2010, and commends them to the Anglican Church of Australia for use and response'.

and one woman arising from mutual promises of lifelong faithfulness. According to *BCP*, God instituted marriage for a threefold purpose. *BCP* understands marriage to be a covenant between a husband and a wife, voluntarily entered into by the public exchange of vows. *BCP* views marriage as 'God's ordinance' for all humanity, as the pattern of relationship established by God from the beginning, and normative for all human 'coupling' relationships that are valid in his sight.

The man/woman nature of marriage is a principle—and not merely a practice—of the doctrine of marriage in *BCP*. Marriage is understood in *BCP* to be the continuing expression of the form of relationship established by God between Adam and Eve (cf. Gen 1:27, 2:18; 2:23–25), and as affirmed by Jesus in Matthew 19. *BCP* understands complementary sexes to be of the essence of marriage.

By virtue of section 4 of the Constitution, this doctrine of marriage arising from the *Book of Common Prayer* is the doctrine of marriage of the Anglican Church of Australia. Because the man/woman principle is fundamental to marriage in *BCP*, a new form of service for 'same-sex marriage' would 'contravene [a] principle of doctrine' of the formularies, unless the doctrine of our Church were to be explicitly changed to allow same-sex marriage.

Can our doctrine of marriage be changed to allow same-sex marriage?

This essay has left open the question as to the doctrine of marriage arising from the 'commands', 'doctrine' and 'discipline' of Christ, and the 'rule and standard of faith' with respect to marriage as established by 'the canonical scriptures'. The answer to this question will determine whether same-sex marriage is *inconsistent* with the Fundamental Declarations (i.e., level 1 doctrine). If this were to be the case, then there is no way to change the Fundamental

Declarations in sections 1–3 to allow same-sex marriage, by virtue of section 66:[12]

> This Church takes no power under this Constitution to alter sections one, two and three and this section other than the name of this Church.

However, even leaving open the level 1 doctrine question, it is clear from the analysis above that the solemnisation of a same-sex marriage would 'contravene [a] principle of doctrine or worship' of the formularies (i.e., level 2 doctrine), and so is currently prohibited by Section 4 of the Constitution. In order to change section 4 to remove this prohibition, it would be necessary to follow the procedure in section 67(1)(c), which requires 'of a majority of the members of each house' together with 'three quarters of the diocesan synods of this Church including all of the metropolitan sees have assented to it by ordinance and all such assents be in force at the same time'.

It would then be necessary to pass a Canon of General Synod to authorise a form of service for same-sex marriage. This would be a Canon touching the 'ritual, ceremonial or discipline of the church', and therefore would need to follow the special bill procedures, which require the support of at least two thirds of each house in 2 successive synods.

Changing the doctrine of marriage? Divorce as a case study

Our constitutional arrangements are very different from those Anglican churches which have changed their doctrine of marriage. Our Constitution makes it very difficult to change any 'doctrine' (so defined).

Divorce provides an important case study for exploring the

---

12 Technically, it could be changed by concurrent Acts of Parliament to amend ss.1–3 of each province's *Anglican Church of Australia Constitution Act 1961*.

process and limits of change, in as much that there has been a significant change in practice in our church (though not, as we shall see, a change in doctrine) in relation to remarriage after divorce.

Under the Canons of 1603, remarriage after divorce was precluded while a former spouse remained alive. This changed for Australian Anglicans in 1985. The relevant Canon of 1603 was repealed, and the *Marriage of Divorced Persons Canon 1985* came into effect, allowing the remarriage of a divorcee where the Bishop of a diocese has given consent.

The General Synod was competent to pass this canon because it was 'not inconsistent' with the principles of doctrine in the *BCP* marriage service. As noted above, the doctrine of marriage of *BCP* is that marriage is the voluntary union of one man and one woman arising from mutual promises of lifelong faithfulness. However, the *BCP* wedding service does not address the situation where there has been a subsequent failure by one spouse to 'forsake all others... so long as ye both shall live'. Does adultery (or abandonment) by one spouse bring the marriage covenant to an end, and thereby leave the 'innocent' spouse free to remarry? The doctrine of marriage in *BCP* does not answer this question, because the wedding service is concerned with what creates a marriage, not what terminates it. To put this another way, the *BCP* wedding service has a doctrine of marriage, but no doctrine of divorce.

Although it now allows remarriage after divorce, the *Marriage of Divorced Persons Canon 1985* has not altered the 'doctrine' of marriage of our Church. Clause 4 limits the power of the bishop as follows (emphasis added).

> Consent shall not be given by a bishop under this canon unless the bishop and the proposed celebrant are satisfied that the marriage of the divorced person would not contravene the **teachings of Holy Scripture** or the **doctrines and principles of this Church**.

The highlighted words recognise the limits imposed by section 4 of the Constitution. This clause only allows divorce where it is consistent with the 'teachings of Holy Scripture'—e.g., adultery (Matt 19:9) and abandonment (1 Cor 7:15)—and where it is consistent with the (unchanged) 'doctrines and principles of this Church.' It would be constitutionally invalid for a Canon to purport to authorise—or for a Bishop to permit—divorce in circumstances which contravene the teachings of Holy Scripture or the doctrines and principles of this Church.

Other ways forward?

Given that, for the reasons outlined above, it would be very difficult for the doctrine of our Church to be changed, would it be possible to leave the doctrine and liturgy of 'holy matrimony' unchanged, but create a new liturgy to bless a civil same-sex marriage? For example, would it be possible to adapt the trial-use 'Blessing of a Civil Marriage' liturgy for use by same-sex couples?

The short answer is 'No'. This is because the *BCP* marriage service expressly 'covers the field' of marriage-like relationships—'so many as are coupled together otherwise than God's Word doth allow are not joined together by God'. This leaves no scope for validating other forms of 'coupling together'. We have already concluded that *BCP* understands that marriage being between a man and a woman is a principle of the doctrine of marriage, and so to declare a blessing upon two people in a same-sex marriage on the basis that it is a valid marriage in the sight of God is to contravene this principle.

What about a service that 'blesses' the same-sex relationship, but does not purport to recognise the relationship as something marriage-like'? The answer to this question depends on another question—does God bless the sexual union of a same-sex couple, or is this a form of '[coupling] together otherwise than God's Word doth allow'? This question—especially as it relates to 'blessing'—will be explored in subsequent essays, and it would be premature to prejudge the answer here. If 'God's word doth allow' a same-sex coupling, then the General Synod has power to pass a canon to authorise a service for the blessing of a same-sex 'relationship' (though not a same-sex 'marriage'). But if God's word 'doth NOT allow' same-sex coupling, then a form of service that purports to declare God's blessing on the couple would be both *inconsistent* with the Fundamental Declarations and *contravene* the Ruling Principles of the Constitution.

A response:
An alternative reading of BCP

Matthew Anstey[1]

On the Interpretation of *BCP*

I am grateful for Michael's detailed study of the *BCP* and more broadly on our Constitution and formularies. With respect to his 'commentary' on the 'the doctrine of marriage arising from the *BCP*', I am in broad agreement with all of his points except point 5, where Michael proposes that the endorsement of heterosexual marriage in the *BCP* entails the rejection of same-sex marriage. Michael's argument can thus be stated in this way: *the BCP endorses heterosexual marriage only*.

But does in fact the affirmation of heterosexual marriage in the *BCP* entail the prohibition of same-sex marriage? I would argue that it does not, as I do also in my chapter on 'The Case for Same-Sex Marriage'. The affirmation of one does not warrant the negation of the other. That is, I argue instead that *the BCP endorses only heterosexual marriage*.

I put forward here four interrelated arguments:

---

[1] The Rev'd Associate Professor Matthew Anstey is a Research Fellow of the Public and Contextual Theology Strategic Research Centre of Charles Sturt University, an Honorary Visiting Fellow at The University of Adelaide and a priest in the Anglican Diocese of Adelaide.

1. Given that homosexual marriage was not a legal option at the time, and that the very possibility of a doctrine of same-sex marriage was not in the thoughts of the church at the time, the *BCP* doctrine of marriage should be taken as pertaining only to 'the *BCP* doctrine of heterosexual marriage'. There is no evidence that same-sex marriage was under consideration in the *BCP* liturgy.
2. Accordingly, the restriction in the liturgy, on which Michael's point 5 is based, namely, 'For be ye well assured, that so many as are coupled together otherwise than God's Word doth allow are not joined together by God; neither is their Matrimony lawful' pertains only to heterosexual marriage. That is, same-sex couples cannot be joined together in heterosexual marriage. We could indeed state that the same prohibition should be operative for same-sex marriage, namely, that opposite sex couples cannot be joined together in same-sex marriage.
3. Michael argues this prohibition rules out same-sex marriage because it only allows what 'God's Word doth allow'. However, those affirming same-sex marriage believe such is allowed by God's word, as argued in a number of essays in this book.
4. The liturgical location of the paragraph containing 'coupled together otherwise' is in the priest's address to the specific couple being married, and has in its intent that this (heterosexual) marriage is legitimate. It is worth quoting at length:

And also, speaking unto the persons that shall be married, he shall say,

I REQUIRE and charge you both, as ye will answer at the dreadful day of judgement, when the secrets of all hearts shall be disclosed, that if either of you know any impediment, why ye may not be lawfully joined together in Matrimony, ye do now confess it. For be ye well assured, that so many as are coupled together otherwise than God's Word doth allow are not joined together by God; neither is their Matrimony lawful.

At which day of Marriage, if any man do allege and declare any impediment, why they may not be coupled together in Matrimony, by God's law, or the laws of this Realm; and will be bound, and sufficient sureties with him, to the parties; or else put in a caution (to the full value of such charges as the persons to be married do thereby sustain) to prove his allegation: then the solemnization must be deferred, until such time as the truth be tried.

Again, this restriction should not be read as pertaining to all forms of coupling, because the liturgical (and legal no less) intent is to ensure that this couple can be legally married and in accord with Scripture (that is, not siblings, not already married, and so forth).

Thus for these reasons, I submit that the *BCP* supports the doctrine of heterosexual marriage and that its rationale, Scriptural warrant, and liturgical forms are written to this end. But its scope does not extend to same-sex marriage. This was neither intended nor even imagined as a possibility.

To put it succinctly, Michael argues that *BCP* endorses heterosexual marriage only but I argue that *BCP* endorses only heterosexual marriage.

On the Canonical Options

Again, I agree with not only much of Michael's interpretation of *BCP*, but also with much of his account the legal processes necessary to instigate changes, notwithstanding future clarifications our church might receive from the Church Law Commission and/or the Appellate Tribunal on these matters.

I wish to present this however in a different manner to Michael, by distinguishing what I believe are the three most plausible and possible (and theologically defensible) forms of change for us to consider. I propose to distinguish these through using three distinct verbal phrases (and their concomitant liturgical expressions and legal statuses), namely **the blessing of the relationship, the recognition of the covenantal relationship**, and **the solemnisation of the marriage.**

Again, in agreement with Michael, each of these three options would require agreement by Synod that each is 'allowed by God's word'.

Let me now explain each option.

1. ***The blessing by the ACA of the relationship*** of a same-sex couple married under law

In this option, a General Synod Canon would institute a liturgy for the blessing of a same-sex couple already married under state law.

This option offers a crucial difference to the next two options from a procedural perspective: if the Canon authorises blessing of a same-sex relationship in a manner that does not entail that it is blessing it as a marriage (or, that it states it explicitly that it is not blessing the relationship as a marriage), General Synod could pass such a Canon without requiring Constitutional change.

2. ***The recognition by the ACA of the covenantal union*** of a same-sex couple married under law

In this option, the couple would, as in the first option, need to be married already under state law. They could then seek liturgical recognition of their union before God and God's people, if such were to be provided for by the ACA. Such an approach is common in Europe, where it goes something like this: every married couple must be and can only be married by the State. Christian couples can thereafter (and this can be years later) have their union recognised in a church in a ceremony. This ceremony has no legal status but provides for Christians a public Christian rite for the recognition of the relationship before God.

This second option for the ACA however would be a variation on the European one, in that ministers could still solemnise heterosexual marriages. (And furthermore, Synod could also decide to cease its solemnisation of heterosexual marriages altogether and thus follow the European model fully.)

According to Michael's analysis, this option would require Constitutional change as per section 67(1)(c). It might be the case however that legal advice determines that this second option could be achieved as per the first option.

3. **The solemnisation by the ACA of the marriage** of a same-sex couple

In this option, the couple would be married under state law through the solemnisation of their marriage by an authorised minister of the Anglican Church of Australia. So it would be legally identical to our current role in marrying couples according the rites of the Anglican Church of Australia, as Australian law only has one type of marriage, which is between two people.

That would not preclude however the preparation of a liturgy for the solemnisation of same-sex marriage, different to that for heterosexual marriage, with distinctive Scriptural texts, prefaces and so forth for this particular form of marriage. Further consideration of the sacramental nature of same-sex marriage would need to be undertaken (as this is not discussed at all in this set of essays).

According to Michael's analysis, this would require Constitutional change as per section 67(1)(c).

SCRIPTURE AND HERMENEUTICS

Scripture and Moral Reasoning

Matthew Anstey[1]

Introduction

I have always loved Scripture, from the first time I read right through the Bible at age ten, through to twelve years of full-time tertiary study, majoring in Biblical Hebrew linguistics, and then onto seventeen-plus years of teaching Biblical studies and languages, including the supervising of many honours and doctoral students. Not only have the stories and the poetry always fascinated me, they continue to shape my life, posing new questions, unsettling old assumptions. I have literally given almost my entire life to pondering the Scriptures, because God as revealed in Christ through the Spirit is in my bones and in this Book.

It is due to this lifetime of immersion that I have come to the position I have on same-sex marriage (chapter 17), and the view of Scripture articulated herein. The reader will see that the lived experience of God's people past and present also figures prominently in both essays, because the Scriptures themselves are a testimony to such experience, in all its evocative calligraphy, sprawled across millennia of cultures and languages, inked through dark stretches

---

[1] The Rev'd Associate Professor Matthew Anstey is a Research Fellow of the Public and Contextual Theology Strategic Research Centre of Charles Sturt University, an Honorary Visiting Fellow at The University of Adelaide and a priest in the Anglican Diocese of Adelaide.

of God's aching silence to irruptions into our lives of that word from God we are unable to say ourselves: 'Today, I have set you free'.

So, I hope the reader has some sense of where I am coming from, as we now turn our minds to the weighty matters before us.

On our current context

The Anglican Church of Australia, like many church denominations around the world, is evaluating its doctrinal position on same-sex marriage. The fact that such evaluation is occurring, and books such as this are being written, speaks to the reality that the church is able to perceive and discern though the Spirit 'the work of God in the world and "decide for God" in response to such discernment'.[2]

That is, the church is doing what it has always done (and what Israel has always done)—being the people of God living out our faith in each historical moment and context, seeking to be faithful to our God, and to be 'response-able', able to respond using our God-given faculties of decision-making, rationality, argument, and reflection, under the guidance of the Spirit.

In this journey, there have been tumultuous upheavals. It is hard to surpass the upheaval of the inclusion of the Gentiles, and the story of this as told in Acts 10–15 especially illustrates precisely my point. As Peter puts it:

> As I looked at it closely I saw four-footed animals, beasts of prey, reptiles, and birds of the air. I also heard a voice saying to me, 'Get up, Peter; kill and eat.' But I replied, 'By no means, Lord; for nothing profane or unclean has ever entered my mouth.' But a second time the voice answered from heaven, 'What God has made clean, you must not call profane.' This happened three times; then everything was pulled up again to heaven. At that very moment three men, sent

---

[2] L. T. Johnson, *The Revelatory Body: Theology as Inductive Art*, (Grand Rapids, MI: Eerdmans, 2015), 17.

to me from Caesarea, arrived at the house where we were. The Spirit told me to go with them and not to make a distinction between them and us. (Acts 11:6–12)

Though this upheaval was tumultuous and its implications far-reaching, there has been no shortage of equally disruptive shifts in the history of the church. It took the church 400 years or thereabouts to settle on its credal affirmations on the Trinitarian nature of God. It took the church 1,500 years for the idea that salvation is the free gift of God to become front and centre to the church's understanding of redemption. It took the church (a staggering) 1,900 years to discern that slavery is nowhere and never the will of God. It took the church and society no less a staggering—one can hardly overstate this—1,950 years give or take to assert the full equality of men and women, notwithstanding that we still must struggle with these issues today in many places.

As a not unimportant aside, this observation of *la longue durée* is important for our current debate, because opponents of same-sex marriage frequently appeal to 'the traditional view of marriage' as if its long shelf-life ought to mean that a change is unlikely to be right (the weight here being on 'traditional'). But this cuts the other way clearly: holding a view for a long time offers no guarantee that the next generation will continue so to do. Hence the longevity of an established position is moot—what matters is how we discern the way forward, to which I now turn.

On the role of Scripture

When the church debates its doctrinal position, there are passionate advocates on each side and passionate appeals to Scripture. Under analysis, it is clear that *the role* Scripture plays in the debate is where the most important differences lie. Hence this volume contains two essays on the role of Scripture, as we seek to interrogate the role Scripture plays in the discernment of the Anglican Church of Australia in its decision regarding the doctrine of same-sex marriage.

Let me be clear about my view from the outset: *Scripture shows us how the people of God come to make moral and theological judgments, rather than providing the substantive content of those judgments.* Hence to be faithful to Scripture in this debate (as in all debates) does not mean we *exegete from Scripture and apply to lived human experience a timeless moral-doctrinal precept* (and such a so-called 'excavative' approach is adopted by opponents to same-sex marriage in this volume), but rather we seek to make our case for the doctrinal position we are arguing *in dialogue with both Scripture and lived human experience*.[3] I propose furthermore that such an approach accords with Scripture itself.[4]

My argument in this essay follows largely the trajectory of Luke Timothy Johnson's *The Revelatory Body: Theology as Inductive Art*, not because it is novel to him (in fact, such an approach to Scripture is common), but because I find his presentation especially cogent and compelling. So, in his words, the role of Scripture is

---

3   Johnson, *The Revelatory Body*, states it this way: 'Scripture ... points readers to the human body as the preeminent place of God's self-disclosure' (38).

4   I dislike the term 'revisionist' to describe those in favour of same-sex marriage because such a revisionist approach often still assumes an excavative perspective, namely, revisionists 'excavate' from Scripture a doctrine affirming of same-sex marriage. A number of scholars who affirm same-sex marriage take this route, such as Branson and Achtemeier. This is not my approach, because I take issue with the notion that it is desirable (let alone coherent) 'to find out what Scripture teaches' on X. For elaborations of the problems with, and the historical origins of, the excavative approach, see Elisabeth Schüssler Fiorenza, *Democratizing Biblical Studies: Toward an Emancipatory Educational Space*, (Louisville, KY: Westminster John Knox, 2009); Susanne Scholz, *The Bible as Political Artifact: On the Feminist Study of the Hebrew Bible*, (Minneapolis, MN: Fortress Press, 2017), and Mark Brett, *Political Trauma and Healing: Biblical Ethics for a Postcolonial World*,(Grand Rapids, MI: William B. Eerdmans, 2016).

summarised thus: 'Scripture is best understood, not as containing revelation, but as participating in revelation'.[5]

On the diversity of Scripture

The Bible, like all areas of life and art and the church, is marked by diversity and differences of views from beginning to end. Diversity is, it seems, part and parcel of the way the world is and it is a helpful way to enter this debate.

In Scripture we are struck by this from the outset with two creation accounts, the first being Genesis 1:1–2:3 and the second Genesis 2:4–25. They differ in a great number of ways. The first occurs over six days, the second has no timeframe. The first is set 'everywhere' and the second in a particular location in the Middle East. The first has man and woman made together on Day Six, the second has the man interacting with God first, and then the woman is made subsequently (and differently). The first ends with the focus on the Sabbath, the second on the man and woman 'leaving and cleaving'. The first has the pronouncement 'it was good' as a core theological assertion and the second early on states 'it was not good for the man to be alone'. Many scholars believe that the first is written by the so-called Priestly School and the second by the so-called Yahwist (who might be an individual, or a School). And so on go the differences.

Such a presentation of two accounts of the same story, or two different views on the same matter, is ubiquitous in the Bible. Here

---

[5] *Ibid*, p. 38. He has published a number of important related papers on this approach, most importantly *Scripture & Discernment: Decision Making in the Church*, (Nashville: Abingdon Press, 1996).

is a small OT sample for consideration, presented in abbreviated form:[6]

1. The Deuteronomists' theology (see Deut 28) is built around the notion of 'if you obey God, God will bless you, if you don't God will curse you'. The Book of Job torpedoes this theological approach by telling the story of Job who obeys God and yet is cursed. The story is not simply about Job; it is a critique of the Deuteronomistic theology.
2. The Deuteronomists centralised worship in Jerusalem (Deut 12) but other traditions state that God's people can worship anywhere they wish.
3. Ezra-Nehemiah ostensibly advocate ethnic purity, especially with regards to marriage. Yet inter-racial marriage is alive and well in the Old Testament (Ruth!).
4. Deuteronomy states: 'I the Lord your God am a jealous God, punishing children for the iniquity of parents, to the third and fourth generation of those who reject me, but showing steadfast love to the thousandth generation of those who love me and keep my commandments' (Deut 5:9–10), but Ezekiel explicitly argues against this: 'The person who sins shall die. A child shall not suffer for the iniquity of a parent, nor a parent suffer for the iniquity of a child; the

---

[6] For a full treatment of the diversity of views in the Old Testament, I recommend Walter Brueggemann, *Theology of the Old Testament: Testimony, Dispute, Advocacy*, (Minneapolis: Fortress Press, 1997). From a systematic theology perspective, I recommend David Kelsey, *Eccentric Existence: A Theological Anthropology* (Louisville, KY: Westminster John Knox Press, 2009) for his masterful engagement with Scripture in the formulation of theology. At a more accessible level, Peter Enns has written a great deal on this topic, see, *How the Bible Actually Works: In Which I Explain How an Ancient, Ambiguous, and Diverse Book Leads Us to Wisdom Rather Than Answers—and Why That's Great News.* (New York: HarperOne, 2019).

righteousness of the righteous shall be his own, and the wickedness of the wicked shall be his own' (Ezek 18:20).
5. Joshua presents the settlement of the Promised Land as a large-scale, relatively successful military-style takeover, but Judges presents it as a fraught, piece-meal, relatively unsuccessful dispersion.
6. Exodus 33:20 states that no one can see God's face, yet earlier in the same chapter (v. 11) it says God spoke to Moses 'face-to-face'.
7. The Day of the Lord is presented as a day of warfare and bloodshed in many texts, and yet as a day of cosmic peace in others. This is starkly represented by two texts that are inverse to each other: Isa 2:4 '...they shall beat their swords into ploughshares, and their spears into pruning-hooks; nation shall not lift up sword against nation, neither shall they learn war any more' versus Joel 3:10, 'Beat your ploughshares into swords, and your pruning-hooks into spears'.

For the New Testament, we have an equally significant list of differences, such as those found in the Gospels, between the Gospels and Paul's writings, and between Paul's writings and the so-called Catholic Epistles.

These differences are not skin-deep, so attempts to minimise or harmonise them not only do a disservice to the texts themselves but they miss the point entirely, namely, that the different theological traditions in the Old and New Testaments *is what characterises* the Scriptures; it is part and parcel of its gift to us.

We see in fact diversity and creativity in every dimension of human endeavour. God grants humanity the ability and no less the responsibility to shape the world in which we live for its well-being, and continues so to do despite our abject failures at such. So in every area, we are on a constant journey of discovery, learning, study, to better understand the world, to address the problems of the world, and to contribute to the future of the world.

The theological rationale for this is located in the freedom and love of God, who as Creator has gifted us with dignity and freedom, through the Spirit. The theological task of discerning the moral rightness or wrongness of same-sex marriage is analogous to the task of investigating the properties of water dynamics, or of seeking a cure for cancer, or in writing a symphony, or so on, in that they all require the full engagement of human rationality and creativity.

On the necessity of lived experience

Diversity in and of itself though does not make the case for the role I am arguing that Scripture should play, though it is not insignificant.

Rather, it is understanding its testimony to God's engagement with the world that is significant. Scripture testifies without hesitation that God is alive and present and engaged with God's world in the midst of our lives through the Spirit. The word of God is spoken not only through Scripture but in and through human experience (a reality that our Pentecostal sisters and brothers have rightly brought back into focus). As Johnson puts it: 'The world of Scripture is one that is answerable to God at every moment; it is a world in which God acts intimately and graciously within creation, above all within the freedom of those created according to the image of God.'[7] The early church's struggle with Gentile inclusion (Acts 10–15) was guided in the end by the undeniable reality of God's Spirit at work in the lives of the Gentiles.

Such recognition of God through the Spirit in our lived experience has throughout history always been the impetus for the re-evaluation of our doctrine. It was the stories coming out

---

7   Johnson, *The Revelatory Body*, 46.

of Nazi Germany that prompted a radical rethink of Christian attitudes to Judaism; it was the stories of the oppression of slaves, of women, of indigenous people, and so forth, that has led to changing in our doctrinal views on these matters. Or in recent years, the contribution to theology by people with disabilities has led to very significant changes in our theology of disability.[8] And very recently, it is the stories of children suffering childhood sexual abuse that have led to changes in the doctrine of confession in the Anglican Church of Australia in 2017.

In each of these cases, it was not exegesis of Scripture that led to the changes; rather, it was the testimony of those on the inside, those affected by the issues, be they faithful members of the church or not. In the debate on slavery, ultimately there was 'the recognition that no matter what Scripture says, owning persons cannot be compatible with the mind of Christ'.[9] Johnson goes on to counter those who might understand this is a rejection of Scripture:

> Rereading and reinterpreting Scripture in the light of human experience that at first appears to be dissonant with Scripture—finding texts that formerly were not seen, discovering new dimensions of commonly read passages, relativising those texts that do not accord with God's new work—is not a form of disloyalty to Scripture. To the contrary, it is loyalty of the highest sort, for it is driven by the conviction that Scripture truly is God-inspired, truly does speak God's word to humans, when it is passionately and patiently engaged by those listening for God's word as well in human experience.[10]

Further below, I will address the specific condemnation of

---

[8] See S. Clifton, *Crippled Grace: Disability, Virtue Ethics, and the Good Life* (Waco, Texas: Baylor University Press, 2018) and Amos Yong, *Theology and Down Syndrome: Reimagining Disability in Late Modernity*, (Waco: Baylor University Press, 2007).

[9] Johnson, *The Revelatory Body*, 50.

[10] Johnson, *The Revelatory Body*, 50.

homosexuality in the Scriptures, but first I wish to further elaborate the role Scripture plays in the formation of our moral judgments.

On moral reasoning and Scripture

At the outset, I put my thesis in this way: *Scripture shows us how the people of God come to make moral and theological judgments, rather than providing the substantive content of those judgments.*

Clear evidence of this is found in the stories and parables found in the Bible. If we limit ourselves just to the stories of Genesis, we find almost a total absence of moral judgment by the narrator. Even stories that cry out for comment, such as the binding of Isaac (Genesis 22), the rape of Dinah (Genesis 34), Hagar's expulsion into the desert (Genesis 16), Jacob's wrestling at Jabbok (Genesis 32), Judah and Tamar (Genesis 38), are notable for their absence of anything like 'And so the moral of the story is...'. In fact, many stories remain morally ambiguous and deeply confronting:

- Does Abraham really tie up his teenage son and draw his knife to sacrifice him? (Genesis 22)
- Does Jacob really not consider anything other than his own well-being when confronted with news of the rape of his own daughter? (Gen 34:30)[11]
- Does Jacob actually wrestle with God skin-on-skin and survive? (Gen 22:28)[12]

---

11 See further M. Anstey, 'Remembering Dinah: Genesis 34,' *St Mark's Review* (2004) 197:31–35.

12 See further M. Anstey, 'Scriptural Reminiscence and Narrative Gerontology: Jacob's Wrestling with the Unknown (Genesis 32),' in E. MacKinlay (ed.), *Ageing, Disability and Spirituality: Addressing the Challenge of Disability in Later Life*, (London: Jessica Kingsley, 2008), 106–117.

- Does the angel of YHWH really tell Hagar to return to a situation of family violence? (Gen 16:9)[13]
- How does it make sense for Judah to declare Tamar righteous after she engaged in prostitution with him? (Genesis 38)

Biblical stories frequently present moral and doctrinal dilemmas in significant tension with other parts of Scripture. As Rabbi Burton Visotsky, who more than most scholars demonstrates how the texts facilitate the development of moral judgment rather than provide the content for such judgments, so lucidly puts it:

> Read simply, in fact, Genesis is an ugly little soap opera about a dysfunctional family. Four generations of that family dynasty are charted, their foibles exposed and all the dirty laundry, as it were, hung out in public for millions to see. It is a story about rape, incest, murder, deception, brute force, sex, and blood lust. The plotlines and characterizations of Genesis are so crude as to call into serious question how this book became and remained a sacred canonical text for two thousand years and more.[14]

Let me conclude though with one of the very few stories in the Old Testament which does have a narratorial moral comment, albeit placed in the mouth the villain of the story (itself a provocative literary feature). Judges 19 tells the shocking story of an unnamed concubine, whose master, a Levite no less, offers her up to be raped and beaten all night to strangers, in place of the virgin daughter of the household where he is visiting (and, yes, such a story really is in sacred Scripture).

The story concludes:

> In the morning her master [the Levite] got up, opened the doors of

---

13 See further M. Anstey, 'Seeing Hagar the Theologian: The Interpretation of Genesis 16,' in G. Garrett (ed), *'Into the World you Love': Encountering God in Everyday Life*, (Hindmarsh: ATF Press., 2007), 17–35.

14 B. Visotsky, *The Genesis of Ethics: How the Tormented Family of Genesis Leads us to Moral Development* (New York: New Rivers Press, 1996).

the house, and when he went out to go on his way, there was his concubine lying at the door of the house, with her hands on the threshold. 'Get up,' he said to her, 'we are going.' But there was no answer. Then he put her on the donkey; and the man set out for his home. When he had entered his house, he took a knife, and grasping his concubine he cut her into twelve pieces, limb by limb, and sent her throughout all the territory of Israel. Then he commanded the men whom he sent, saying, 'Thus shall you say to all the Israelites, "Has such a thing ever happened since the day that the Israelites came up from the land of Egypt until this day? Consider it, take counsel, and speak out."' (Judg 19:27–30)

What is especially distressing about this story is in the details: that her hands are 'on the threshold', depicting her desperate attempt to flee from the rapists, that her master stumbles over her, not noticing at first she is even there on the ground, and most shocking of all, that the narrator notes only that she fails to answer, not that she is dead, suggesting she might have been dismembered alive. Little comfort comes from the next chapter in which we read that the Levite says otherwise: 'she was raped and died' (Judg 20:5; Then again, should we believe him?)

And then, a final comment, which an astute reader will take as addressed to the reader rather than those in the storyworld: 'Consider it, take counsel, and speak out' (NRSV). The readers (as the verbs are all plural 'you') here are enjoined to consider this story together and speak out. Clearly the people of God, in choosing to include this story in the canon, judged it as important for the well-being of the community. Thank God that they did, and that they retained the stories above, and so many other difficult stories.

And the point is this: Scripture itself, here and as shown above, leaves the reader with little guidance. The stories are not told so as to convey a moral precept but to evoke and provoke reflection in ways that lead to moral development. And in this one story where the narrator does subtly comment, we are asked to figure it out amongst ourselves and then to share our reflections (note that to whom we are to speak, and about what, and for what ends, and so forth, is left unspecified). Many of Jesus' parables are like this—the point is in the theological conversations they generate rather than any particular propositional content to be conveyed (otherwise, we could just have propositions and no stories or parables).

Johnson's central argument is not only that the stories are told in such a way as to leave moral discernment to the reader, but in such a way that repeatedly gives witness to God's presence in the lives of people, experienced in ways that lead to a re-evaluation of our view on God and God's work in the world.

On the Scriptures concerning homosexuality

I have made the case that Scripture does not provide the content of our doctrinal and moral judgments, but rather testifies to the way the people of God go about making such judgments in the light of God's ongoing presence in the lives of God's people and the world. Thus we are now able to address the elephant in the room: the seven or so Scriptural texts on homosexuality, all of which depict it as sinful. It is difficult in my view to read them otherwise.[15]

---

15   So in this, I follow W. Loader, *The New Testament on Sexuality*, (Grand Rapids: Eerdmans, 2012) who affirms homosexuality but argues the Scriptures do not. When I say 'very difficult', I do think there is a case for arguing that the actual sort of same-sex relationship we are considering in the twenty-first century is outside the purview of the Scriptural authors, but equally, we must admit that the Scriptural authors might well have been just as condemning of these, were they a reality in their time.

Again, Johnson is characteristically forthright:

> I think it important to state clearly that we do [with regard to homosexuality], in fact, reject the straightforward commands of Scripture, and appeal instead to another authority when we declare that same-sex unions can be holy and good. And what exactly is that authority? We appeal explicitly to the weight of our own experience and the experience thousands of others have witnessed to, which tells us that to claim our own sexual orientation is in fact to accept the way in which God has created us. By so doing, we explicitly reject as well the premises of the scriptural statements condemning homosexuality—namely, that it is a vice freely chosen, a symptom of human corruption, and disobedience to God's created order.[16]

Thus affirming same-sex marriage in my view is not to dismiss Scripture but indeed the opposite, to take it with the utmost seriousness. The rationale for our rejection of the view espoused in these seven texts is grounded then in Scripture itself, in its witness to Christ and the nature of God, and in its taking with the utmost seriousness the testimony of the presence of God in the lives of God's people. We are thus *not* rejecting the word of God, but discerning and embracing the word of God.

And even if these seven texts were all in lavish praise of homosexuality, extolling its virtues, that too would not determine our moral judgment on the matter. (For the Scriptures do not condemn slavery, yet we must do so.) What matters always is that we make a coherent and cogent case to discern the mind of Christ on each issue. I find this liberating – to engage deeply in Scripture and the experiences of God in our lives, in order to arrive at a theologically coherent and morally defensible position.

---

16   https://www.commonwealmagazine.org/homosexuality-church-0.

Finally, I wish to comment on method: many of those opposed to same-sex marriage claim that approaches such as mine view and interpret Scripture in a way that is (radically) different from theirs. I dispute such an accusation; I would submit that both approaches are essentially the same (and so then, their claim to be 'following the clear teaching of Scripture alone' is not true in practice).

I encourage the reader to consider this for themselves, by reflecting upon the ways in which both sides present their arguments in this book: is it not the case that each of us puts forward in much the same way a rational, coherent, moral-doctrinal argument, with reference to Scripture, tradition, and experience? I strongly believe that this is the case, and I state this clearly because I will never accept the claim that the position I am advocating requires abandoning the Scriptures.

Conclusion

For the matter before us, I am arguing that to be faithful to Scripture means to engage in a considered conversation about the doctrine of same-sex marriage, taking Scripture with the utmost seriousness as a witness as to how the people of God undertake such discernment. This requires listening to how God's people have responded to (new) manifestations of God's presence in their lives, so as to discern together the mind of Christ on this issue. And clearly, the lived experience of gay and lesbian Christians is paramount to our deliberations.

In sum, in the light of God's full revelation, our responsibility is to discern what is compatible with the mind of Christ. (It is to this end that my other essay in this volume is directed.)

Or to put it the way Scripture does in the most haunting of all its texts:

Let us consider it, take counsel, and speak out.

Attentively Reading Scripture

Mark D Thompson[1]

The Success of the Written Word

Most of our communication, including our written communication, succeeds. When I leave an affectionate note for my beloved on the dining room table, or send a quick email to a work colleague, or draft a chapter for a book, I do so with the quiet confidence that those who read my work will understand what I have written. And they do, most of the time. That does not mean it is impossible to be misunderstood. Nor does it mean that every writer writes clearly enough to be understood. However, it is important to acknowledge at the outset, with the evidence of experience, that most of the time most of what we write is accessible to most of those who read it. What is more, where a lack of familiarity with the subject matter, the use of overly technical language, or a particular writing style makes reading more difficult, these are rarely ever insuperable barriers. A little background research and the use of a dictionary enables progress to be made. I write this chapter confident that what I am endeavouring to convey will in fact be conveyed.

Nevertheless, it is possible to misread or, we might say, to read

---

[1] The Rev'd Canon Dr Mark D Thompson is Principal of Moore College, Sydney and the head of its Department of Theology, Philosophy and Ethics. His doctorate was awarded by the University of Oxford. He is a Canon of St Andrew's Cathedral, Sydney.

against the grain of a text. This can be done for comic effect, as when a car manual is used to provide the lyrics for a familiar tune on a popular television program. It might be the result of a lack of vital information, e.g., what kind of literature are we reading? It might be through the neglect of vital information, i.e., the context of the passage being read—the words said immediately before these words or the rest of the story in which it is embedded. It might even be deliberate, as a reader seeks, for whatever reason, to subvert what is written in the text, e.g., seeking to look behind the text to what is not written. Misreading is possible but this does not overturn the simple fact that most of our written communication succeeds most of the time.

But what about Christian reading and, in particular, the reading of the Bible? On the face of it we might suggest that the plethora of commentaries and the variety of exegetical opinions on some biblical texts testifies to something much more complex. Some may conclude on this basis that the message of the Bible is not clear, or not clear on the subject being addressed at a particular point, and that, to some degree or other, guidance is necessary if the texts are to be read profitably and we are to approach anything like an exegetical consensus. However, such a conclusion is not the only conclusion we might reach in the light of this evidence, nor is it a necessary one. The variety in comment, interpretation and application might not arise from problems within the text at all. Nor need we conclude that the meaning of the biblical text (i.e., what God intends to communicate to us in these words) is beyond us and we are more likely to misread than to read as the Bible was intended to be read. Thomas Cranmer (1489–1556), a chief architect of the Protestant Church of England, wrote of those who were reluctant to read Scripture for fear of the danger of error or confusion. In Articles 6 and 20 of what would become the 39 Articles of Religion and in the first of his Homilies, *The Fruitful Exhortation to the Reading and Knowledge of Holy Scripture,* he provided what have good claim to be the foundational principles of a genuinely *Anglican* reading of Scripture.

> **Article VI:** Holy Scripture containeth all things necessary to salvation: so that whatsoever is not read therein, nor may be proved thereby, is not to be required of any man, that it should be believed as an article of the Faith, or be thought requisite or necessary to salvation ...[2]

> **Article XX:** The Church hath power to decree Rites or Ceremonies, and authority in Controversies of Faith: And yet it is not lawful for the Church to ordain any thing that is contrary to God's Word written, neither may it so expound one place of Scripture, that it be repugnant to another. Wherefore, although the Church be a witness and keeper of holy Writ, yet, as it ought not to decree any thing against the same, so besides the same ought it not to enforce any thing to be believed for necessity of Salvation.[3]

> **Homily 1:** And if you be afraid to fall into error by reading of holy Scripture, I shall shew you how you may read it without danger of error. Read it humbly with a meek and a lowly heart, to the intent you may glorify God, and not yourself, with the knowledge of it; and read it not without daily praying to God, that he would direct your reading to good effect; and take upon you to expound it no further than you can plainly understand it. For, as St. Augustine saith, the knowledge of holy Scripture is a great, large and high place, but the

---

2 'Thirty-nine Articles of Religion', in *The Book of Common Prayer* (Oxford: Oxford University Press, 1913), 704.
3 'Thirty-nine Articles of Religion', 712.

door is very low; so that the high and arrogant man cannot run in, but he must stoop low and humble himself that shall enter into it. Presumption and arrogancy is the mother of all error: and humility needeth to fear no error. For humility will only search to know the truth; it will search and will bring together one place with another; and, where it cannot find out the meaning, it will pray, it will ask of others that know, and will not presumptuously and rashly define any thing which it knoweth not. Therefore the humble man may search any truth boldly in the Scripture without any danger of error.[4]

The 39 Articles, which include an endorsement of the *Book of Homilies* (Article XXXV), remains the confessional document of Anglicanism, and so is included in The Constitution of the Anglican Church of Australia. The Articles provide us with a strong statement of the identity of Scripture as 'God's Word written', the final authority of biblical teaching, the boundary condition of recognising and honouring the coherence and unity of biblical teaching, and the stance of the reader: humility, prayerfulness, a concern for the glory of God, and restraint in exposition. What is particularly noteworthy is that these statements about Scripture and its use are richly theological. They relate this text and our use of it to the person and activity of God.

The Danger of a Non-Theological Account of Reading

While there has been a long history of serious reflection on the nature of Christian reading of the Bible, both prior to and following on from the Reformation, it has often been construed in philosophical rather than theological terms. The genuinely human and therefore creaturely dimension of the text has been taken as a cue that the reading

---

[4] *Certain Sermons or Homilies Appointed to be Read in Churches* (repr. London: SPCK, 1864), 7.

of Scripture is a subset of a much wider practice of reading.[5] Other non-theological factors are allowed to set the character and trajectory of the task in a way which has eclipsed the God-breathed and so Spirit-attended character of this text and the specifically theological factors which are its proper ground and explanation. In this, much modern biblical hermeneutics stands in some contrast to the confidence and theological preoccupation of Cranmer's articles and homily.

Too often the result of this has been a subtle shift in what is in fact the final authority in matters of faith and practice. Historical reconstruction, sometimes plausible, sometimes not, and sometimes without sufficient evidentiary warrant, can be treated as determinative when it comes to the meaning of a text. In extreme cases, this appeal to a history beyond the text can be used to circumvent what is actually in the text. A speculative reconstruction of precisely what was going on in the church at Rome or Ephesus, or indeed in the mind of the apostle, becomes a final authority in understanding what Paul wrote in his letter to the Romans or to the Ephesians or to Timothy. In such a light, what is actually written might be qualified beyond recognition or even overturned, without realising that this process has in effect undermined the authority of 'God's Word written'. Each biblical text does indeed have a historical location, but the history that is necessary for understanding a biblical text is in the text. We ought to be very wary of appeals to circumstances or attitudes of the apostle Paul, for instance, which are not explicit in the text of his epistles and which have the effect of discounting or overturning what *is* actually written there.

Strangely, an analysis and application of contemporary literary

---

5   See J. B. Webster, 'Hermeneutics in Modern Theology: Some Doctrinal Reflections', pp. 47–86 in *Word and Church: Essays in Church Dogmatics* (Edinburgh: T. & T. Clark 2001) and his insistence that 'the Bible as text is the *viva vox Dei* addressing the people of God and generating faith and obedience' (p. 58).

convention, be it in terms of form and genre, rhetoric and style, or structure and linguistic device, insightful though this undoubtedly is, may also become an alternative to a simple attentive reading of what is written in its immediate and biblical-theological context.[6] So the references to the empty tomb in the resurrection narratives might come to be regarded as literary devices rather than a record of genuine historical events. Appeals to literary artifice or editorial intrusion might be used to dismiss what has been written and in such cases the capacity of a reader to discern these things has taken precedence over the authority of the text.

A reader's personal experience or the broader cultural consensus might function in this way as well. It is possible to give these factors a priority in determining the meaning and relevance of a text rather than allowing the text to correct personal or cultural experience and bring about that cardinal Christian virtue, repentance. So, a twenty-first century emphasis on freedom of sexual expression and the right of self-determination may lead the reader to insist that if the biblical text is to have any value or relevance today it must not be saying what it appears to be saying.[7]

Moreover, larger theological constructions and systems too can be given a priority to such an extent that they swamp a reading that is disciplined by the details of the text. A classic example is

---

[6] 'Biblical theological' is understood here as the unfolding message of the Bible from Genesis to Revelation. See the works of Donald Robinson, Graeme Goldsworthy and, in a more popular vein, Vaughan Roberts.

[7] Far more honest, yet deeply troubling, is historian Diarmaid MacCulloch's conclusion, 'This is an issue of biblical authority. Despite much well-intentioned theological fancy footwork to the contrary, it is difficult to see the Bible as expressing anything else but disapproval of homosexual activity, let alone having any conception of a homosexual identity. The only alternatives are either to try to cleave to patterns of life and assumptions set out in the Bible, or to say that in this, as in much else, the Bible is simply wrong.' D. MacCulloch, *Reformation: Europe's House Divided 1490–1700* (London: Penguin, 2003), 705.

the felt need in some theological circles to find a detailed covenantal scheme in texts in which neither the language nor concept of covenant is immediately obvious, such as Genesis 1–2. It is even possible in some cases for the voice of God to become confused with the voice of our favourite theologian or theological system, such as 'the Reformed faith' or 'the Catholic tradition'.

The answer to each of these opportunities for misreading is an attentive reading of what is actually there in front of us in the biblical text.

Over the past thirty years, hermeneutical guides and textbooks have become longer, more detailed, and, in some cases, more prescriptive. The impression can be given that reading and understanding the Bible is a complex and difficult enterprise which ought not to be attempted by the uninitiated. The question has been raised whether we have been witnessing a hypertrophy of hermeneutical theory which obscures the primary stance of humility, faith and repentance before the written word of the living God.[8] Too often and too quickly the comment is made that the meaning of this or that passage is uncertain or that the point at issue is 'a matter of interpretation'. In contrast, the Danish philosopher Søren Kierkegaard (1813–1855) once wrote, 'The Bible is very easy to understand. But we Christians are a bunch of scheming swindlers. We pretend to be unable to understand it because we know very well that the minute we understand, we are obliged to act accordingly.'[9] The language is strong but Kierkegaard's point is still well taken. Reading is a moral

---

[8] '[I]nterpreters and their acts are to demonstrate the mortification and vivification which are the basic forms of baptized human existence and action in the domain of the resurrection.' J. B. Webster, 'Resurrection and Scripture', 32–49 in *The Domain of the Word: Scripture and Theological Reason* (London: Bloomsbury T. & T. Clark, 2012), 46.

[9] S. Kierkegaard, *Provocations: Spiritual Writings of Kierkegaard* (ed. C.E. Moore; Farmington, PA: Plough Publishing House, 1999), 201.

activity as well as an intellectual one. When it comes to reading the Bible, it is also, and primarily, a spiritual activity. Are we willing to obey what is in fact written in the biblical text or do we think we know (or our culture knows) better? Will we take seriously the words God has given to us or will we seek a way to evade, manipulate, or explain away what is written? These are serious questions and they admit of no middle ground where we can pretend to accept mutually contradictory positions with the explanation they are merely 'interpretative differences'.

Outline of a Theological Account of Reading

The activity of reading and understanding the Bible needs to be understood in an explicitly theological frame. God's communicative activity is basic to the nature and use of the Bible. Even more basic is the character and capacity of God as a communicator. The Bible presents God himself as the first to use human language in addressing the man and the woman in the Garden of Eden (Genesis 1–2). He uses words which they understand and are able to repeat to each other (and to the serpent, though with a sinful interpolation—Gen 3:3). God is also the first to transpose his spoken word into a written text (Exod 24:12; 31:18). Neither human words nor a human text are barriers to God's communicative act. God is an effective communicator, whatever the medium or agency he chooses. Furthermore, neither human sin (Genesis 3, 4) nor the fracture of human language following work on the Tower of Babel (Genesis 11) make it impossible, or even difficult, for God to communicate to his human creatures. God expects Abraham to hear and understand his call (Genesis 12), similarly with Moses (Exodus 3), David (2 Samuel 7) and the first audience of the prophets, despite the passage of years and the differences of context. Similarly, the Lord Jesus Christ expected those to whom he spoke and those with whom he debated to have read and understood the Old Testament texts which he cites. 'Have you not read?' he asked repeatedly (Matt 12:3, 5; 19:4; 22:31). 'It is written' he said with an undeniable finality (Matt 4:4, 7, 10; 11:10; 21:13; 26:31). God has made his mind known and he has done so in a way which is effective. Even when that word is rejected, and other words are manufactured or believed, it is not because there is something intrinsically problematic about the biblical text. It is rather because of the hardness of the human heart.

It has long been part of the classic Christian confession that God has spoken and his word needs both to be heard and heeded. God does not speak to no purpose. His word always accomplishes its purpose (Isa 55:10–11). This is the case whether the medium is the speaking of the prophet or the written words of the biblical text. The little remembered Swiss theologian Benedict Pictet (1655–1724) challenged the idea that God's word is not clear or that it is accessible only through the sophisticated hermeneutical manoeuvres of the experts by drawing attention to what such a conclusion would mean for our doctrine of God.

> Once more; either God *could not* reveal himself more plainly to men, or he *would not*. No one will assert the former, and the latter is most absurd; for who could believe that God our heavenly Father has been unwilling to reveal his will to his children, when it was necessary to do so, in order that men might more easily obey it?[10]

Either God's word is in need of clarification by our techniques because God was incapable of communicating clearly, in which case his omnipotence and omniscience dissolve before our eyes, or he chose not to communicate clearly, in which case his grace and

---

10   B. Pictet, *Christian Theology* (trans. F. Reyroux; Weston Green: Seeley and Sons, 1833), 48. Despite the Doctrine Commission's preference for gender inclusive language, the generic use of 'men' has been retained to preserve the integrity of the original quotation, understanding that the referent clearly includes both women and men.

goodness towards those he has redeemed is partial at best, compromised at worst. However, might there not be a further possibility, that the situation of his human creatures has so materially changed that God's word committed to writing two millennia ago needs revision or qualification? This strategy is no better, since it compromises God's eternal omniscience. God's word does not 'go out of date' because he knows the end from the beginning and he always speaks the truth (John 17:17; Titus 1:2). Nothing catches God by surprise. He has no need to change his mind as if he did not have the information then that we have now. Once again, the guarantee of Scripture's ongoing truthfulness is the person and character of the God who has given it to us. As Bishop N. T. Wright has pointed out, 'the phrase "authority of Scripture" can only make Christian sense if it is a shorthand for "the authority of the triune God" exercised somehow through Scripture'.[11] To adopt approaches to reading that dismiss or evade what is actually written, including adopting a trajectory which would take us to a place diametrically opposed to what is actually written, end up being an assault upon God. That is why they must be rejected by the disciples of the Lord Jesus Christ.

Attentive Reading, Repentance and Human Sexuality

The Bible is the word of God given to us through the conscious and creative agency of human authors whose humanity—including both their finitude and fallenness—was in no way a barrier to God's clear communication of his character, will and purpose for people in all ages. Ultimately what we say about the Bible and the accessibility of its message has profound consequences for our doctrine of God. Can God be God and fail to communicate to his

---

11   N. T. Wright, *Scripture and the Authority of God* (London: SPCK, 2005), 17.

creatures? The stance we take as we approach the reading and study of the Bible is reflective of the stance we take towards God himself. Do we expect to be addressed by God in and through these words? Are we willing to be challenged and corrected by what he has to say to us? Are repentance and faith—inextricably linked as they are—properly foundational to our reading of the Bible? As English Anglican theologian John Webster (1955–2016) put it,

> Above all, faithful reading is an aspect of *mortificatio sui*, a repudiation of the desire to assemble all realities, including texts, including even the revelation of God, around the steady centre of my will. To read—*really* to read—is to submit to the process of the elimination or correction or conversion of false desire, for it is that false desire—sin—which more than anything else is destructive of the communicative fellowship between God and humanity …[12]

This must be the case in the matter of human sexuality and marriage as everywhere else. When Jesus taught that marriage was intended from the beginning to be between a man and woman and that the one-flesh relationship God had created was not to be undone (Matt 19:4–5), he expected that his words would be understood. When Jesus' authorised apostle, Paul, wrote to the Romans that sexual activity between two people of the same sex was unnatural and under judgment (Rom 1:26–27), it was not as if God was oblivious to the struggle of those who are same-sex attracted. When the same Paul listed 'men who practise homosexuality' among those who 'will not inherit the kingdom of God' (1 Cor 6:9), or described them as those who do what is 'contrary to sound doctrine' (1 Tim 1:10), it was not reflective of a cultural bias on the part of the apostle but the unchanging word of the living and loving God who 'does not wish that any should perish, but that

---

12   J. B. Webster, 'The Dogmatic Location of the Canon' 9–46 in *Word and Church*, 43–44. The Latin phrase *mortificatio sui* means 'putting yourself to death'.

all should reach repentance' (2 Pet 3:9). These are not isolated or obscure proof texts but reside in the mainstream of biblical teaching from Genesis 1–2 with its joining of a man and a woman as one flesh, to its unequivocal condemnation of all sexual activity outside of that context (Leviticus 18; Col 3:5–6), its positioning of the faithful, loving marriage of a man and woman as an analogue of Christ's relation to the church (Eph 5:25–27), and the exclusion of 'the sexually immoral' from the blessing of the new heaven and new earth (Rev 21:8). It is the consistent teaching of the Spirit-inspired Scriptures which insists the stakes are very high when it comes this issue: it is a salvation issue. This is why a departure from this teaching has been recognised as an act of schism, a separation from the church of God or, in the words of the Primates of the Anglican Communion, it has resulted in a 'tear in the fabric of our communion at its deepest level'.[13]

We need to be careful that hermeneutical theory does not become a device to avoid what God has clearly and repeatedly caused to be written 'for our instruction' (Rom 15:4). Most of our spoken and written communication succeeds. How much more God's! Since that is so, we need to be repentant, humble yet confident, in our determination to be directed by God's effective communication of his person, character and purposes. There is no middle ground where conflicting opinions on this issue can exist peaceably side by side. If God has spoken and effectively communicated to us that sexual behaviour between two members of the same sex is contrary to his will for humankind, then any attempt to bless this behaviour,

---

[13] The expression was first used in a communique from the Anglican Primates following their emergency meeting at Lambeth Palace on 16 October 2003. The full text of the communiqué can be found online at http://www.globalsouthanglican.org/index.php/blog/comments/a_statement_by_the_primates_of_the_anglican_communion_meeting_in_lambeth_pa (accessed 28 Jan 2019).

or the unions in which it occurs, amounts to a repudiation of God's authority over the lives of his people and, indeed, over all his creatures. That is why this has been a presenting issue in the current deep and enduring tear in the fabric of the Anglican Communion. The real issue is whether we shall live and teach according to God's written word or our own personal or cultural preferences.

How does the Old Testament help us think about marriage and especially same-sex marriage?

Meg Warner[1]

The Old Testament can be terrifically annoying. We Christians so often think of it as a book of laws—directions for living, if you like. And then, when we go to the Old Testament ('OT') to see what its rules, laws and directions on a certain subject might be, we find that they are missing. It would be so much more straight-forward if the various books of the OT would just give us a series of definitions of their central concepts. As a general rule, however, they do not. And that is true in the case of marriage. In fact, the OT has quite a lot to say about marriage: the Torah has a whole series of instructions,[2] the Prophets use the imagery of marriage to great effect, and Genesis is packed full of extraordinary illustrations of what marriage might look like. Nowhere, however, do we find a definition of marriage.[3]

In this essay I want to explore what the OT Scriptures *do* have

---

[1] Dr Meg Warner is Visiting Lecturer at King's College London and Honorary Research Fellow at the University of Exeter. She is a Reader (LLM) in the Diocese of London, a member of the General Synod of the Church of England and author of SPCK's 2016 Lent Book, *Abraham: A Journey through Lent*.
[2] 'Instruction' is a better translation of 'Torah' than 'law'.
[3] Some Christians consider that Gen 2:24 functions as a definition of marriage. I will come back to this verse in the latter part of this essay.

to say about marriage, and how they might be helpful for us as Christians today as we struggle to discern God's will for marriage, including same-sex marriage. Most of this paper will focus on OT Scriptures that paint a picture of how marriage was understood during the OT period, considering how that picture compares with the conception(s) of marriage that we hold collectively today and how we might seek, faithfully, to represent that picture in our own context. Toward the end of the paper I will look more specifically at God's plan for relationship between men and women as it is depicted in the creation narratives (Genesis 1–3), as many Christians look to these narratives as a kind of interpretational key for considering issues of human relationship and sexuality.

Marriage in the OT and in its context

There can be no doubt that marriage functions as the primary structure for personal relationship in the OT Scriptures, as it does in our own time, providing a foundation for procreation and for building families. Nevertheless, there is no place where the text prescribes what marriage will be. Nor is there any one Hebrew word that is invariably used in the OT to mean 'marry'.[4] In fact a variety of models or arrangements are presented as marriage, as is the case in most cultures, ancient and modern. Deuteronomy includes provisions about a number of specific aspects of marriage, such as betrothal, adultery and divorce, but it doesn't say what it considers marriage to be. Instead, it assumes that its readers already know what marriage is. In other words, Deuteronomy (like the other books of the Torah) 'borrows' the understanding of marriage from its context. It doesn't set out to prescribe the boundaries of marriage, or a procedure for becoming married. Nevertheless, one can, by

---

4   A number of colloquialisms are used to indicate marrying, including 'to take' and 'to lift'.

reading between the lines, infer that the authors of Deuteronomy understood marriage to be, in its essence, a socially-recognised commitment between a man and a woman, and they wrote about it on that basis. The authors of Deuteronomy wanted to put in place specific rules, or provisions, about marriage that would apply exclusively to Israelites, such as rules about divorcing one's wife (eg, Deut 24:1), about marrying a woman who has been taken in battle (Deut 21:1–14), or about re-marrying a woman from whom one had previously been divorced (Deut 24:1–4). Nevertheless, they were content to adopt the general understanding of marriage that the Israelites brought with them from the surrounding culture.

The *Mohar*

Some of these revisions or additional stipulations relate to matters that are not standard elements of marriage in the West today. One such example is the '*mohar*', or bride price. The *mohar* was an amount of money that a man would pay to his prospective father-in-law. It was not unlike the dowry system, except that dowries are paid by the *bride's* family to her prospective husband. The *mohar* system is reflected in a number of OT stories, usually in the context of trickery or enticement. For example, in Genesis 34 a Hivite prince seduces or rapes Jacob's daughter, Dinah, and wishes to marry her, saying 'Put the marriage present and gift (*mohar*) as high as you like, and I will give whatever you ask me; only give me the girl to be my wife' (Gen 34:12). Dinah's brothers eventually agree to the marriage, but only as a ruse. Jacob, himself, had been tricked into working for two blocks of seven years as a *mohar* to Laban in order to marry Laban's daughter Rachel (Gen 29:22–30). In 1 Samuel 18 Saul 'tricks' David into marrying his daughter Michal, and when David objects that he cannot afford to pay the kind of *mohar* that a king might expect, Saul insists that he wishes no *mohar* apart from one hundred Philistine foreskins.

Just as there is no general definition of marriage in the OT, nor is there a definition or description of the *mohar*. It is simply assumed that readers will be familiar with it. There are, however, two 'laws' or 'instructions' that mention the *mohar*:

> **Exod 22:16–17** When a man seduces a virgin who is not engaged to be married, and lies with her, he shall give the bride-price (mohar) for her and make her his wife. But if her father refuses to give her to him, he shall pay an amount equal to the bride-price for virgins.

> **Deut 22:28–29** If a man meets a virgin who is not engaged, and seizes her and lies with her, and they are caught in the act, the man who lay with her shall give fifty shekels of silver to the young woman's father, and she shall become his wife. Because he violated her he shall not be permitted to divorce her as long as he lives.

These provisions come into play when a man has sex with an unmarried, unbetrothed, woman. In each case the man must be prepared to pay the *mohar* and marry her. In the Exodus provision the girl's father may refuse the marriage, but is still entitled to the payment. The Deuteronomy provision appears to apply in situations in which the seduction has been violent.[5] Here, the girl's father does not have the option of refusing the marriage, but the man must pay the *mohar* and may never divorce the woman. Both provisions strike the modern reader as abhorrent. There is a sense

---

5   It is not easy to say with certainty whether the two provisions were understood to respond to different situations, or whether the Deuteronomy provision was designed to supersede the Exodus provision. See, generally, Bernard M. Levinson, *Deuteronomy and the Hermeneutics of Legal Innovation* (New York/Oxford: Oxford University, 1997).

in which each treats the daughter as property to be bought and sold, and, Deuteronomy in particular, sentences her to life imprisonment in the home of her seducer/rapist.

Surprisingly to us, the intent of these provisions is essentially pastoral. Yes, the outcome is likely to be dreadful for the young woman involved, but we need to understand a little of the background to appreciate the pastoral intent. First, where our own society is focused strongly on the interests of the individual, in OT times society had a communal focus; family and community were more important than individuals. These provisions promoted the well-being of the woman's family, as well as the woman herself. A public seduction prior to marriage would almost certainly render a young woman unmarriageable. The provisions saved the woman's family from the shame and burden of an ageing unmarried daughter, and also secured the bride-price. Secondly, women in the OT period could not, in any event, function as individuals. A woman needed to 'belong' to a man, whether that man be her father, her husband, or her brother(s). Without a man to protect and provide for her a woman had no hope for safety or security. Even a woman doomed to live in the home of her attacker had a degree of security and a personal identity through marriage.[6]

The Incest Laws

I have already noted that passages alluding to the *mohar* suggest

---

[6] I have argued elsewhere that Genesis 34, the story of the sexual assault of Dinah, is like an ethical case study that explores whether this 'remedy' (particularly in its Deut 22:28–29 version) is available to a girl's father when her seducer or attacker is a foreigner. The two potential answers to this question are represented by the contrasting responses of Dinah's father and brothers. Dinah's ultimate fate is, apparently, to spend the remainder of her life in the care of her brothers; M. Warner, 'What if They're Foreign?: Inner-Legal Exegesis in the Ancestral Narratives' in M. G. Brett and J. Wöhrle (eds.), *The Politics of the Ancestors* (Tübingen: Mohr Siebeck, 2018) 67–92.

a sense in which women in the OT period were treated like property and passed from one man to another in procedures akin to business transactions. This sense is implicit also in the incest provisions in Leviticus 18 and 20, which are probably an expansion of the single incest provision in Deuteronomy, found in 22:30.[7] Deut 22:30 provides that a man should not marry his father's wife, *thereby violating his father's rights*. Similarly, Lev 18:8 provides, 'You shall not uncover the nakedness of your father's wife; it is the nakedness of your father.' In other words, a man should not marry his father's wife because she belongs to his father, or because her sexuality belongs to him. To be sure, consanguinity is an evident and strong concern in Leviticus 18 and 20, but the sense that a woman (or her sexuality) 'belongs' to a man with whom she is in relationship—father, husband, bother, uncle etc.—is also undoubtedly present.[8] Perhaps the most chilling fact about Leviticus 18 and 20 is that neither includes a provision prohibiting sexual contact with one's daughter. Is it that the taboo is so obvious that it doesn't need stating,[9] or that in having sexual contact with his daughter a man is violating nobody's rights but his own?

Marrying 'out'

Even if incest, or 'marrying in', is the subject of the bulk of two chapters of Leviticus, it is not the marital taboo that receives most attention in the OT. That honour belongs to 'marrying out', or,

---

[7] C. Nihan, *From Priestly Torah to Pentateuch* (FAT II, 25; Tübingen: Mohr Siebeck, 2005), 549, argues that the Leviticus provisions are an expansion of this verse.

[8] In using the word 'belong' I mean to allude to belonging in both a familial and a mercantile sense. The latter may seem far-fetched, but both these incest provisions, and those concerning the *mohar*, discussed above, suggest that a daughter was, *among other things*, an asset to be realised.

[9] As D. Lipton, *Longing for Egypt and other Unexpected Tales* (HBM 15; Sheffield: Sheffield Phoenix, 2008), suggests.

in other words, marriages between Israelites and non-Israelites, and in particular between Israelite men and non-Israelite women ('intermarriage'). It appears that this was a hot topic particularly in the period following the return from exile in the fifth and fourth centuries BCE, and probably also later. We see this especially in the books of Ezra (see chapters 9–10) and Nehemiah, as well as in later books such as Malachi, although it is also prohibited in Exodus (e.g., Exod 34:11–16) and Deuteronomy (e.g., Deut 7:1–4), while narratives including Numbers 25 and Genesis 21; 26–28; 34 engage with the issue.

It is not entirely clear why intermarriage was such a prominent issue, or precisely what harm was being objected to.[10] Possibly the rationale changed over time, or was different in different quarters. Ezra didn't specify what it was about the intermarriages he observed that made him so appalled, except that the 'holy seed' had mixed itself faithlessly with the people of the land (Ezra 9:2). Exod 34:11–16 and Deut 7:1–4, among other texts, link intermarriage with cultic prostitution and the worship of gods other than YHWH. I have argued elsewhere that Gen 21:8–14 alludes to Ezra's direction to send away the foreign wives and their children in Ezra 9–10, as Mark G. Brett has also done.[11] In OT times in Israel the inheritance of land passed through female rather than male lines, so that if a man married a non-Israelite woman his land would pass to her

---

[10] See C. Frevel, (ed.), *Mixed Marriages: Intermarriage and Group Identity in the Second Temple Period* (LHBOTS 547; New York: T&T Clark, 2011).

[11] Warner, 'What if They're Foreign?', 70; M. G. Brett, *Genesis: Identity and Politics of Procreation* (London: Routledge, 2000), 76–78. In 'What if They're Foreign' I argue that Genesis 21 is like Genesis 34 in that it presents an ethical dilemma, this time about inheritance. Deut 21:15–17 provides that when a man has two wives, one whom is loved and the other hated, if his firstborn is the son of the unloved wife he may not deprive her child of his right to a double inheritance portion. Gen 21:8–14 raises the question—does this still hold good if the firstborn is the son of a foreign woman?

family, and thus away from Israel (for an intra-Israelite example see Num 36:1–9). It may be, then, that Gen 21:8–14 functioned in its time as a critique, exposing hypocrisy in the piety surrounding the intermarriage issue, especially as manifested in Ezra-Nehemiah.

Polygamy

Ironically, polygamy is *not* obviously an issue in the OT. Numerous OT characters are presented as having multiple wives, without any narratorial censure, even when their particular expression of polygamy offends against other marital norms. Polygamy is especially to be found in Genesis, but is also a notable part of the world of the monarchic narratives (Solomon is a serial offender). In Genesis Abraham initially has two wives, Sarah and Hagar (Gen 16:3), but later he takes a third wife, Keturah (Gen 25:1) and, apparently, a number of concubines (Gen 25:6). Esau marries two Hittite women, Judith and Basemath (Gen 26:34), to the consternation of Rebekah (in particular), but not explicitly of the narrator.[12] Esau's brother, Jacob, initially has two wives also, admittedly as a result of trickery rather than design (Genesis 29), who happen to be sisters (*contra* Lev 18:18). He additionally marries and has children with the handmaids of both wives, in arrangements that recall that made between Sarah and Hagar. Isaac and Joseph manage with one wife each, but Joseph's is Egyptian. In none of these cases does the narrator specifically comment on these multiple wives/sexual partners.

It is notable that the 'mini-code' of marriage instructions in Deuteronomy 24 doesn't say anything explicit about polygamy. Instead, at least two provisions of Deuteronomy presume polygamy as a given. Deuteronomy 21:15–17 protects the inheritance of the firstborn. The passage sets out rights of inheritance when a man

---

[12] Brett, *Genesis*, 88; M, Warner, *Re-Imagining Abraham: A Re-Assessment of the Influence of Deuteronomism in Genesis* (OTS 72; Leiden/Boston: Brill, 2018), 51.

has sons by two wives—one loved and one hated.[13] Deuteronomy 25:5–10's provisions about levirate marriage also seem to assume polygamy as a possibility. There is no consideration given in these verses as to whether already being married might be a bar to a man marrying the wife of his dead brother and procreating on his behalf. Indeed, vv. 9–10 outline the humiliating ritual that will ensue when a man refuses to honour his dead brother in this way.

Mind the gap

I have discussed four specific elements of the OT understanding of marriage: the *mohar*, incest laws, intermarriage and polygamy. I could have picked a number of other elements for my purposes, but there is not room here to undertake an exhaustive appraisal of what the OT has to say about marriage. What may have become apparent, nevertheless, is that while the examples I have explored reflect an understanding of marriage in some respects not unlike our own (i.e., marriage as lifelong commitment between men and women, and with provision for divorce), these same examples also reflect an understanding of marriage that is vastly different from our own. You can probably imagine how, in our post-#MeToo world, a sermon that treated women as property, railed against inter-ethnic marriage, or sanctioned polygamy, would be received!

Just as in the London tube, there is a 'gap' between the OT's understanding of marriage (if, indeed, such a thing can be expressed in the singular) and our own. There are elements of it that most of us simply could not countenance. Indeed, most of us were horrified by the interpretation of Genesis' conception of marriage and procreation presented in HBO's recent dramatization of Margaret Atwood's classic dystopian novel, *A Handmaid's*

---

13 Note that Hebrew doesn't distinguish between wife and woman – the same word, *ishshah*, serves for both.

Tale. What that means is that we need to be cautious in how we adopt the OT's provisions about marriage in our own context. Even the most traditionalist of today's Anglicans is likely to baulk at the idea of marriage as property-transaction, for example, and polygamy has been an awkward issue for Anglican Australians and US Episcopalians working especially closely with some African sisters and brothers.

This does not necessarily mean that the OT cannot help us in our thinking about marriage today. However, it does mean that we need to exercise care about the ways in which we claim the OT as authority in this regard, in order to ensure that we don't 'pick and choose' in a manner that is selective and, even, to adopt the language of today, 'random'. When you think about it, it is extraordinary that we see reflected in the OT Scriptures a picture of marriage that has such a high degree of continuity with our own. This venerable institution has weathered thousands of years of practice and reflection, and it still provides our primary framework for family life—even if our conception of 'family' has changed enormously.

Same-sex marriage

One of my briefs for this essay is to give special consideration to what the OT might have to say about same-sex marriage. The foregoing discussion ought to give us pause for thought in this regard. The first thing to note is that the OT does not say anything explicit about same-sex marriage, in the sense that we understand it. It *does* have some things to say about sex between men, but it doesn't contemplate that two people of the same sex might wish to pledge themselves to one another in marriage. It is difficult to deny that Lev 18:22 and 20:13 state that for a man to 'lie with' another man as he would with a woman is contrary to God's will.[14] Arguably, the only other OT passages that address the issue are Genesis 19 and Judges 19. I have written about these narratives at length elsewhere,[15] concluding that they are stories principally focused on questions of hospitality and not on matters of sexual ethics. For example, the desire of the men in Genesis 19 'to know' the visitors to Sodom, I argue, is presented as a caricature of grotesque inhospitality matching the caricature of grotesque hospitality found in Lot's offer of his virgin daughters to the angry mob.

Lev 18:22 and 20:13 cannot, however, be dismissed so readily. They say on the face of it that for a man to lie with another man is contrary to God's will for humans. Here, it seems, we *do* have a clear provision that says that sex between men is contrary to God's will. How then, bearing in mind 'the gap' I identified above, should we go about applying this provision in today's world and what considerations should we take into account?

The first point to note is that Lev 18:22 and 20:13 apply only to men. There is nothing at all in the OT about God's will concerning sex or marriage between women. Could we extrapolate and apply these same provisions to women? For a series of reasons such a move would be inappropriate. We have already seen the major discrepancy between the ways in which men and women lived in the OT world. For a start, a family unit including only women could not have functioned. Even in the OT's most women-focused book, Ruth, the 'business' of the relationship between Ruth and Naomi is to find Ruth a husband. A related reason is just as cogent. The superiority of men in the OT world was valued and respected. For a man

---

14   A number of scholarly articles have argued, with varying degrees of success, that these verses mean something subtly different from this.
15   'Were the Sodomites sodomites?' in N. Wright (ed.), *Five Uneasy Pieces: Essays on Scripture and Sexuality* (Adelaide: ATF, 2011), 1–9; Warner, *Re-Imagining Abraham*, 145–155.

to disrespect his masculinity by becoming 'feminised' (whether intentionally or not) was a matter of shame (see, for example, 2 Sam 20:4–5). It is highly probable that this sense of shame is at least part of what lay behind the prohibition in Lev 18:22 and 20:13—sex between two men 'as with a woman' requires one partner to adopt the 'feminine', receptive, role. The shame of this would have been sufficient to warrant a blanket prohibition. In our own culture a connection between shame and the feminization of males is not unknown, but it is being subjected to enormous challenge as sexual boundaries, and binaries, move and shift before our eyes it seems, and as we are learning that this sort of shame can be extremely damaging. For these reasons, it should not be argued that what the OT says about men should be applied also to women.

Restricting our focus, therefore, to men—there are at least two general considerations that should deter us from adopting Lev 18:22 and 20:13 as a blanket prohibition on sexual activity or intimate relationships between men in our own context. The first is that the current emphasis in some quarters upon opposition to homosexuality as a marker of faithful Christianity is out of all proportion to the OT witness. I have identified these two verses (subject to what I say about Gen 2:24 below) as the only provisions unambiguously proposing a bar on sex between men in the OT. In my discussion of intermarriage, above, I said that intermarriage was the most regularly attested sexual offence in the OT and listed a series of OT books that address the issue. Most of us no longer recognize a religious or cultural taboo against marriage between partners of different ethnic backgrounds. To the contrary, mostly we pride ourselves on our openness to such examples of globalization and tolerance. Why, then, place such emphasis on two verses? Admittedly, the language of 'abomination', *to'eyvah*, in those verses is strong—stronger than language used for most sexual aberrations. However, the same language is used also in respect of cross-dressing (Deut 22:5), re-marrying a former spouse (Deut 24:4) and using incense (Isa 1:13) and our churches don't maintain religious objections to such activities, indeed some are positively encouraged!

The second reason why we should be hesitant about interpreting Lev 18:22 and 20:13 as a blanket prohibition against sexual intimacy or marriage between males today is that to do so risks ancillary adoption of principles of sexual ethics that most, or all, of us would find unacceptable. As I have already shown, many aspects of the sexual ethics underlying the OT's provisions about marriage are a product of their own time and circumstances and run counter to today's principles, assumptions and morality of sexuality. As we've seen, an underlying principle of the relationship between men and women in OT times was that women were, at least in some senses, the property of the men to whom they were related by birth or marriage. Additionally, a woman required relationship with a man in order to have security and to be able to function in society. Those principles no longer hold sway in the West, at least, and the change has been hard-won. Even if some of us may struggle with more recent trends around gender identity, it is difficult to imagine that *any* of us would wish—knowingly—to affirm the commodification of women. Indeed, such an affirmation would run counter to the Scriptures in other respects. An adoption of Lev 18:22 and 20:13 as a blanket prohibition on sex or marriage between men today, however, does just this.

I would like to touch on just one further reason why a blanket adoption of Lev 18:22 and 20:13 as a prohibition against same-sex marriage today is problematic, and it concerns procreation. The Bible's very first blessing, found in Gen 1:28 incorporates an imperative to procreate and to fill the earth. The full imperative, 'Be fruitful and multiply, and fill the earth and subdue it; and have dominion over the fish of the sea and over the birds of the air and over every living thing that moves upon the earth', is modified in later iterations,[16] but Genesis 1:28 nevertheless implicitly marks-out procreation as a, if not the, central vocation of humanity. The rest of Genesis goes on to narrate the spread of people across the known world, filling and subduing it, and suggests that marriage is generally the context in which procreation is to occur. (There are other models presented—Abraham has children with his concubines as well as with his wives (Gen 25:6), while there is no explicit record of Eve and Adam marrying prior to bearing their sons.) Genesis was written during a period when numbers of people, and especially Israelites, were small, while land and resources were relatively plentiful. The Israelites' small numbers made them vulnerable. Today, conversely, what makes human beings vulnerable is our large numbers and the growing scarcity of resources. We have been fruitful and multiplied and filled the earth and subdued it, until the earth cannot take much more. An adoption of the imperative to be fruitful and multiply, therefore, that does not take into account the impact of changed and changing context can be no safer than a blanket adoption of Lev 18:22 and 20:13 as divine prohibition against sexual intimacy between men. This must give us pause if we are inclined to argue that the centrality of procreation to the purpose of marriage militates against same-sex marriage.

Genesis 2:24

Therefore a man leaves his father and his mother and clings to his wife, and they become one flesh.

I began this essay with the proposition that the OT contains no definition of marriage. Some will wish to argue that Gen 2:24,

---

16   See, for example, Gen 9:1,7; 28:3; 35:11; 48:4.

reproduced above, defines marriage. I have written at length about Gen 2:24 and marriage, first in '"Set in Tradition and History": Gen 2:24 and the Marriage Debate', published in *Pieces of Ease and Grace*,[17] and later in 'Therefore a Man Leaves his Father and his Mother and Clings to his Wife: Marriage and Intermarriage in Gen 2:24'.[18] In both places I challenge the idea that Gen 2:24 functions as a prescription of marriage (or a proscription of homosexuality, or of the several other sexual practices against which Gen 2:24 has been brought to bear at different times, including divorce, incest, bestiality, polygamy and intermarriage). I propose, therefore, to make only brief remarks about Gen 2:24 here.

First, the idea that Gen 2:24 prescribes life-long union between one man and one woman as the model of marriage uniquely acceptable to God, proscribing other models, does not fit at all well with the remainder of the witness of Genesis. The marriages of the ancestors, for example, reflect a range of alternative models. As already noted, Abraham has two wives concurrently (one of whom is apparently his half-sister—Gen 20:12 cf. Lev 18:9) and a number of concubines, Esau also has at least two wives (Gen 26:34), while Jacob has four, two of whom are sisters (Genesis 29–30 cf. Lev 18:18). Significantly, none of these arrangements is disapproved by the narrator or any of the characters, *except* in relation to the ethnicity of the marriage partner(s) (principally in the cases of Abraham and Hagar—Gen 21:8–21, Esau and his Hittite wives—Gen 26:34 and Dinah and her Hivite seducer—Genesis 34).

Secondly, while it is tempting to read Gen 2:4b–25 as the story of God's introduction of the phenomenon of gender into creation,

---

17   M. Warner, '"Set in Tradition and History": Gen 2:24 and the Marriage Debate' in A. Cadwallader (ed.), *Pieces of Ease and Grace* (Adelaide: ATF, 2013), 1–15.
18   M. Warner, 'Therefore a Man Leaves his Father and his Mother and Clings to his Wife: Marriage and Intermarriage in Gen 2:24' *Journal of Biblical Literature* 113 (2017): 269–289.

to do so overlooks the principal thrust of the narrative. After the mounting grandeur and overwhelming 'goodness' of the creation account of Gen 1–2:4a, Gen 2:5 presents a situation of lack—nothing is yet growing in the earth because YHWH has not yet caused it to rain and because there is nobody to till (*'ezer*, lit. 'serve') the ground. Then a stream rises up and YHWH creates an earth creature (*adam*) to till the ground (*adamah*) (Gen 2:6–7). However YHWH announces, in Gen 2:18, that it is not good for the adam to be alone. The idea that something should be 'not good' is shocking after Gen 1–2:4a, in which each new element of creation is pronounced 'good' or, finally, 'very good'. So YHWH makes a second earth creature— a woman (*ishshah*) alongside the man (*ish*)—to be his helper/opposite number (*'ezer kenegdo'*). What becomes apparent when the story is set out in this way is that human beings are subsequent, and secondary, to the principal character in the story, the earth. To see the focus of the story as being the explanation of gender and model for marriage is so androcentric as to miss the point, which is that the earth comes first and we are here to serve it. If you like, we have a competing primary vocation here—not to procreate (as in Genesis 1) but to serve the earth. *For this reason, it is not good that the earth creature—the 'adam'—should be alone* (Gen 2:18). Here is a final reason why we should not insist upon an interpretation of Gen 2:24, Lev 18:22 and 20:13 that prohibits same-sex marriage. If we read Gen 2:24 as an explanation of what marriage *must be*, rather than an explanation of how men and women (or earth-creatures) *are* (as I argue in the essays noted above), effectively limiting the availability of marriage and intimacy to certain people while excluding others, we risk bringing about the *one* thing that Genesis 2 explicitly says that YHWH God hates—the aloneness of God's creatures.

Much attention has been given to the creation narratives, and to Gen 2:24 in particular, as a key to the interpretation of God's will for marriage in the Scriptures, both Old and New. When read carefully, they point not to an exclusive or prescriptive model of marriage, but to God's will that his creatures might experience companionship in a shared vocation to serve his creation.

Conclusion

How, then, do the OT Scriptures help us to think about marriage, and especially same-sex marriage? What they do *not* do is to offer us a road map or an exclusive model for marriage. Instead, they show us how marriage has been central to the endeavours of human beings over the centuries to be in right relationship with one another and with God. They reflect the way in which marriage has adapted and changed to fit new circumstances and understandings of God, the world and the human condition over time. This observation helps us to see and understand the need for immense caution in adopting principles, or even directives, from the biblical text and imposing them upon our own lives, or the lives of others.[19] To take a position of support for same-sex marriage means adopting some practices or principles that differ from practices and principles reflected in the text. However, to follow such practices and principles, or to seek to reflect them indiscriminately in our relationships today, may mean acting in ways that are anomalous or oppressive in our context, or that are in conflict with more generalised biblical principles that have weathered the tests of time. These include the revelation that God wills companionship, intimacy and joy for his creatures in their service of his creation.

---

19   Anyone uncertain about this would do well to consider the experiences of South Africa and what the Dutch Reformed Church in that country has had to say about its experience of formulating, and then abandoning, apartheid as a biblical principle. Richard Burridge's analysis is especially helpful: R. A. Burridge, *Imitating Jesus: An Inclusive Approach to New Testament Ethics* (Grand Rapids, MI/Cambridge: Eerdmans, 2007), 347–409.

Belonging to God in Relational Wholeness: A Conservative Perspective on the Old Testament's View of Marriage and Same-Sex Intimate Relationships

Katherine M Smith[1]

From creation to new creation, Scripture presents God's view of his world and so invites us to align our view of the world, and so our lives, with his. It is remarkable that God, who is complete in and of himself, and who is utterly other, chooses to reveal the constancy of who he is through the means of an imperfect people and in a broken world. While cultures change, historical ages pass by, Scripture from the Old to the New testifies that God's character and his purposes are unchanging. For this reason, as this essay unfolds a conservative perspective on the Old Testament's view of marriage and same-sex intimate relationships, I will be taking a biblical-theological approach, tracing this issue through Genesis—Deuteronomy, into the New Testament briefly, and then to today. Since most passages that touch on the issue of marriage and same-sex intimate relations in the Old Testament are dependent upon canonical and theological contexts for meaning, I will

---

[1] The Rev'd Dr Katherine Smith is the Branch Director for CMS South Australia with the Northern Territory.

explain these contexts before approaching the particular passages that pertain to the issue of marriage. The danger of this type of essay is that some readers might find the following compounds their sense of exclusion; my hope though is that readers will find encouragement and hope in the compassion and whole relationship that is offered in Christ.

1. Creation and Marriage in the Book of Genesis

The First Creation Narrative in Genesis 1:1–2:3

The first creation narrative in 1:1–2:3 presents the grandeur of the pre-existent Creator, who spoke his creating intent, and who created by command (1:3, 6, 9, 11, 14, 20, 24, 26). By virtue of being the Creator, God has authority to determine what represents order and also what is good for his creation. This is the context in which God creates humanity in 1:26–28. In contrast to the creation stories of the other nations, this first of Israel's creation narratives evinces the generosity and goodness of the sovereign God who provides for humanity to flourish.[2] God announces his intention in 1:26 to make humanity in his image for the purpose of having dominion among all living things. Verse 27 then conveys, in three clauses, that God accomplished what he intended. The first and second clauses emphasise, by use of the collective singular, that God created humanity in his image, while the third clause then makes a distinction within how God created them—male and female. Just

---

[2] For example, read Tablet VI of the Babylonian creation story 'Enuma Elish' where Ea creates humanity from the murder of another god and creates with the intent of oppression. An accessible translation of Enuma Elish ('The Epic of Creation') can be found in *Myths from Mesopotamia*, trans. S. Dalley, rev. ed (Oxford: Oxford, 2000), 228–277. For further explanation, see J. H. Walton, *Ancient Near Eastern Thought and the Old Testament: Introducing the Conceptual World of the Hebrew Bible* (2nd ed., Grand Rapids: Baker, 2018).

as God creates in days 1–5 by instilling and sustaining distinction within his creation, so also humanity is created in day six with distinction in their unity. Then, in v.28, God's declaration as he assigns humanity's purpose in his world—being fruitful, filling, subduing, and having dominion—are words of blessing; an outworking of God's active favour for humanity with the goal that they flourish and have an honoured place in his world. He desires good for his creation.

The Second Creation Narrative in Genesis 2:3–4:26

In the second creation narrative in 2:3–4:26, we witness a relational God who once more acts for the good of humanity and his world. At the beginning, we watch as God forms the man (2:5–7), plants a garden of delight (*eden*) where life flows to the rest of the world (2:8–14), and places the man in this garden to work and serve within it (2:15). In this context, YHWH's command to the man in 2:16–17 is also for humanity's good as he gives abundant freedom with one exception; the man can eat of *every* tree in the garden, except for *one*—the tree of knowing good and evil. God's command is not jarring; it is natural for YHWH, who created the man, to command, expecting obedience from his creation, and naming consequence in the instance where man does what is prohibited. This same goodness of God that commands is the same good that observes in 2:18 that the man's 'aloneness' is not good (2:18), and second, provides for the man's need by creating woman of the same essence as him (2:22).

The man's song as God brings the woman to the man in 2:23 is meant to instil joy. Finally, here is a helper who is the same as the man! The man's declaration affirms that the woman is a fitting helper for the man to remedy his aloneness. The Hebrew text then uses the strong conjunction 'therefore' at the beginning of 2:24 to connect the man's response with the narrator's summary that 'a man (*ish*) shall leave his father and his mother and be united (*dabaq*) with his wife (*ishshah*)'. For the first time in Genesis 1–2, the Hebrew text chooses to use the noun *ish* ('man/husband'), rather than *adam* ('man'), to form a wordplay with *ishshah* ('woman/wife'). Whereas the noun *adam* is a generic term pertaining to being human, the two nouns *ish* (man/husband) and *ishshah* (woman/wife) are relational terms that emphasise the distinction of being man and woman, husband and wife. The narrator's statement in context functions to establish the norm for family within Israel's worldview. Furthermore, the verb used to convey 'he shall be united' (*dabaq*) describes the permanency of the kinship relationship between the man and the woman.[3] The final clause of 2:24 then accentuates the special kind of unity that exists in this relationship; the husband and wife have unity from being the same 'matter' and also by becoming one flesh together.

While the term 'marriage' is absent in Gen 2:24, the concept is not. The purpose of ancient Near Eastern creation narratives as a genre is to form the worldview norm for the people-groups to whom the narrative belongs. As such, Gen 2:4–25 is part of a creation narrative (Gen 2:4–4:25) belonging to Israel, intending to form their worldview as a nation, particularly with regards to their relationship with YHWH, with the land that they are associated with, and in relationship with one another in community. A man forming a permanent relationship of oneness with a woman, as husband and wife, is the concept of marriage that is to form Israel's norm within community under God's kingship. A critical part of this worldview is that this norm established by Gen 2:24 is part of God's creative purposes. It is not the function of ancient Near

---

[3] B. K. Waltke, *Genesis* (Grand Rapids: Zondervan, 2001), 90; G. Wenham, *Genesis 1–15* (WBC 1, Dallas: Thomas Nelson, 1987), 71.

Eastern creation narratives to clarify what is not the norm; this is the role of law. The very fact that same-sex intimate relationships are not included in this picture is an instance where absence is evidence that same-sex relationships are not to be part of the norm for God's covenant community.

The wholeness of relationship between the man and the woman in Genesis 2:23–25 was shattered when the woman desired what belonged in God's domain—the ability to know good and evil—and she let this desire lead to the action of taking what was prohibited (Gen 3:1–6). The woman desiring and taking what has not been given to her, and so breaking command, is the desire for autonomous wisdom; that is, wisdom with self as the referent and not God.[4] The tragedy of the scene is that the snake distorted the goodness and generosity of God by depicting him as withholding good from the man and the woman; and the woman believed. This has immediate relational consequences for the man and the woman after they both ate what was prohibited. They felt and acted out of shame, and they hid from God's presence. The man's joy over the woman turns to blame and anger, not only directed at the woman, but to God too. Furthermore, the breaking of God's command has consequence, which YHWH conveys in 3:14–19. For the woman, the consequence is relational disorder with her husband; she will desire him and yet he shall rule over her (3:16). Furthermore, the loss of relational wholeness with God would have been torturous for the man and woman to remain in a place where God is present. And worse is a prolonged life in this unwhole condition in God's presence if they had eaten from the tree of life (3:22). So, God acted in

---

4 See also J. Sklar, 'Pentateuch' in *T&T Clark Companion to the Doctrine of Sin*, ed. K. L. Johnson and D. Lauber (London: Bloomsbury, 2016), 6 Waltke, *Genesis*, 86; J. H. Walton, *Genesis* (NIVAC, Grand Rapids: Zondervan, 2001), 214–215; Wenham, *Genesis 1–15*, 75.

both grace and justice when he separated the man and the woman from his presence when he exiled them from the garden (3:23–24).

As Genesis 4 narrates Adam and Eve's life outside of the garden, the narrator depicts sin's mastery over humanity as family disorder causes violence. In the first instance, Cain killed his brother (4:8–10). In the second instance, Lamech boasted in the murder of another human (4:23). In this context, polygamy arises in 4:19 for the first time and, again, this is not a coincidence. The emergence of polygamy along with an escalation of sin's consequences suggests that polygamy is also a part of sin's mastery and, as the narrative progresses beyond this second creation narrative, becomes part of a disordered world.[5]

Marriage and the Message of the Book of Genesis

As Genesis connects the world's beginnings (1:1–9:29), with the beginnings of the nations (10:1–11:9) and of Israel (11:10–50:26), the message of the whole book is that the sovereign creator who is able to bring life from nothing is Israel's God who can bring good from evil intent. From Noah to Joseph, God chose to accomplish his purposes through relationally frail and sinful humans to demonstrate that, when his purposes are achieved, it is God's work and his alone. At every turn in the narrative, those whom God chose to work through endanger the covenant promises, whether it be Abram and Isaac lying to foreign kings (12:10–20; 26:1–16), sibling rivalry (25:22–34; 27:1–28:9), wives and sibling jealousy caused by polygamy (29:9–30:24), or a father-in-law's sexual offence with his daughter-in-law (38:12–26), just to name a few. In each instance, where marriage and sexual offence are part of the strife and conflict in the narrative, it is wrong to assume that God approves

---

5   See also Wenham, *Genesis*, 112.

of their behaviour because there is an absence of rebuke or justice. Rather, a focus of the narrative is to demonstrate that God chooses to bring good from the sinful desires and actions of others.

The above though is detail in the larger picture of Genesis 12:1–50:26 where YHWH promises Abram the gifts of land, nationhood (people), and relationship, for the sake of blessing the nations (12:1–3; 15:1–16; 17:1–8). The purpose of each gift is to recreate order within the four relational dimensions that were disordered by human sin in Genesis 3; the YHWH-human relationship (3:8–13), YHWH-land relationship (3:17), human-land relationship (3:17–19), and human-human relationship (3:8–13, 16). By means of YHWH's promise to create a nation through Abram, to gift land to this nation, and to establish a relationship with him, God initiates his purpose to restore his order within each relational dimension first within Israel.[6] As we will see in the following sections, this is significant for instructions about marriage and same-sex intimate relationships in Exodus, Leviticus and also Deuteronomy.

2. Redemption, Covenant, and Marriage in Exodus and Deuteronomy

God's instruction about marriage within the law sections of Exodus and Deuteronomy are grounded in the identity-forming event of God's redemption of Israel in Exodus 12–14. When YHWH rescued Israel from Egypt, his redemption of the fledgling nation transferred the Israelites from Egyptian slavery to being YHWH's servants (Exod 3:7–12; 19:1–6). This is evident also at the beginning of the Decalogue (i.e., Ten Commandments) in Exodus 20:1–7.

---

[6] C. Wright, 'Preaching from the Law' in 'He Began with Moses...': Preaching the Old Testament Today, ed. G. J. R. Kent, P. J. Kissling, and L. A. Turner (Nottingham: IVP, 2010), 52–53. For a more detailed explanation, see C. J. H. Wright, Old Testament Ethics for the People of God (Nottingham: IVP, 2010), 23–102.

Significantly, the Decalogue does not launch immediately into prohibition, but begins in 20:2 by declaring the identity of the one commanding; namely, YHWH, who brought Israel from the land of Egypt, from the house of slavery. This is crucial for two reasons. First, this is a reminder that YHWH, as the one who redeemed Israel, is their Covenant-King and so has authority derived from his status to set instruction within his nation. That is, he has the status to command what represents relational order and to define relational disorder within his people. Second, the relationship between YHWH and Israel is already established by God's work of redemption and so God's instruction is founded first and foremost in his grace.[7] The function of the law then is primarily about establishing order within the young covenant community at Sinai, as the nation begins to form its norms relating to YHWH and to one another, and as God begins his plan to extend this restored order to the world.

In this context, the Covenant Code has a small section of instruction in 22:16–17. These verses exist in the Covenant Code to protect an unmarried young woman who is not engaged to be married (*betulah*), who allows a man to seduce her, and so consents to sexual relations.[8] In this situation, the man has a duty to marry her and so preserves relational order within the community. However, the girl's father is not obligated to accept the man's duty-bound offer of marriage and so preserves the girl from a life-long situation married to her seducer if that is not the father's wish. Irrespective of the instruction's particulars, 22:16–17 assumes the basis of marriage between

---

7 See C. Wright, 'Preaching from the Law', 47–58, for an excellent overview of how Old Testament is established in past grace and anticipates future grace.
8 See also T. D. Alexander, *Exodus* (AOTC, London: Apollos, 2017), 498, who understands the young girl to be consenting to sexual activity.

a man and a woman, and that the status and security of the young girl is to be protected either by the duty-bound man or her father.[9]

The pithy instructions in Exodus 22:16–17 recur again in Deuteronomy 22:28–29, although in a different context and with a slightly different idea. The context in Deuteronomy is Israel poised at the edge of the Promised Land and YHWH, through Moses, is exhorting Israel to choose faithfulness as they enter and settle in the land. Due to this major development, all of Deuteronomy's instructions are addressed in more detail than what is contained in Exodus. In Deuteronomy 22:28–29, the particular situation addressed is a man forcing himself upon a young woman, rather than the man seducing a consenting young woman, as per Exodus 22:16–17. Again, the purpose of this instruction is to restore, as much as can be, a traumatic situation. The focus in the instruction is upon the offending man and his obligation towards the girl he has violated and towards her father. What is not said—and does not need to be said because it has already been established in Exodus 22:17, and Deuteronomy 22:28–29 builds on Exodus 22:17— is that the father still maintains the right to refuse the duty-bound marriage to the offending man.[10] The violated girl is not duty-bound to enter into the marriage with the offender through the father's refusal. Again, much could be said about the horror of this offence, but the instruction in the context of Deuteronomy is to protect the community's vulnerable, and the intent in this instance is to protect the young girl and relational order within the girl's familial community.

This particular instruction in Deuteronomy 22:28–29 occurs within a wider set of instructions in 22:13–30 about sexual relationships. The first situation in vv.13–21 is where a man takes a wife,

---

9   See also D. Stuart, *Exodus* (NAC, Nashville: B&H, 2006), 509–510.
10   See also D. I. Block, *Deuteronomy* (NIVAC, Grand Rapids: Zondervan, 2012), 526; J. G. McConville, *Deuteronomy* (AOTC, Leicester: Apollos, 2002), 342.

has sex with her, and motivated by hate, seeks to ruin her reputation by saying she was not a virgin (vv.13–14). There are two outcomes in this situation. If the girl is vindicated, then the outcome against the man protects the girl (vv.15–19). However, the second outcome is that the husband's accusation proves true, in which case the community enacts the death penalty (v.21). While today's culture would find this unpalatable, what we learn theologically from this is that the girl's sexual activity outside of the marriage relationship is considered an offence by God and so she is guilty. The impurity caused by the offence needs to be removed from the father's household. Such is the seriousness of sexual offence that, in the law, there is no provision for an offering to remove impurity caused by sexual offence on behalf of the guilty; the girl herself must bear her own penalty. This is true too of the following situations where a man has consenting sex with his neighbour's wife (v.22), when a man has consenting sex with an engaged young woman (vv.23–24), and when a man forces himself on an engaged young woman (vv.25–27). In this last situation, in vv.26–27, the priority of vindicating and caring for the vulnerable is once more demonstrated by the clear instruction that only the man bears the penalty as the guilty party, and not the innocent young woman (v.27).

What is evident from the above situations is that each seeks to restore a situation created by relational offence connected to marriage and sexual relationships. The underlying principle that has been offended in each case is the idea of belonging between husband and wife in a marriage relationship. Where sexual offence introduces unwholeness or disorder into a present or future marriage relationship, the seriousness of the offence is such that the guilty must suffer their own penalty, which is, in these instances, death.

3. Marriage and Same-Sex Activity in Leviticus

To understand Leviticus' view of marriage and same-sex activity, we need to return to the context of the fledgling nation at Sinai and the conclusion of the book of Exodus. In Exodus 40, Moses finishes the tabernacle, and YHWH's presence, which to this point was like a consuming fire at the top of Sinai (see Exod 24:17), fills the tabernacle so that he can dwell in the midst of his people (Exod 25:8–9, 40:34–35). YHWH's holy presence is no longer at a distance, but is now residing amongst his rebellious people (see Exodus 32–34). This marks a partial reversal of Genesis 3. No longer is humanity exiled from God's presence, although the tabernacle itself still forms a physical barrier. Due to this reversal, God makes provision, through the book of Leviticus, for Israel's life to be preserved with him, a holy God, dwelling in their midst (e.g., Lev 15:31, 26:3–13). The primary means by which Israel's life is to be preserved is by ensuring that Israel is set apart in a condition of wholeness and integrity, that is, in purity (Lev 1:3–16; 4:1–5:19; 11:1–16:34; 18:1–20:27). Becoming impure leads to exclusion from God's presence, so God provides ritual actions to ensure that anyone who becomes impure can be restored once more to his presence (e.g, Lev 11–15). Leviticus 1–16 focuses upon these provisions for Israel's life in the camp at Sinai and as Israel travels to the land. Leviticus 17–20, however, extends these provisions to Israel's future life in the land.

In this context, Leviticus 18 and 20 address the issue of relational disorder in the Israelite community, including the issue of sexual offence. In Leviticus 18:6–23, the prohibitions begin with the principle in v.6 that no one should approach a family member for sexual relations, after which vv.7–18 give concrete examples.[11] Verses 19–21 then address sexual offence outside of family relationships,

---

11　G. Wenham, *Leviticus* (NICOT, Grand Rapids: Eerdmans, 1979), 253.

culminating in vv.22–23 with prohibitions about sexual relations outside of male-female intimate acts. Verse 22 is clear in syntax and meaning: a man is not to engage in sexual acts with another man as with a woman. It is a prohibition of male-male same-sex sexual acts. This is an instance though, due to the kind of writing genre that Leviticus 18 exemplifies–a law list–that an absence of a parallel prohibition of female-female same-sex sexual acts does not mean evidence of absence. Although a prohibition of female-female intimate relationships is absent, this absence does not mean that there is freedom for women to engage in same-sex sexual activity; the principle and spirit of the prohibition still applies.[12]

The list of instructions in Leviticus 20:9–21 unfolds using different logic from Leviticus 18 and functions by listing penalties for relational offence, rather than conveying prohibitions. Notably though, the list begins in 20:9 with the penalty for anyone who curses his father or mother, after which 20:10–21 then addresses the penalties for sexual offence. Within this list, 20:13 outlines the penalty for a man engaging in sexual activity with another man, and again, the penalty is death. There is no other way around the syntax and meaning of this verse. In every instance of sexual offence addressed in vv.10–19, the guilty bear their own penalty which, for the most part, is death.[13]

Significantly though, each set of instructions addressing sexual offence in Leviticus 18 and 20 is bracketed by exhortations conveying YHWH's intent (18:2–4, 24–30; 20:7–8, 22–26). In 18:2–4 and 24–30, YHWH's desire is for his people to follow his ways in the land and not to adopt the impure actions of the Canaanite nations,

---

[12] For further explanation, see K. Smith, 'Ordered Relationships in Leviticus' in *Marriage, Family and Relationships: Biblical, Doctrinal and Contemporary Perspectives*, ed. T. A. Noble, S. K. Whittle, and P. S. Johnston (London: Apollos, 2017), 33–35.

[13] For further explanation, see Smith, 'Ordered Relationships', 36–38.

since the consequence would be exile. By doing what is prohibited, Israel would no longer be distinct from those nations as a people belonging to YHWH, and so would experience exclusion from the land. The exhortation in 20:7–8 and 20:22–26 extends this to persuade Israel to set themselves apart for two reasons; first, as a people who belong to God, they are to reflect his character, namely his holiness. Second, YHWH himself has acted to set them apart, namely through his work of redemption. With these sections of exhortation framing the prohibitions in Leviticus 18 and then the list of penalties in Leviticus 20, it is clear that the intent of the instruction is for Israel to relate to YHWH in a way that expresses their status of being set apart in relational wholeness as a people who belong to him. Sexual offence of any kind, not just same-sex sexual activity, causes relational disorder with YHWH that requires the guilty to bear their own penalty. There is no provision for an offering or sacrifice to remove this penalty from the offender, such is the seriousness of the offence to the holy God who dwells in the midst of his nation. The only way for Israel to have life with a holy God living in their midst is to be a people who belong wholly to him and who reflect wholeness and completeness in their family, marital, and sexual relationships.

4. Summary: The Torah's View of Marriage and Same-Sex Intimate Relationships

From Genesis to Deuteronomy, the conviction of God's instruction about marriage is consistent. In God's created order and as he begins to recreate order through Israel, marriage is a permanent commitment between a man and a woman where there is a mutual belonging. Where legal instructions address situations where a present or future marriage relationship (i.e., where the young girl is engaged) is compromised, the offence of these situations is considered to be so because the action opposes a particular dimension of the marriage relationship and causes relational disorder. Furthermore, a constant theme throughout the Torah is that God can command and expect obedience from his people because, firstly, YHWH is the sovereign creator and, secondly, he is Israel's covenant redeemer-king. His desire as he restores order among his people is that his people reflect relational order in community that testifies to their status as a people who are set apart to belong to God. In this context, it is evident that sexual offence, including same-sex sexual activity, is contrary to God's purposes for his people and his work of sanctifying them through his work of redemption.

The rest of the Old Testament builds on the Torah's understanding of marriage, particularly in Wisdom Literature and also in the use of marriage in the Prophets as a metaphor for covenant obedience between YHWH and his people. However, there is very little said in the Writings and the Prophets about same-sex intimate relationships because the assumption is that the norm, even when Israel's and Judah's rejection of God leads to exile, is that marriage is between a man and a woman. The Torah's instruction from Genesis to Deuteronomy establishes the foundations of Israel's worldview and is the measure by which the Writings and the Prophets either motivate faithfulness or indict covenant unfaithfulness.

5. Moving Forward into the New Testament and to Today

Throughout the Old Testament, there is the dynamic of God being present among his people (Gen 1:1–2:24), then the exile of humanity from God's presence (Gen 3:23–24), to God creating a nation so as to begin restoring relational order and to return his presence among his people (Gen 12:1–3; Lev 26:11–13). However, Israel persisted in covenant unfaithfulness in the land—and as a consequence was removed from the land and exiled to Babylon—and God's presence departed from the temple before Jerusalem was destroyed (Ezek 8–10). In an extraordinary act of reversal, we learn in the New Testament that God became flesh and dwelt among his people, to redeem those who believe in him from every tribe and nation, putting an end to the exile (John 1:1–5; Rev 5:6–14; 21:1–27). Through his ascension and rule at the right hand of God, Jesus has sent his Spirit to reside among his people (Acts 2:14–40), which is only possible because Jesus' blood shed for us purifies and removes our offence (Eph 1:3–2:22). Where there was no provision for sacrifice to bear the penalty of particular kinds of offence, like sexual offence, Jesus' offering of himself on our behalf is a perfect and complete sacrifice that removes the penalty of these offences from us who are guilty. There is no longer condemnation in Christ (Rom 8:1–4). This present reality for believers in Jesus is the reason why we have an imperishable hope of life beyond the grave in the new creation community where God will reside permanently amongst his people (Rev 21:1–27).

Also, through the blood of the cross, Jesus has redeemed us from the powers of sin and death so that these powers no longer have mastery over us (Heb 2:14–18). We are redeemed to belong to the Lord Jesus and so we are a people called to be set apart for him. We have this status of being set apart—that is, being holy—through the work of Christ bringing us from darkness and into the light. Yet those who have this status, and so belong to Jesus, have the responsibility of reflecting this status within an unbelieving world by being distinct in our relational wholeness and completeness with one another, through the peace Jesus has gained for us with God (1 Pet 1:13–2:12). Because of what Jesus has achieved on our behalf, and because those who believe are free from condemnation, we must not persist in acting on desires that are contrary to God's desire for his people who belong to him (Rom 6:1–14; Col 3:1–17). If we do, we despise the grace that redeemed us. This is as true of acting on same-sex sexual desire, as it is for an unmarried person acting on their sexual desire for someone of the other sex, or a married person acting on their sexual desire for someone other than their husband or wife. This is a challenge for every believer in Jesus, whose desires are in tension with biblical teaching because of sin at work in us, irrespective of sexual orientation. Yet we also know that God desires our good in Jesus and part of this good is that we are called to trust that God will sustain us in Christ as we deny the desires that are contrary to God's purposes for those who belong to him in Christ.

Therefore, although the gospel does not make distinctions between gender or race, and those who are in Christ are new creations awaiting the completeness of the new creation, the boundaries of distinction within the unity of being human still remain in a marriage relationship while we await Christ's return. The Old Testament does not countenance the option of same-sex unions because the very notion of same-sex sexual acts is contrary to God's purposes for his people to be set apart to belong to him. This is also true of adultery, sex outside of a marriage relationship, and failing to honour one's parents. It is critical to remember that we are all culpable, and we are not saved by putting off our sinful desires; we are saved by the once-for-all and finished work of Christ on our behalf. But knowing the costly gift of grace we have received in Christ, we seek to offer our bodies as whole and living sacrifices to God, seeking renewal in the image of Christ, and longing for Jesus' return. We do this, though, in the reality that we live in the already and the not yet; where our nature is being renewed each day, and we become aware of another facet to our sinfulness and a new struggle comes to light. Thus, an outworking of the conservative view of marriage must, while speaking in grace and truth, seek to engage an unbelieving world in the mess and realities of their marriage and sexual relationships and let the gospel transform brokenness into wholeness and life with kindness, gentleness, and patience.

Marriage, Headship and the New Testament

Dorothy A Lee[1]

A key question confronting the church in the area of sexual relationships is whether male headship is integral to Christian marriage. The answer affects both the shape of heterosexual marriage and—as I will argue in this paper—is also pertinent to the question of of homosexual unions. Does marriage demand wifely compliance or is it is intrinsically egalitarian? If obedience, on the one hand, is deemed on biblical and theological grounds to be essential to marriage, then mutual heterosexual relationships are ruled out, as are homosexual unions. If patriarchal structuring, on the other hand, can be shown to be a distortion of marriage from the perspective of New Testament theology and not grounded in a preordained 'order of creation', then new possibilities emerge for all equal and non-submissive partnerships.

Marriage in the ancient world and today

The context of marriage in the ancient Greco-Roman and Jewish worlds was very different from modern Western culture. Marriages

---

[1] The Rev'd Canon Professor Dorothy A. Lee FAHA is Stewart Research Professor of New Testament at Trinity College, University of Divinity. She is licensed as a priest in the Diocese of Melbourne, and is a Canon of St Paul's Anglican Cathedral, Melbourne, and of Holy Trinity Anglican Cathedral, Wangaratta.

were generally conducted between an adult man of around thirty years of age and a woman (girl) of between thirteen and sixteen. The man was usually the superior, not only in years, but also in education and adult life experience. The wider culture viewed the eldest male as the head of household with considerable authority, including over other adult members, male as well as female, along with children and the household slaves. Even the religion practised by the extended family was determined, and its rituals carried out, by the male head of house.[2]

Marriages were organised within kinship clusters which were primarily concerned with property, children, and the honour of the extended family. While Jewish marriage recognised the place of love, affection and sexual desire, the provision of children and the well-being of the wider kinship group played a larger role. Romantic love and soul friendship were not a necessary part of marriage and may indeed have been relatively rare, particularly since arranged marriages were the norm.

In today's world, by contrast, wives are now considerably older, better educated and much more worldly-wise than their ancient equivalents. In most contexts in the Western world, they are not required to obey their husbands. Marriage is no longer the uneven yoking together of two people with minimal choice within a male-oriented context, but a mutual and egalitarian, freely chosen partnership. In the 1995 *Prayer Book for Australia (APBA)*, for example, there are no vows promising wifely obedience.[3] In the previous book (*AAPB*), vows of wifely obedience were present in the first marriage form but not the second, the first form replicating the

---

[2] For a fuller description, see especially G. D. Fee, 'The Cultural Context of Ephesians 5:18–6:9' *Priscilla Papers* 16 (2002), 5–7.

[3] *A Prayer Book for Australia* (Anglican Church of Australia, Broughton Publishing, 1995), First Order, 648–649; Second Order, 660–661.

wife's promise to obey in *BCP*.[4] There is, however, a significant exception to the trend away from differentiated promises. A recent resource book from one Diocese encourages wifely obedience in a way that seems to go further than the *Book of Common Prayer*. Using imagery from Ephesians 5—interpreted in a certain way—it prays that the wife may cultivate 'the unfading beauty of a gentle and quiet spirit in submitting to her husband'.[5] The example is anomalous in the general view of Christian women, including within Anglicanism. The prayer books of other national Churches in the Anglican Communion include identical vows for wife as for husband: both are required to love, cherish and protect, and neither is summoned to obey or be submissive to the other.

In the contemporary context, it is hard to make sense of why a woman of around the same age as her husband, with an equivalent level of education and life experience, should have to obey him. Arguments from the so-called 'order of creation' in Genesis are sometimes used to bolster specific texts within the New Testament. But these arguments contradict the wider impulse of the gospel, as well as reason and experience. If, in creation, God has ordained the submission of wife to husband, the same 'order' ought logically to apply to all walks of life. It would mean that women should never exercise leadership or authority over men. That this is fallacious is evident from the many social and public contexts in which women exercise competent and effective leadership. Ironically, this same freedom may be accorded to women even in contexts

---

4   *An Australian Prayer Book* (General Synod of the Church of England in Australia, St Andrew's House, Sydney: 1978), First Order, 549–550; Second Order, 561–563.
5   'A Service for Marriage Form 2' in *Common Prayer: Resources for Gospel-Shaped Gatherings* (Archbishop of Sydney's Liturgical Panel, Anglican Press, 2012), 129.

where obedience and submission are required of them in home and church. The level of contradiction here is blatant.

Furthermore, past generations could give a 'reasonable' account of why authority resided with males as against females. Women were considered more emotional than men and less capable of rational thought. Their personalities were by definition thought to be gentle, passive and nurturing rather than courageous, active and outgoing. Women, in this worldview, lacked the necessary qualities for leadership. It belonged, for the most part (and allowing for exceptions), in the male domain. Such a gender binary is not derived from biology and is of limited (if any) value, and so there is no longer any external reason in calling for wifely obedience. The Bible is not irrational; God's commands have a firm basis in human experience, and diversity of context needs always to be taken into account in interpreting the sacred text.

There is a further aspect to wifely obedience in today's context. If wives are called to cultivate a gentle and quiet spirit in submission to their husbands, there is the danger that they are rendered powerless if they experience abuse within the marriage. A gentle and quiet spirit does not readily speak out against injustice. Many wives in Christian households, including those married to clergy, have begun to disclose the abuse they have endured, the biblical texts quoted at them to justify it, the disempowerment they have experienced and the discouragement they have received from clergy to escape the marriage.[6]

---

[6]   See Julia Baird & Hayley Gleeson, 'Raped, tracked, humiliated: Clergy wives speak out about domestic violence, ABC News, http://www.abc.net.au/news/2017-11-23/clergy-wives-speak-out-domestic-violence/9168096. Last accessed 10 August 2018.

Marriage in the New Testament

In the Gospels Jesus speaks positively of marriage, commending its life-long nature and sanctity (Mark 10:1–12; Matt 5:31–32; Luke 16:18–10), while making allowance for divorce in serious circumstances (Matt 19:1–9).[7] Yet nowhere does Jesus support marriage as a patriarchal institution. Indeed, he quotes the second creation account where the husband leaves his family in order to become 'one flesh' with his wife (Mark 10:7–8/par.; Gen 2:24). In gender terms, this pattern is counter-cultural: it is not the wife's role to surrender her natal family but the husband's. Ironically, in contexts of patriarchal marriage, the opposite is the case: the wife leaves behind her family and kinship to join that of her husband, a custom reflected in the Western tradition of the woman's change of surname upon marriage to that of her husband.

The 'household codes' in the New Testament epistles outline the responsibilities of household members to one another.[8] They originate originally with Aristotle who believed that men were more rational than women and thus more fitted for leadership.[9] In these biblical texts, slavery as an institution is not directly questioned and marriage seems to involve a ranking of status between husband and wife.[10] In Ephesians, in particular, the relationship between husband and wife is analogous to the relationship between Christ and the church (Eph 5:22–33).

---

[7] Here Jesus allies himself more closely with the Pharisaic House of Shammai, which was strict on the conditions that allowed for divorce, as opposed to that of Himmel which permitted divorce for trivial reasons, thereby condemning women (who could not initiate divorce) to public shame and permanent separation from their children.

[8] See esp. Col 3:18–4:1; Eph 5:21–6:9; 1 Tim 2:8–15, 5:1–2, 6:1–2; Titus 2:1–10; 1 Pet 2:18–3:7.

[9] D.L. Balch, *Let Wives Be Submissive: The Domestic Code in 1 Peter* (Chico, CA: SBL Scholars Press, 1981), 33–49.

[10] Shi-Min Lu, 'Woman's Role in New Testament Household Codes: Transforming First Century Roman Culture' *Priscilla Papers* 30 (2016), 9–10.

According to Gordon Fee, the actual structure of marriage is not the issue in these codes but rather the theological precepts enshrined within them. As such, they contain underlying principles of mutual submission, love and respect—principles that are ultimately grounded in the equality and mutuality of women and men through baptism into Christ (Gal 3:27–28).[11] There is a parallel here with slavery. Modern interpreters do not regard the ownership and obedient submission of slaves as something to be affirmed, though that too falls within the purview of the household codes; on the contrary slavery itself is widely and vehemently opposed in Christian circles. Respect, mutuality, faithfulness, and self-giving, sacrificial love are the core principles of marriage in these texts, notwithstanding the limiting social realities of the early church struggling to survive in a context of empire with all its idolatrous demands and threats.

Even the analogy between Christ and the church still finds a place in contemporary theology by pointing to the unique and 'sacramental' character of marriage between Christians. Interpreted as symbol rather than allegory—where the meaning is not located in the particulars but rather in the whole[12]—the imagery conveys a sense of Christian marriage as the mystical union between Christ and the church, the union of love and covenant fidelity. The symbolism need not be used to reinforce gender hierarchy but rather, in the light of Galatians 3:28–29, has the capacity to reinforce the union between

---

11   Fee, 'Cultural Context', 7–8.
12   The distinction between symbol and allegory goes back to S.T. Coleridge who believed that 'whereas allegories merely substitute fictional images for abstract ideas, symbols convey something beyond or greater than themselves precisely because of what they are in themselves' (N. Halmi, 'Coleridge on Symbol and Allegory' in F. Berwick (ed.), *The Oxford Handbook of Samuel Taylor Coleridge* (Oxford: Oxford University Press, 2009), 345–358; https://www.academia.edu/6999259/_Coleridge_on_Allegory_and_Symbol_in_The_Oxford_Handbook_of_Samuel_Taylor_Coleridge_ed._Frederick_Burwick_Oxford_University_Press_2009_345_58, 5. Last accessed 28 Jan 2019.

male and female in Christ, just as the epistle also confirms the unity between Jew and Gentile effected through the cross (Eph 2:11–22).

Homosexuality in the ancient world and today

On the second issue of same-sex partnerships, the idea of marriage between two persons of the same gender in the ancient world was virtually inconceivable. There is evidence of same-sex activity, particularly among the Greeks. Strictly speaking, the ancient world knew little of homosexuality as an exclusive orientation of life, although it could recognise deep relationships between people of the same sex.[13] Men and boys with homosexual experience were also expected to enter into marriages and relationships with women.[14] In fact, bisexuality was more the reality than homosexuality. Furthermore, many homosexual unions were, by our current social standards and indeed by biblical standards, abusive and exploitative. Older men might have sexual relationships with teenage boys as an expression of power and patronage. Pederasty was not uncommon in the ancient world and regarded as a matter, not of commitment, but of sexual unrestraint and domination, even where there were strong feelings on the part of the older man towards the boy.

A further factor is that the receptive partner in penetrative homosexual sex was regarded in the ancient world more generally

---

13   The speech of Aristophanes in Plato's *Symposium,* with its focus on the nature of love, envisages life-long relationships between people of the same sex, but he argues for it on the basis of a creation myth in which three types of human were originally made: male, female, and androgynous. All of these beings are cut in half by Zeus, so that each now longs for wholeness and union with his or her other half, a longing that may include but yet goes beyond sex. Diotima, however, whom Socrates quotes at length, critiques Aristophanes' speech in favour of Platonic love which is grounded in love of the divine (http://classics.mit.edu/Plato/symposium.html; last accessed 28 Jan 2019).

14   The lyrical poetry of Sappho (c. 630–570 BCE) is homoerotic, unusual for its focus on female-female love— though even she was said to be married with a daughter, and the young women whom she lauds also go on to marry.

as playing the female part, which was seen as passive. In the same way, women were viewed, not only as sexually passive—where men by contrast were sexually active initiators—but also as the recipients and nurturers of the male seed *in utero*. In values of honour and shame, pertaining particularly to men, the female role was shameful for the male to play and led to a significant loss of honour. Furthermore, homosexual practice had no procreative purpose, which was a significant factor among those who disapproved of homosexuality. These attitudes are widespread in Jewish writings, as well as in some Greco-Roman texts.[15]

While many philosophers admired self-restraint in matters of the body—including food and sexuality—the sexual exploitation of males by males was common enough in the ancient world, including of slaves who had no civic rights. The physical abuse of slaves, both male and female, was widespread and fell within the rights of the *paterfamilias*, the father of the family, who had—at least in Roman law—the power of life and death over household members, thus also legitimising sexual abuse. In a 'culture marked by aggressive bisexuality', Judeo-Christian ethics that confined sexual desire to marriage was liberating by comparison, and must have seemed thankfully so to many Christian slaves.[16]

In the contemporary Western world, by contrast, a different kind of homosexual relationship has now become visible, one which need not be either abusive or promiscuous. Homosexual Christians who have lived in faithful partnerships for decades—without the

---

15 The first century Jewish philosopher, Philo, shares this view and is generally highly negative about homosexuality; see W. Loader, 'Reading Romans 1 on Homosexuality in the Light of Biblical/Jewish and Greco-Roman Perspectives of its Time' *Zeitschrift für die Neutestamentliche Wissenschaft* 108 (2017), 124–127; 135–137.

16 R. Jewett, 'The Social Context and Implications of Homoerotic References in Romans 1:24–27' in D.L. Balch (ed.), *Homosexuality, Science, and the 'Plain Sense' of Scripture* (Grand Rapids: Eerdmans, 2000), 240.

comfort and security of being blessed by the church—believe that the Christian community should extend covenant blessing, and even marriage, to them in order to confirm and support their partnerships in the public setting of the Christian assembly. This call comes from across the breadth of Anglicanism and is not confined to any one part of the church.[17] At the very least we need to listen carefully to our sisters and brothers in the faith and take seriously their experience and their reading of the Bible.

A number of theological arguments, based on careful reading and interpretation of Scripture, support the view that gay relationships do not in themselves contravene the spirit of the gospel. One such argument is that Jesus himself has nothing to say on the subject of same-sex relationships and that the New Testament more widely has little to say. It is sometimes assumed on the basis of Jesus' teaching that marriage must always be the union of one woman and one man, but this is an inference from texts that have no principle of exclusion. A further argument is that the key test of spiritual authenticity is a life lived in love, justice and mercy (e.g., Matt 7:15–20; Gal 5:16–21; Jas 1:22–27). If homosexual partners display the fruit of the Spirit in their lives, including their life together, is this not a point in favour of the church's thanksgiving and blessing? So at least a previous Bishop of Gippsland asserted in the charge to his Synod in 2012.[18]

Homosexuality and the New Testament

There are only a handful of New Testament texts that seem to condemn homosexual activity, and these have been taken

---

[17] See e.g. the English organisation, 'Accepting Evangelicals', who support same-sex relationships from a biblical perspective: http://www.acceptingevangelicals.org/. Last accessed 25 Jan 2019.

[18] M. Porter (ed.), *A Man Called Johnny Mac: Selected Writings of Bishop John McIntyre* (Northcote Vic: Morning Star/ Diocese of Gippsland, 2015), 125–131.

traditionally as outright condemnations of same-sex unions. Of these four texts, one is unlikely to be referring to homosexuality in general. Jude speaks of sinful people 'engaging in sexual promiscuity and going after strange [lit. other] flesh' (Jude 1:7). This is the third example of divine judgement in Jude, preceded by the disobedience of the exodus generation (1:5) and the rebellion of certain angels (1:6). In this context, 'strange flesh' most likely refers to non-human flesh, that of the two angels visiting Lot whose hospitality is desecrated by his fellow citizens' desire for sexual violence.[19] In any case, if Jude has in mind the homosexual intentions of the inhabitants of Sodom and Gomorrah, he is condemning acts of gross sexual aggression and violence.

Two other references from the Pauline school belong in a catalogue of wrong-doers (1 Cor 6:9–11; 1 Tim 1:9–10). There are two descriptive terms employed in these texts: *malakos* and *arsenokoitês*. The former means literally a 'soft person' while the second pairs two words meaning 'male' and 'bed'.[20] Both are difficult to translate since they are rare and widely disputed. The 'soft' may refer to people who live in luxury (cf. Matt 11:8/Luke 7:25), are in some way effeminate or are morally lax, including sexually. It may refer to the passive partners in anal intercourse. In 1 Corinthians 6, the term follows the condemnation of idolaters who will not inherit the kingdom.

The second term is more difficult. The NRSV translates *arsenokoitai* as 'sodomites', but the TNIV and ESV go further, translating it explicitly as 'those/men who practise homosexuality' (the assumption being that Lev 18:22 and 20:13 are in mind here). By contrast, the KJV gives a different translation: 'nor effeminate, nor abusers

---

19   R.J. Bauckham, *Jude, 2 Peter* (WBC; Waco: Word Books, 1983), 53–54.
20   Note, however, that etymology is a poor guide to meaning; see J. Barr, *The Semantics of Biblical Language* (Oxford: Oxford University Press, 1961), 107–160.

of themselves with mankind'. Paul's usage is the first in Classical literature and its meaning is not at all plain, so the confidence of modern translators is remarkable. There are no earlier examples and later writers either quote Paul without defining the term or use it in different ways, including in relation to women and rape.[21]

Even if Paul's meaning here is the condemnation of sodomy (in accord with the NRSV's translation), which is itself debatable, there is a further problem of interpretation. In the more immediate sense, the sin of Sodom was not sodomy per se, as we have seen, but rather the act of violence threatened against guests to whom hospitality was a sacred duty (Gen 19:1–11; cf. Ezek 16:48–50).[22] In the broader sense, we need to be aware that, in today's context, not all gay couples practise literal sodomy in their relationship. And what of heterosexual couples who do? These complicating factors make the translation more difficult to pinpoint with any precision.

The context in both passages assists in discerning the broader meaning, however, even if we cannot as yet be sure of the specifics. Lists of vices were conventional rhetorical tools in ancient literature. What is condemned here is the behaviour of those who are idolatrous, violent, indifferent to others, and sexually promiscuous. Alan Cadwallader, who argues that the case of the man living with his stepmother lies behind the list in 1 Corinthians, defines *arsenokoitês* more generally as one who 'acts dishonourably and violently in a sexual intrusion upon the body of another'.[23] In the

---

21 A. Cadwallader, 'Keeping Lists or Embracing Freedom: 1 Corinthians 6:9–10 in Context' in *Five Uneasy Pieces: Essays on Scripture and Sexuality* (Adelaide: ATF Press, 2011), 50–61.
22 Note that rape is always, first and foremost, an act of violence and power rather than simply uncontrolled desire/lust. See, e.g., L. Pennington, 'Rape is Always an Act of Violence' *Huffington Post UK 2014*: https://www.huffingtonpost.co.uk/louise-pennington/ched-evans-rape-is-always-an-act-of-violence_b_5990092.html. Last accessed 27 Jan 2019.
23 'Keeping Lists', 60.

New Testament world, the most prevalent form of such intrusion (rape) was the abuse of boys—in other words, pederasty.

The passage in Romans 1:26-27 is particularly significant, though its meaning is debated. Paul speaks of those who reject their natural orientation to indulge in promiscuous acts, motivated by passions that seek their own self-gratification. In imagery that is intemperate and ungovernable (fire, burning, consuming), Paul condemns these examples of abusive and uncontrolled sexual license on the part of women and men.[24] In their frantic search for self-gratification, such people are behaving in ways that are contrary to nature, according to Paul. The language used is that of exchange (*ellaxan, metellaxan*, 1:23, 25, 26), where natural behaviour is substituted for what is unnatural: murder, faithlessness, rebellion and gossip (1:29–31), all of which flow from the worship of pagan gods. Idolatry, indeed, is the main issue here,[25] with Paul using typically Jewish reactions to homosexuality; the sexual issue is in part a rhetorical ploy to expose Jewish hypocrisy in regards to the Law. The list is set, in other words, within the revelation of divine wrath (1:17), most immediately against Gentile conduct widely despised by Jews and based on idolatry (1:20–23), but in fact designed to expose Jewish and thus cosmic human sinfulness, whether or not it lays claim to moral superiority (2:1–5).[26]

A fundamental issue of interpretation is what is meant here by

---

24 Loader, 'Reading Romans 1', 131–135.
25 See, e.g., the evangelical gay website, GayChristian101, and the article 'Does Romans 1:26-27 condemn homosexuals?' which argues that Paul has the orgiastic cult of Cybele in mind here: https://www.gaychristian101.com/does-romans-12627-condemn-homosexuals.html. Last accessed 26 Jan 2019.
26 W. Countryman argues that Paul sees homosexual behaviour as falling under the rubric of 'uncleanness' (*akatharsia*) which, along with dietary laws and circumcision, is now superseded by Christian faith (*Dirt, Greed, and Sex: Sexual Ethics in the New Testament and their Implications for Today* (London: SCM, 1988/2001),110–116. Against this, Loader argues that Paul sees these acts as sinful ('Reading Romans 1', 120–122).

'natural' and 'unnatural'. It is possible that Paul has in mind heterosexual persons who indulge in licentious and predatory behaviour towards others of the same gender. It is unlikely that he knows anything of homosexuality as 'an abiding personal psychological orientation',[27] nor of those whose sexual orientation 'is not the result of deliberate perversion, but something natural to them.'[28] In his Jewish context, Paul does not envisage homosexual partnerships that are exclusive and grounded in Christian virtue; the alternatives in Greco-Roman society fill him with dismay. On this basis some commentators argue that neither Romans nor any other book of the New Testament can be used to condemn the homosexual orientation that is natural to individuals today.[29] Loader, by contrast, argues that Paul has in mind not only homosexuals but also the mindset behind them.[30]

There are Christians who, in opposing homosexual practice, have argued that there is no sin is being homosexual per se, but only in acting on it. This conclusion does not quite follow logically. If there is no sin in being homosexual and gay people are innocent in this respect, why do they suddenly incur guilt by entering into loving and covenanted partnerships? Is there no 'remedy' for their natural, sexual desires as there is for heterosexuals, with the result that they are left throughout their lives 'to burn' with unfulfilled passion rather than 'to marry' (1 Cor 7:9)?

---

27 B. Byrne, *Romans* (Collegeville: Liturgical Press, 1996), 70.
28 W. Loader, *The New Testament with Imagination: A Fresh Approach to Its Writings and Themes* (Grand Rapids: Eerdmans, 2007), 91. See also Peta Sherlock, 'Reading Romans as Anglicans: Romans 1:26–27' in *Five Uneasy Pieces*, 39–44.
29 See, e.g., A.J. Hultgren, *Paul's Letter to the Romans: A Commentary* (Grand Rapids: Eerdmans, 2011), 95–103, 616–620.
30 Loader, 'Reading Romans 1', 147. Loader sees Paul as holding a typically Jewish view that opposes homosexuality in any form, citing in particular Philo; yet Paul and Philo have very different views of sexuality within marriage—for the latter, e.g., its sole purpose is procreation.

If the latter is the case, there must be by definition something intrinsically distorting about homosexuality in itself, for Christians and non-Christians alike. Otherwise, why would a gay relationship be sinful? As with the issue of wifely obedience, the Bible is not irrational, issuing commands simply in order to evoke an unquestioning obedience from human beings. Biblical injunctions make sense at a human level and we need to be ready to argue for them in relation to human experience and well-being. As with wifely submission, there is no argument to support the view outside of a narrow interpretation of a small number of biblical texts where the wood is lost for the trees. The 'onus of proof' lies with those who support such submission and oppose homosexual unions to demonstrate how these negative commands contribute, specifically, to human thriving and social well-being, and to proffer clear reasons that can be demonstrated on the grounds of experience, as well as on biblical grounds.

The issue here is essentially how we are to interpret the Bible in relation to reason and human experience.[31] C.S. Lewis has famously written of the intrinsic (though not absolute) value of experience in his autobiography:

> What I like about experience is that it is such an honest thing. You may take any number of wrong turnings; but keep your eyes open and you will not be allowed to go very far before the warning signs appear. You may have deceived yourself, but experience is not trying to deceive you. The universe rings true wherever you fairly test it.[32]

Experience and reason are both integral to the interpretation of Scripture. There is, of course, a mutuality to such interpretation

---

31 L.T. Johnson, *The First and Second Letters to Timothy* (AB; New York: Doubleday, 2001), 170.
32 *Surprised by Joy: The Shape of my Early Life* (New York: HarperCollins, 1955), 177.

because, as we interpret the Bible, it too interprets us to ourselves. But this mutual interpretation takes place within the concrete realities of human life and in acknowledgement that the world itself belongs to God and has the capacity to reveal God: the capacity, in other words, to disclose truth. None of this is to deny the primal authority of Scripture. Rather, as biblical Christians, we are called to be ready 'for a defense [*apologia*] to anyone requesting from you a reasoned account [*logos*] of the hope within you' (1 Pet 3:15). We are given the capacity to reason and make sense of biblical faith. It is not a matter of *credo quia absurdum* ('I believe because it is absurd') but rather of *fides quaerens intellectum*: 'faith seeking understanding' through reflection on Scripture via the dual lens of reason and experience.[33]

Conclusion

One of the classic divides in biblical interpretation stands between those who believe Christians should confine themselves to what Scripture explicitly commands—a view associated popularly with Puritanism—and those who believe that Christian behaviour may legitimately move beyond Scripture but not against it. In the latter case, rather than hunting for obscure or infrequent texts that might be turned into commands, regardless of context, it seeks biblical values and principles that will guide Christian conduct in new settings that the Bible itself may not envisage. Homosexuality as both an orientation of nature and a desire for loving and loyal commitment belongs within this latter category, as do a number of

---

33 The former saying has been wrongly attributed to Tertullian (E. Osborn, *Tertullian: First Theologian of the West* [Cambridge: Cambridge University Press, 1997], 48–64), while the latter is associated with Augustine and Anselm. See also the 'Methodist Quadrilateral' which, deriving from John Wesley and his Anglican background, includes experience alongside reason, tradition and Scripture, the latter having primacy: see, e.g., http://www.umc.org/what-we-believe/glossary-wesleyan-quadrilateral-the. Last accessed 19 Jan 2019.

other contemporary issues. The capacity to support and celebrate same-sex unions might then be seen as a trajectory not explicitly endorsed by the biblical text but not overtly condemned by it either.

The argument of this essay is that the gospel principles of the New Testament present a model of marriage and partnership that dismantles male-dominated structures, valuing instead mutuality, fidelity, respect and love, without domination or subjugation. These principles overthrow notions of paternalistic marriage and challenge the necessity of wifely obedience. They also open the way for covenantal relationships that are not based on gender but strive for the same gospel values in their union. The overcoming of male-oriented and discriminatory structures enables the redemptive voice of the New Testament to be heard anew, with all its challenge and hope, in our present context.

Family Ties: Marriage, Sex, and Belonging in the New Testament

Claire Smith[1]

> Then the angel said to me, 'Write this: Blessed are those who are invited to the wedding supper of the Lamb!' And he added, 'These are the true words of God.'
>
> Rev 19:9

> I saw the Holy City, the new Jerusalem, coming down out of heaven from God, prepared as a bride beautifully dressed for her husband.
>
> Rev 21:2

The heavenly marriage

Marriage is mentioned explicitly or implicitly in most books in the New Testament.[2] It is evident in the mention of specific married

---

1 Dr Claire Smith is a writer and theologian, and a member of St Andrew's Cathedral, Sydney. She received her doctorate in Biblical Studies from the University of Western Sydney/Moore College.

2 It is not found in Galatians, Philippians, 1 & 2 Thessalonians, Philemon, 1, 2, & 3 John. However, references to sexual immorality in the NT assume a common understanding of sanctioned sexual activity within heterosexual marriage: Gal 5:19; 1 Thess 4:3–7. The following footnotes cite only one reference per book, however, most books include multiple references.

couples.³ It features in historical narratives.⁴ It is the focus of specific teaching.⁵ It is the backdrop to discussions of singleness and celibacy, widowhood, divorce, and adultery.⁶ It is used to illustrate theological truths.⁷

That is, the New Testament is not silent about marriage, neither is marriage peripheral. It is both background noise and headline news. And it is good. Human marriage is blessed by Jesus' presence at the marriage of Cana where he performed his first messianic sign (John 2:1–11),⁸ and elsewhere its practice and purpose are embraced, endorsed, and explained with rich theological themes.⁹

So that when the New Testament ends with a marriage—the eschatological marriage of the Lamb and his bride as the culmination of God's redemptive purposes foreshadowed by Isaiah (Isa 62:4–5)—it does not come as a surprise or beg explanation (Rev 19:6–9; 21:2, 9–10). We know what marriage is, and that it is joyous, good, pure, and beautiful—at least, this heavenly marriage is, notwithstanding the weaknesses of human marriage this side of the fall.

The New Testament consistently points towards this end-time marriage. In the Gospels, it is seen in the bridegroom sayings (Matt 25:1–13), including some where Jesus is the identified as the groom

---

3 E.g., Acts 5:1–10; 2 Tim 4:19.
4 E.g., Matt 1:18–25; John 4:16–18.
5 E.g., Col 3:18–19; 1 Tim 5:14; Titus 2:3–5; Heb 13:4; 1 Pet 3:1–7.
6 E.g., Mark 10:2–12; Luke 20:27–36; 1 Cor 7:1–40; Jas 1:27; 2 Pet 2:14; Jude 7.
7 E.g., Rom 7:1–3; 2 Cor 11:2; Eph 5:22–33; Rev 21:2, 9–10.
8 Cf. *The Book of Common Prayer*, The Form of Solemnization of Matrimony.
9 In this way, marriage is inherently different from slavery. Slavery is assumed as an existing social practice, which the New Testament writers seek to regulate (Eph 6:5–9; Col 3:22–4:1; 1 Tim 6:1–2; Titus 2:9–10; 1 Pet 2:18). Slavery as an institution is not blessed or endorsed or grounded in creation or theological themes. Unlike marriage, slaves are to gain their freedom if that is possible (1 Cor 7:21). The only slavery about which the NT speaks positively is our slavery to Christ in holy obedience (Rom 6:16–22; 1 Cor 7:23; Eph 6:6; 1 Pet 2:16).

(Matt 9:14–17; Mark 2:18–22; Luke 5:33–39; John 3:27–30), and in those parables where the kingdom is likened to a wedding banquet (Matt 22;1–14; Luke 14:7–24). It is glimpsed when Jesus assumes the role of the bridegroom-host meeting the needs of the guests at the wedding at Cana (John 2:1–11; cf. 3:27–30).[10] In the epistles, Paul speaks of having betrothed the Corinthian Christians to one husband, Christ (2 Cor 11:2),[11] and uses the marriage of Christ and the church as the archetype for human marriage (Eph 5:23–32).

Yet despite being thematically and theologically embedded in the New Testament, there are clearly cultural aspects to the practice of marriage. These include the betrothal of Joseph and Mary which could only be ended by divorce (Matt 1:19),[12] the lamp-holding virgins awaiting the groom (Matt 25:1–10), certain conventions around wedding banquets, invitations, and clothing (Matt 22:1–12), and, probably, a head-covering worn by wives symbolising marriage (1 Cor 11:4–10).[13] None of these are now part of our practice of marriage.[14]

So, the question arises: Is the New Testament writers' treatment of marriage, including their understanding of sexual immorality[15]

---

[10] D. A. Carson, *The Gospel According to John* (Leicester, England: Inter-Varsity Press, 1991), 172–73, cf. 169.

[11] B. S. Rosner, *Paul, Scripture, and Ethics: A Study of 1 Corinthians 5–7* (Grand Rapids, MI: Baker Books. 1994), 132, also notes that '[s]piritual marriage imagery also lurks in the 'atmosphere' of 1 Corinthians 7:32–35, where pleasing the Lord and pleasing one's marriage partner are compared.'

[12] A. Köstenberger and D. W. Jones, *God, Marriage, and Family: Rebuilding the Biblical Foundations*, 2nd ed. (Wheaton, IL: Crossway Books, 2010), 375, fn. 13.

[13] B. W. Winter, *Roman Wives, Roman Widows: The Appearance of New Women and the Pauline Communities* (Grand Rapids, MI.: Eerdmans. 2003), 77–96.

[14] Historical studies also suggest that girls typically married young (from 14 years on), whereas men were closer to 30. This would be unacceptable today (in fact, illegal). See S. Baugh, 'Marriage and Family in Ancient Greek Society', in *Marriage and Family in the Biblical World*, ed. K. M. Campbell, (Downers Grove, IL: InterVarsity Press, 2003), 107.

[15] E.g., *porneia, moicheia, koite, ekporneuo*.

and the metaphor of the end-time marriage, simply a culturally located expression of God-ordained covenant-love relationships that can take different forms in different cultures?[16] Could it be that the sexual dimorphism of marriage as we meet it in the Bible is nothing more than a cultural trope?

To focus the question: Does the New Testament allow for marriage or sanctioned sexual relationships between two people of the same sex?

Marriage from the beginning

Often these questions are approached, whether to argue for or against same-sex sexual activity and relationships, through a handful of texts in isolation from the rest of Scripture (i.e., Gen 19:1–38; Lev 18:22; 20:13; Rom 1:24–27; 1 Cor 6:9–11; 1 Tim 1:9–10; Jude 6–7).[17] But that is to miss the wood for the trees.

These are not isolated texts. They are part of the fabric of biblical revelation, which begins with a human marriage (Gen 2:23–24, cf. Gen 1:27) and ends with the marriage of the bride and the Lamb, and where the structure of the former is based on the latter.

In fact, there is a consistent understanding of marriage throughout the Bible—even with the many post-fall aberrations, including polygamy, adultery, divorce, and, with death, the experience of widowhood—namely, that marriage is the union of two people of opposing biological sex, and that this sexed complementarity is essential not incidental to the nature and purpose of marriage.

---

16   E.g., Simon Taylor, 'A Positive Biblical Approach to Equal Marriage', *Modern Believing*, 58.1 (2017): 41–53.

17   E.g., Nigel Wright (ed.), *Five Uneasy Pieces: Essays on Scripture and Sexuality* (Hindmarsh, SA: Australian Theological Forum, 2012), where the teaching of Genesis 1–2 on marriage, Jesus' teaching on marriage and divorce (Matthew 19; Mark 10), apostolic instructions on marriage (1 Corinthians 7; Ephesians 5; 1 Peter 3), and the eschatological marriage of Revelation are not listed in the Index of Biblical References (pages 89–92).

In the New Testament this is most clearly articulated in Jesus' response to the Pharisees as they sought to trap him by drawing him into disputes between rival rabbinical schools about the scope of Deuteronomy 24:1 and the grounds for divorce (Matt 19:3–9; Mark 10:2–12). Jesus knows the dissolution of marriage can only rightly be understood in light of its original nature and purpose before sin and brokenness corrupted the human heart, and the provision of divorce was needed. So, as we might expect, he begins there.

But he also does something unexpected. Instead of simply citing the explanation in Genesis 2:24 that follows the marriage of the first man and woman—equals of the same flesh and bone, with complementary sex and gender—he places that statement in the context of the even earlier statement that humanity was created by God in his image, male and female (Gen 1:27; Matt 19:4).

In doing so Jesus shows there is a creational logic to the nature of marriage.[18] It is not just that one person chooses to leave the family home and be joined to another, and their bodily sex is not significant. Rather, 'from the beginning' the Creator created humankind as sexually differentiated beings, male and female, and 'for this reason' a man and woman are joined in marriage—two equal and complementary image-bearers joined by God to be 'one flesh', united in a covenantal relationship unlike any other. One flesh in their exclusive sexual union, in the new family unit they create, in their companionship, and potentially, in offspring.[19]

That is, the very nature and purpose of marriage require that there be only two, and that the two are male and female. Moreover, the ability of human marriage to explain or reflect rich theological

---

18   Cf. 19:5 'Therefore' (*eneka toutou*); 19:6 'So' (*hōste*).
19   G. Wenham, *Genesis 1–15* (Waco, TX: Word, 1987), 71.

truths—such as, the union of Christ and the church[20]—demands that the sex and gender differences within human marriage are real not illusory, stable not fluid, and fixed not interchangeable.

Note, too, that Jesus does not say '*in* the beginning', which might allow for differences this side of Genesis 3, but '*from* the beginning'.[21] Despite the tragic effects of the fall, what God first intended for marriage is still now his design, in all cultures and all times.

It is not that other expressions of committed sexual partnerships were unknown in the ancient world. They were, including committed, consensual, same-sex peer relationships, and notions of same-sex marriage, and same-sex sexual orientation.[22]

Yet despite this, Jesus and the apostles after him maintain the enduring authority and goodness of God's creation design for marriage as between one man and one woman, and as the only proper domain for the expression of sexual desire and intimacy (cf. Matt 5:28; Heb 13:4). More than that, they are not unaware or neutral about other types of sexual activity. Without exception, every reference to alternative sexual expression in the New Testament is negative, including every reference to same-sex sexual activity.[23]

Thus, when Paul traces the consequences of our rebellion and

---

20 Other examples are the metaphor of the Lamb and his bride, and the structured relationships of man and woman (likely, husband and wife) and Christ and God, in 1 Cor. 11:3. See R. E. Ciampa and B. S. Rosner, *The First Letter to the Corinthians*, PNTC, (Grand Rapids, MI: Eerdmans, 2010), 508.

21 Cf. *ap' archēs*. Rightly, ESV. William Loader, *The New Testament on Sexuality* (Grand Rapids, MI.: Eerdmans, 2012) 275, notes the words are both a reference to time, and 'by implication to first principles of God's will'.

22 E.g., Plato, *Sym*, 179D–180B; 181B; Aristotle, *Eth. Nic.* 1148b, lines 28–34; Suetonius, *Galba* 22; Photois, *Bibliothêkê*, 94.77a–b (after Iamblichos); Suetonius, *Nero* 28. See Branson Parler, 'Worlds Apart?: James Brownson and the Sexual Diversity of the Greco-Roman World', *TrinJ.* 38NS (2017): 183–200. Preston Sprinkle, 'Romans 1 and Homosexuality: A Critical Review of James Brownson's *Bible, Gender, Sexuality*', *BBR* 24.4 (2014): 515–28, here 522–27. Loader, *Sexuality*, 322–324.

23 Robert Gagnon, *The Bible and Homosexual Practice: Texts and Hermeneutics* (Nashville, TN: Abingdon Press, 2001), 87–90, 229–339.

rejection of God through human history, sexual impurity—including same-sex sexual activity—is emblematic of the progressive spiritual and moral decline of all humanity (Rom 1:24–27). At each step, in judgement, God delivered humanity over to wrongly directed worship, lusts, passions, and conduct.

The glory of God was exchanged for images resembling human beings, birds, animals and creeping things. The truth of God was exchanged for a lie and created things were worshipped rather than the Creator. Natural sexual relations (*physiken chresin*) were exchanged by females and males for those contrary to nature (*para physin*). Men gave up natural relations with women and committed shameless acts with one another, and women did likewise with other women (cf. *homoios*).

But what 'nature' does Paul have in mind, and how do women and men act against it? It is not that these sexual acts have no procreative potential.[24] Neither is it heterosexuals acting against their 'natural' orientation by engaging in homosexual acts.[25] It is not simply 'excessive' passion that is at issue.[26] The 'nature' Paul has in mind is the natural created order, which is evident in the many linguistic and thematic links to Genesis 1 that run through the text.[27] It is the way that God designed his creation to work.[28]

Accordingly, the sexual relations that are 'contrary to nature' are

---

24 Loader, *Sexuality*, 311. However, his claim that 'we should feel free to reach different conclusions from Paul if the evidence suggests that this is appropriate' (p. 321) does not adequately recognise the authority of Holy Scripture, cf. page 499.
25 Loader, *Sexuality*, 313, 326. Sprinkle, 'Romans 1 and Homosexuality', 518–526.
26 Loader, *Sexuality*, 305–7, 312.
27 E.g., 'ever since the creation of the world' (v. 19); 'image' and 'likeness' (v. 23); 'mankind and birds and animals and creeping things' (v. 23); 'Creator' (v. 25); 'female' (v. 26, 27); 'male' (v. 27). See esp. Gen 1:26–27.
28 Robert Jewett, *Romans*, Hermeneia (Minneapolis, MN: Fortress Press, 2007), 177.

those that are contrary to the created order and God's purposes for it as revealed in Scripture.[29] It is men and women doing with their own sex what God intended only to be done with the opposite sex[30]—and that within marriage, as the rest of Scripture makes clear.

This broader Scriptural canvas lies behind Paul's references to homosexual practice in 1 Corinthians 6 and 1 Timothy 1. Both texts identify the high spiritual stakes involved, not just for same-sex sexual activity, but for other forms of unrepentant sin, including sexual immorality generally, idolatry, adultery, drunkenness, theft, and greed. Indeed, those who do these things are unrighteous, and will not inherit the kingdom of God.

Paul uses two words for same-sex sexual activity in 1 Corinthians 6:9, both function as plural nouns for people characterised by particular behaviour, and their proximity means they help interpret the other.

The first word (*malakoi*) in its broadest sense denotes 'soft' and could be used, for example, to describe clothing. The same word could also refer to a 'soft' or 'effeminate person', and was used this way to refer to the passive male partner in a same-sex sexual act.

The second (*arsenokoitai*) appears to be a new word Paul may have coined, as it has not been found in earlier texts from classical antiquity. It brings together two words—*arseno* (male) + *koit* ('bed' often with sexual connotations)—which appear together side by side in Leviticus 20:13 (cf. 18:22) in the Greek Old Testament (LXX), in relation to God's prohibition of same-sex sexual activity.[31]

This background to the new word, and Paul's indebtedness to the

---

29 Loader, *Sexuality*, 313–15.
30 Loader, *Sexuality*, 311.
31 The origin or history of a word (etymology) does not always determine its meaning. However, with compound neologisms, where a new word is formed out of two or more existing words, the meaning of the original component words typically inform the meaning of the new word.

Jewish Scriptures give us its meaning.[32] It refers to the active partner in male same-sex sexual acts, and includes consensual sexual acts between adults, and cannot be limited to cultic settings or pederasty.[33]

When Paul uses this same word (*arsenokoitais*) again in 1 Timothy 1:10, in the context of Old Testament law, same-sex sexual activity is again on view and—together with other forms of disobedience to the law—is proscribed as being contrary to sound doctrine, and the gospel. It refers to all same-sex sexual activity as a specific form of 'sexual immorality' (*pornois*), which is listed immediately beforehand, and cannot be limited to exploitative practices of the slave trade.[34]

The final text to consider appears in the letter of Jude. The cities of Sodom and Gomorrah are included as Old Testament examples of those who sinned and received the due penalty for their sins (Jude 7). Their sins are listed as 'sexual immorality' (*ekporneusasai*) and pursuing 'other flesh' (*sarkos heteras*).[35] The reference is to the tragic episode in Genesis 19, where the men of the cities demanded Lot deliver over his two visitors to them so they might 'know' them sexually.[36]

However, whatever other sins the men of Sodom and Gomorrah sought to commit—such as inhospitality and violence—Jude names sexual immorality. Indeed, the offending conduct is said to be 'in the same manner' as the preceding example of the 'sons of God' in Genesis 6 who had sex with human women, so sexual sin is clearly on view.

---

32 This includes Paul's demonstrated familiarity with the LXX.
33 Loader, *Sexuality*, 331–32. Bruce W. Winter, *After Paul Left Corinth: The Influence of Secular Ethics and Social Change*, (Grand Rapids, MI: Eerdmans, 2001), 116–120.
34 Gagnon, *Homosexual Practice*, 332– 336
35 Cf. 'unnatural desire' (*NIV*).
36 Lindsay Wilson, 'Let Sodom be Sodom! Another Look at Genesis 19', in *Sexegesis: An Evangelical Response to* Five Uneasy Pieces on Homosexuality, eds. Michael Bird and Gordon Preece (Sydney South: Anglican Youthworks, 2012), 48–64, here 54–59.

But what is the nature of their sexual sin? While part of their sin was the desire to profane angelic beings, the men of the cities were unaware the visitors were angels. Rather, they desired them as 'men', and so it is difficult to exclude the active desire for same-sex intercourse from their sin.

This discussion shows that while the New Testament addresses same-sex sexual activity specifically in only a handful of texts, it does so consistently from the position that, like all sexual activity outside of God-ordained marriage, it is sin to be avoided and rejected.

The lived experience of marriage

However, for all the goodness of marriage in the New Testament, it is not picture-perfect. There are challenges and failures on view that are only too familiar to us.

There are husbands who need to be told to love their wives, to treat them as equal co-heirs of grace, and not to treat them harshly (Eph 5:24; Col 3:19; 1 Pet 3:7). There are wives who need to be told to respect their husbands (Eph 5:33; 1 Pet 3:2). There are believers married to unbelievers, needing reassurance their marriages and children are holy, and needing encouragement to persevere in the marriage (1 Cor 7:12–16). There is marital breakdown and desertion (1 Cor 7:10–11, 15).

There is also frank acknowledgement some have fallen or will fall short of God's ideals of celibate singleness or faithful marriage, and need the healing restoration of his love, forgiveness and grace (Luke 7:36–50; John 4:7–42; 1 Cor 6:9–20). Those of us who have failed are given hope.

Neither is the New Testament teaching on marriage captive to its own culture. In a culture where men had the sexual advantage, Paul advocates a radical equality between wife and husband in sexual relations, such that a husband's body belongs to his wife, and a wife's to her husband, and where, as equal moral agents, they are mutually obliged to serve each other, and meet the other's needs, so Satan might not tempt them (1 Cor 7:2–5).[37]

As in all matters of life, believers are to use their bodies in ways that honour the Lord. This includes sexual purity. As broken and fallen people, our unconscious desires and our conscious 'sex lives' are set on rebellion against God's purposes and commands (Rom 1:24–27; 3:9–18; 8:7). Yet all who trust in Christ are to put off the old sinful person and put on the new person, which is being transformed by Christ (Rom 13:12–13; Eph 4:17–24; Col 3:5–10), and we are to help one another do so (Gal 6:1–2, cf. 1 Cor 5:1–13).

Those who are married are to love their spouse (Eph 5:25; Titus 2:4), and be faithful and pure in mind and body (Eph 5:3; 1 Thess 4:3–8), and those who are unmarried are to abstain from all sexual activity or marry rather than burn with passion (1 Cor 7:8–9; 1 Tim 5:11–15). Any sexual activity outside of heterosexual marriage is contrary to God's will and our good (Heb 13:4). This is as true for sexual lust (Matt 5:27–28), as it is for all heterosexual extra-marital sexual activity, and all same-sex sexual activity.

When the New Testament tells believers to 'flee sexual immorality' (1 Cor 6:18), this is what is on view. And it was culturally radical. The first Christians stood out from their surrounding culture because of their sexual purity (1 Pet 4:2–5). It should be no different for Christians today.

The future of marriage

But we must avoid making human marriage into an idol or cure-all. It is good, but it is not ultimate—not in this life or the next.

The fate of Ananias and Sapphira remind us that a close

---

37 Winter, *After Paul*, 227–30.

marriage is not necessarily a God-honouring one (Acts 5:1–10). The provision of divorce (in certain circumstances) reminds us that this side of the fall, the fracture of divorce is sometimes an appropriate response to human sin and brokenness. Indeed, history and experience tell us that human marriage is not uniformly good.

Moreover, the New Testament speaks very highly of singleness for both women and men—particularly, with the freedom and focus it allows to serve Christ wholeheartedly (1 Cor 7:6, 28–38). We must not forget that Jesus lived the perfect human life, and yet he never married, or had sex. While Peter and other apostles were married, Paul was not.

But Jesus is realistic about the challenges that singleness and sexual abstinence present. He speaks positively of the lives of those who cannot or do not marry, including those who forego marriage for the sake of the kingdom, but at the same time acknowledges it is not an easy path, and not one that everyone can follow (Matt 19:11–12).[38]

Regrettably in our sex- and romance-fixated society and family-focused churches, we can make that even harder. Virginity and chaste singleness are not esteemed, and the experience of being single can be not just that of being unmarried, but of being alone or even unlovable. This is a serious failure of Christian fellowship.

The truth is that none of us is alone. Faith in Christ recalibrates all our relational bonds, in such a way that our union with him takes precedence over all human ties, even those of marriage and blood (Luke 14:20–26). Christ is the essential locus of our identity, notwithstanding the human relationships that make up our lives.

More than that, our true family is the new spiritual family of

---

38 'This saying' (19:11) refers to the disciples' statement that 'it is better not to marry' (19:10). D. A. Carson, 'Matthew' in *Expositor's Bible Commentary*, Vol. 8, F. E. Gaebelein (ed.), (Grand Rapids, MI: Zondervan, 1984), 419.

brothers and sisters[39] united in Christ by the power of the Spirit (Rom 8:12–17)—a family to which all those who trust in Christ belong equally, irrespective of marital status, race, sex, sexual orientation, age, ability, wealth, status, previous sins, or any other consideration (cf. Gal 3:28; 1 Cor 6:11). As sisters and brothers in Christ we belong to one another, and are called to love each other, and share our lives, our homes, our time, our material possessions, our griefs and joys with each other for the sake of Christ.

These relationships and family bonds will continue into the next life, but human marriage will not (Matt 22:29–30). Its purposes in this world, and its purpose as a gospel signpost to the eternal marriage of Christ and the church will have been fulfilled.

Until then, marriage between a man and a woman, as he established it from the beginning, will continue as God's gracious gift for the good of all people—believers and unbelievers, individually and communally—and human sexuality will continue as a precious gift from him, to be expressed only within the bonds of marriage as he designed it.

The best way to love our unmarried and same-sex attracted sisters and brothers is not to turn away from or add to God's pattern for marriage so clearly set out in Scripture, nor to doubt the goodness of the boundaries he puts around our sexuality. It is humbly to accept the wisdom and kindness of his will for us, to seek his help to ensure the marriages among us are strong and faithful, and as Christian communities, to live together as brothers and sisters in Christ in such a way that those who are unmarried know deeply that they are loved and belong.

---

39   Including as spiritual mothers and fathers in the Lord, cf. Rom 16:13; 1 Tim 5:1–2.

HISTORY, THEOLOGY AND ECCLESIOLOGY

Christian Marriage:
A Concise History

Muriel Porter[1]

Then the Lord God said, 'It is not good that the man should be alone;
I will make him a helper as his partner'. Genesis 2:18 (NRSV)

Marriage, according to the second creation account, was established as an institution to give human beings the closest form of companionship.[2] This second 'creation blueprint' has been more honoured in the breach than in the observance. Marriage has veered far from this original ideal throughout human history, and changed significantly many, many times up to the present.

This 'blueprint' was not followed faithfully in the story of the Israelites, with the Old Testament recording few couples in a monogamous, let alone genuinely companionate, marriage. The

---

1   Dr Muriel Porter OAM is a Melbourne laywoman, author, journalist, and academic. She gained her doctorate in church history from the University of Melbourne. She is an honorary research fellow of the University of Divinity, and an adjunct lecturer at Trinity College Theological School, a college of the University of Divinity.

2   In the first account of creation (Gen 1: 26–28), humankind is created as both male and female together at the same time. That the humans in this account are commanded to 'be fruitful and multiply' can be read as giving procreation the reason for the different genders, but so too can the partnership of men and women commanded together not only to fill the earth but also to subdue it through their dominion over 'every living thing that moves upon the earth'.

patriarchs and most of the kings of Israel had multiple wives and concubines. In the Christian era, until very recent times, marriage has been unrelentingly patriarchal, with wives treated in law as subordinate to their husbands, rather than equal partners. Until the late nineteenth century, married women in both the United Kingdom and Australia, for instance, had no legal status. They could not own property, take action in a court of law, sign contracts, have legal custody of their own children, or even legally hire servants. In law, the husband and wife were one person—and the husband was the one.[3] More seriously, this gave husbands the legal right to discipline their wives with physical violence, and also to rape them—a situation changed only very recently. In 1891, British law finally abolished the right of a husband to 'moderately correct' his wife by physical punishment, a right that had previously been enshrined in canon law.[4] Legislation against rape in marriage began to be introduced in Australia only from 1976; it was not illegal in all Australian states and territories until 1994.[5]

Although civil law did not recognise egalitarian marriage until recently, companionate marriage was increasingly expected in the English-speaking world from the eighteenth century on and so came closer to the second Genesis ideal. It remained, however, far from equal in Anglican teaching (as revealed in Anglican liturgies) until well into the twentieth century. Anglican marriage rites began to dispense with the bride's vow to obey her husband only in the 1928 Church of England revision of the *Book of Common Prayer*. *An Australian Prayer Book* (1978) dispensed with it in the second

---

[3] 'Out of his shadow: The long struggle of wives under English Law', The High Sheriff of Oxfordshire's Annual Law Lecture, 9 October 2012, 9, https://www.supremecourt.uk/docs/speech-121009.pdf, accessed 18 September 2018.
[4] 'Out of his shadow', 13.
[5] http://www.auswhn.org.au/blog/marital-rape/ accessed 19 September 2018.

order of marriage; it is absent from both marriage services in *A Prayer Book for Australia* (1995).[6] The permission given for artificial contraception in marriage by the 1958 Lambeth Conference of bishops[7] released marital sexual activity from requiring procreative intent, so increasing its role as an expression of love. Anglican acceptance of divorce and remarriage—a huge and controversial change that had threatened Anglican church unity over many decades[8]—further cemented companionship as the primary reason for marriage. In the twenty-first century, 'mutual companionship, help and comfort'[9] is now clearly the primary reason for marriage in Australia, and is the first 'cause' of marriage in *A Prayer Book for Australia*.[10]

Until these recent changes, Anglican marriage rites had consistently made procreation the primary reason for marriage. The *Book of Common Prayer*, through its various editions beginning with the first edition of 1549, always listed procreation first, with sexual control ('remedy') second, and companionship a poor third reason

---

6   It has however re-emerged, in a far stricter form than in any previous Anglican liturgy, in the second form of marriage in the Diocese of Sydney's *Common Prayer: Resources for Gospel-shaped Gatherings* (Sydney: Anglican Press Australia, 2012). The bride is asked to promise to 'submit' herself to her husband (125).

7   A decade before the Vatican banned artificial contraception in *Humanae Vitae*, the Lambeth bishops declared that family planning was "a right and important factor in Christian family life": Resolution 115, *The Lambeth Conference 1958*, (London: SPCK, 1958).

8   See Muriel Porter, 'Scripture and the breaking of Communion', in Scott Cowdell and Muriel Porter, eds, *Lost in Translation? Anglicans, Controversy and the Bible*, (Melbourne: Desbooks, 2004), 143–149. The Australian General Synod canon on remarriage of divorced persons was not passed until 1985.

9   *An Australian Prayer Book*, (Sydney: The Standing Committee of the General Synod of the Church of England in Australia, 1978), 548.

10 This is not the case in *Common Prayer*, where it is second to sexual control in the first marriage order (117), and third after sexual control and procreation in the second order (124).

for marriage.[11] In the main, they were following the pattern of the pre-Reformation church, itself based on St Augustine of Hippo's highly influential treatise *On the Good of Marriage*, written in about 401CE. Procreation was the first 'good' of marriage for Augustine, sexual fidelity the second, and 'the sacramental stability of the marital household within the city of God' the third.[12] Augustine's third 'good' became 'mutuall societie, helpe, and coumfort' in the 1549 *Book of Common Prayer*.[13]

The 'causes' remained in the order established in 1549 in Anglican marriage rites until the first Australian prayer book, one of the first modern revisions in the Anglican Communion. In the second form of marriage in *An Australian Prayer Book* 1978, sexual control rather than procreation became the first purpose of marriage, discreetly termed as 'the proper expression of natural instincts and affections with which [God] has endowed us'.[14] Companionship became the second purpose, while procreation was relegated to third place.[15]

It took until the second Australian prayer book—*A Prayer Book for Australia* 1995—for companionship to become the primary reason for marriage. It is in first place in both the first and second orders of matrimony.[16] Other Anglican prayer book revisions have followed

---

11   *The Book of Common Prayer: The Texts of 1549, 1559 and 1662*, ed. Brian Cummings (Oxford: Oxford University Press, 2011), 64.
12   John Witte Jr., *From Sacrament to Contract: Marriage, Religion, and Law in the Western Tradition*, second edition, (Louisville: Western John Knox Press, Kentucky, 2012), 67.
13   *The Book of Common Prayer*, Cummings, 64.
14   *An Australian Prayer Book 1978*, 560.
15   *An Australian Prayer Book*, 560–561.
16   *A Prayer Book for Australia 1995*, (Sydney: Broughton Books, 1995), 647; 658.

suit; for example, in the marriage service in *Common Worship*, the Church of England's collection of liturgies published in 2000.[17]

Had Archbishop Cranmer and his fellow bishops listened to an eminent Continental reformer exiled in England in the year the first English prayer book was published, the second creation order of reasons for marriage might have been honoured from the outset in Anglican liturgies. At the time the Regius Professor of Divinity at Cambridge University, Martin Bucer was invited by his bishop, the Bishop of Ely, to offer a commentary on the new prayer book.[18] On the marriage service, Bucer, who was one of the first reformers to marry, wrote:

> … I should prefer that what is placed third among the causes for marriage might be in the first place, because it is first. For a true marriage can take place between people who seek neither for children nor for a remedy against fornication…Yet since "the two are one flesh" and live unto God as one person, it follows that without that union of minds and bodies and possessions… it is no true and real marriage before God. And so it is that in the first institution of marriage, to which the Lord Christ taught us always to look back, God did not say that its purpose was children, or a remedy, but this: "It is not good for man to be alone, let us therefore make a help for him, to be with him".[19]

Bucer's words fell on deaf ears. As we have seen, it took more than 400 years for Bucer's preference to be implemented.

In its mainstream liturgies, the Anglican Church has now at last

---

17 https://www.churchofengland.org/prayer-and-worship/worship-texts-and-resources/common-worship/marriage#mm095, accessed 14 September 2018.
18 Given conflicting notations on an original manuscript and the first printed version of Bucer's commentary, the *Censura*, it is not clear whether it was the Bishop of Ely or Thomas Cranmer, Archbishop of Canterbury, who invited Bucer to write the commentary. See E. C. Whitaker, *Martin Bucer and the Book of Common Prayer* (Great Wakering, Essex: Alcuin Club, Mayhew-McCrimmon,1978), 2–3.
19 E. C. Whitaker, *Martin Bucer and the Book of Common Prayer*, 120–121.

openly recognised that most people need partners in a relationship blessed by God. The mutual society, help and comfort provided by a partner enables most people to live fulfilling lives. According to the Genesis 2 blueprint, the companionship and support of a partner is at least as important as a sexual relationship or parenthood, and has in fact always been implicitly recognised by the Christian Church. Christian marriage has not been denied to people unable, because of age or disability, to have either sexual relations or to procreate. This, I hold, is true for same-sex attracted people as for heterosexual people. It is worth remembering that God, having initially, and unsuccessfully, offered Adam 'every animal of the field and every bird of the air' (Gen 2:19–20) as potential partners, resorted to creating Eve out of Adam himself—bone of his bones, and flesh of his flesh (Gen 2:23). In the Genesis account here, in the context of creating a companionate relationship, Eve's human one-ness with Adam could be considered as more important than her different gender.

If the sixteenth century English reformers did not give mutual support the Genesis 2 priority, they nevertheless recognised that the overwhelming majority of people needed marriage for the proper expression of their sexuality. As we have seen, they made sexual control the second reason for marriage.

As with the Continental reformers, they knew only too well the dangers of enforced celibacy. They saw the evidence all around them in the promiscuous lives of clergy barred from marriage. They still saw celibacy as the holier state for clergy—they were after all men of their time—but they insisted that only those few who had the God-given charism of celibacy should refrain from marriage. They enthusiastically adopted St Paul's dictum that it was 'better to marry than to burn' (1 Cor 7:9), and made that their main defence of clerical marriage.[20]

The promiscuity of the clergy was common knowledge, and caused lay people to view them with disdain. (At the time, ordination was required not merely for those with genuine priestly vocations but for men employed in academe and many forms of government service.) For the reformers, this promiscuity was not only scandalous, but a danger to the Gospel. How could clergy preach the Gospel while they themselves were openly immoral? How could they build up a godly society while they were living a flagrant lie?[21] As Martin Luther put it, obligatory sexual abstinence was 'wanton wickedness' and a 'devilish tyranny' that no bishop had the right to require.[22] Clerical marriage was critical for their reform agenda that re-cast the clergy's primary role as that of preacher rather than cultic priest. To give credence to their teaching, the reformers almost all married, even if sometimes reluctantly.[23]

Their view of marriage was not very exalted, however. It was still a poor second to chastity for those who had the charism. This is hardly surprising, as these men were in the vanguard

---

20 See M. Porter, *Sex, Marriage and the Church: Patterns of Change* (Melbourne: Dove, 1996).
21 See M. Luther, *Commentary on I Corinthians VII* in Hilton C. Oswald (ed.), *Luther's Works* (St Louis, Concordia, 1973).
22 T. A. Fudge, 'Incest and Lust in Luther's Marriage: Theology and Morality in Reformation Polemics', *Sixteenth Century Journal*, 34/2 (2003), 323.
23 S. E. Ozment, 'Marriage and the Ministry in Protestant Churches', *Concilium*, 8, 8, (1972), 52,42. 'Luther gave three reasons for his marriage: to please his old father, Hans, to spite the devil and the pope, and to give witness to his faith. Luther rejoiced that he had testified to the gospel... ', Thomas A. Fudge, 'Incest and Lust in Luther's Marriage', 319. Fudge cites Luther's letters written to friends shortly after his marriage to the former nun, Katherine von Bora, in June 1525.

of a paradigm shift in Christian thought. They were the heirs of more than a thousand years of teaching that exalted virginity over marriage.

The early Church, strongly influenced by Greco-Roman expectations of cultic purity, had abandoned the Judaic expectation of marriage for all, and had quickly developed a strong preference for sexual abstinence.[24] Certain teachings of Jesus (for example, 'eunuchs for the sake of the kingdom', Matt. 19:12) and Paul ('It is well for a man not to touch a woman', 1 Cor 7.1) were harnessed to support these positions, but it is highly probable that these were not the origins of the new views, but rather convenient support for them. Monastic communities were one development from this teaching. From the fourth century on, there was a growing expectation that clergy, *while married*, would abstain from all sexual activity for cultic purity reasons.[25] This coincided with the increasing practice of daily Eucharistic celebrations. In other words, clergy at this early stage were not expected to be unmarried, just abstinent. Clergy were thus elevated to a higher, superior caste to lay people who were not expected to be able to maintain abstinence within marriage.

The exaltation of sexual abstinence and total virginity developed, in some quarters, into an almost hysterical denial of any value in marriage, with a consequent horror of female sexuality. There are undeniable overtones of cultic purity concerns in these teachings. This became explicit in claims that only a sexually pure—that is,

---

24 For a full excursus on the development of church teaching on marriage, see J. Witte Jr, *From Sacrament to Contract* and M. Porter, *Sex, Marriage and the Church*.

25 Canon 33 of the Synod of Elvira, Spain, required married clergy to be abstinent. Bishop Ossius of Cordova, a member of the Elvira Synod, tried to make this a universal law of the Church at the 325 Council of Nicaea. See Samuel Laeuchli, *Power and Sexuality: The Emergence of Canon Law at the Synod of Elvira* (Philadelphia, Temple University Press, 1972).

abstinent—priest could handle the bread and wine on the altar.[26] This accompanied an increasing tightening of the rules about clergy marriage in the eleventh and twelfth centuries, with clergy marriage declared invalid for the first time by the Second Lateran Council in 1139. Until then, most 'lower' clergy—that is, parish priests—had been married men with families; only monastics and clergy in higher ranks were expected to be unmarried.

The sixteenth century reformers had all been either secular clergy or monastics, so the exaltation of virginity and celibacy was ingrained in them. It is hard at this remove to understand just how radical was their decision not merely to allow clerical marriage but to promote it. All traditional church teaching was against them, including current biblical interpretation. They were opposing everything they had been taught about sexuality and marriage. It is hardly surprising then that they had no realistic vision of married life. They saw it as difficult, messy, and unpleasant, even if it was essential for people who could not maintain sexual chastity. Even so, the old taboo lingered. Peter Martyr (Vermigli), an Italian reformer who lectured on the theological acceptability of clerical marriage at Oxford University in the face of considerable opposition in 1548, nevertheless recommended that married people should refrain from sexual activity at times, particularly when the sacraments were to be administered or received.

The reformers' views were virulently opposed by traditionalists. The debate about clerical marriage in England continued

---

26 'If, therefore, our Redeemer so loved the bloom of perfect chastity that he was not only born of a virgin womb, but also fondly handled by a virgin foster-father, and this while he was still an infant crying in the cradle, by whom, I ask, does he wish his Body to be handled, now that he is reigning in all his immensity in heaven?' Peter Damian, eleventh century monk and Doctor of the Church. Pope Pius XII quoted these words approvingly in his 1954 encyclical on priestly celibacy. B. Verkamp, 'Cultic purity and the Law of Celibacy', *Review for Religious*, 30, (1971), 217.

from the 1520s until it was given a degree of security in the Thirty-nine Articles of Religion, approved by Parliament in 1571. It was finally legalised in 1604. The earlier 1549 legalisation permitting clerical marriage had been swiftly overturned by Mary I in 1553, resulting in wholesale deprivations and humiliations of married clergy. During the reign of Edward VI, and then in the first half of Elizabeth's reign, married clergy had attracted great opprobrium. They were denounced as sinful, lustful and heretical, and not just by theologians. Peter Martyr and his wife, for instance, were subjected to sustained abuse in Oxford from the townspeople.[27] Allowing clergy to marry caused more controversy in England than any other Reformation change.[28] It was a deeply significant change but, regardless of the opposition it faced, in time it became not just acceptable but expected. Opening the door to same-sex marriage, while controversial and disturbing for some now, will in time become one more accepted development in the history of Christian marriage.

The reformers' promotion of clergy marriage inevitably began too to usher in a new theology of marriage. As Martyr had said in the telling opening sentence of his Oxford lectures, 'It is now a thing worthy to be noted, that married folks are not despised of God'.[29] Puritan theologians from the late sixteenth century on became strong advocates of the importance of mutuality in marriage. For them, marriage was first and foremost a covenant between two people. This view would eventually open the way for an acceptance

---

27 P. McNair, 'Peter Martyr in England' in *Peter Martyr Vermigli and Italian Reform*, J.C.McLelland (ed.), (Ontario, Wilfrid Laurier University Press, 1980), 101.

28 J. K. Yost, 'The Reformation Defense of Clerical Marriage in the Reigns of Henry VIII and Edward VI', *Church History*, 50, 2, (1981), 164.

29 P. Martyr (Vermigli), *The Commonplaces of the Most Renowned and Divine Doctor Peter Martyr*, A. Marten (ed.), Short Title Catalogue 24669, London, 1583.

of divorce by Protestant churches, for if the mutuality died, then so did the marriage.[30]

It is worth noting that, while the reformers could and did point to an earlier tradition of married clergy in the Christian Church as a justification for the change they were implementing, they quietly introduced a major innovation in allowing clergy to marry *after* ordination. The early Church practice, still maintained by the Orthodox churches, was that clergy who wished to marry had to do so *before* ordination. This may be connected to the notion of married clergy remaining abstinent; presumably they could theoretically consummate their marriages and have children before ordination, then live abstinent lives while remaining married after ordination.

Not only the sixteenth century reformers recognised the rarity of a genuine vocation to chastity. In the wake of the child sexual abuse scandal, many in the Roman Catholic Church are increasingly recognising that fact. The Royal Commission into Institutional Responses into Child Sexual Abuse has drawn attention to it, providing the impetus for growing calls for Rome to make clerical celibacy voluntary.[31] How realistic or fair, then, is it to require Christian same-sex attracted people without a vocation to chastity to live effectively under a chastity vow?

In conclusion

Christian marriage in Australia in the twenty-first century is

---

30   See J. T. Johnson, *A Society Ordained by God: English Puritan Marriage Doctrine in the First Half of the Seventeenth Century* (Nashville, Abingdon Press, 1970).

31   See D. Cahill, '"....And What Would God Think?": Rebuilding Pastoral Health and Integrity after the Royal Commission into Institutional Responses to Child Sexual Abuse', Keynote address to the Health and Integrity Conference, University of Divinity, Melbourne, 27 August 2018, 5–6.

very different in many respects from the patterns, rules and expectations of earlier centuries. The expectation in society, and in its presentation in contemporary Anglican liturgies, honours the Genesis 2 ideal of marriage as first and foremost for mutual companionship, help and comfort. Thanks to the determined advocacy of the sixteenth century Reformers, it is also now accepted by Anglicans and Protestants, and increasingly by Roman Catholics, that people should not be expected to reject marriage unless they have what the reformers claimed was the rare God-given charism of chastity.[32] On both these grounds, Christian marriage can and should be opened to same-sex attracted people desiring to live openly before God in loving, faithful, monogamous partnerships.

---

32   For instance, the 16th century English reformer Robert Barnes maintained that chastity given by God changed men's physical nature, eliminating sexual desire, and that this was a very rare gift given to very few. Striving to live single without this gift was a waste of time, he maintained. Robert Barnes, 'That by God's Word it is Lawful for Priests... to Marry Wives', *Supplication*, in *The Whole Works of W. Tyndale*, J. Frith and Dr Barnes, John Foxe (ed.), Short Title Catalogue 24436, London, 1573, 313; 323.

For Better or for Worse: The Changing Shape of Marriage in Christian History

Claire Smith[1]

Introduction

Ecclesia reformata, semper reformanda ('the church is reformed, and always being reformed') is the Protestant principle that embeds change in the church, both in doctrine and practice. It captures the mind of the Reformation even if the motto was coined by Dutch theologians after the first wave of European reformers.[2]

Quoted in full, however, the principle 'the church is reformed, and always being reformed according to the word of God' (*ecclesia reformata, semper reformanda secundum verbi Dei*) is a double-edged sword. On the one hand, it means that not all change is desirable, because not all change is consistent with the written word of God. On the other, it means that resistance to change for the sake of preserving the past will not do either, particularly if what is being preserved is contrary to the word of God.

Marriage is a case in point. It is beyond dispute that marriage

---

1 Dr Claire Smith is a writer and theologian, and a member of St Andrew's Cathedral, Sydney. She received her doctorate in Biblical Studies from the University of Western Sydney/Moore College.
2 Andrew Atherstone, 'The Implications of *Semper Reformanda*', Anvil 26/1 (2009) 31, available at https://biblicalstudies.org.uk/pdf/anvil/26-1_031.pdf Accessed 20 December 2018.

has changed since the first century, both inside and outside the church—and, within the church, done so in both belief and practice. That observation alone tells us little about the merits of such changes. If it is possible for the church to err (Articles xix, xxi), the same is certainly true of all secular cultures.

The merits of the status quo or change are determined by the word of God alone. This is the Protestant principle of *'sola Scriptura'*, the sola on which all other Reformation 'solas' hang. This is why the last phrase of the motto quoted above is so important—it is reform *according to the word of God*.

Scripture alone is to rule over the change, both by identifying what needs to be changed, and by informing what and how change is to occur.

As Australian Anglicans we acknowledge as much in the Fundamental Declarations of the Anglican Church of Australia, which state that 'This Church receives all the canonical scriptures of the Old and New Testaments as being the *ultimate rule and standard of faith* given by inspiration of God'.[3]

That is, we believe that God rules his people and his church through his Spirit, by his Word.

The early church

We see this happening even within the pages of the New Testament. It seems that early in the life of the church ambivalence quickly arose about the goodness and appropriateness of marriage, sex and childbearing (cf. 1 Cor 7:1–9; 1 Tim 4:1–4; cf. 1 Tim 2:15; 5:11–14; Tit 2:3–5).

It is difficult to know the exact origins and nature of this

---

3   *The Constitution of the Anglican Church of Australia*, Part I, Fundamental Declarations, clause 2. Available at https://www.anglican.org.au/data/1._The_Constitution_of_the_Anglican_Church_of_Australia-2016.pdf Accessed 31 October 2018. *Italics* added.

ambivalence—how much it was due to the philosophical or religious beliefs of the day or a misunderstanding of Christian teaching about the body and sexual intimacy, or other factors.[4]

Certainly, the New Testament is clear that the liberalising sexual trends of Graeco-Roman culture were not compatible with Christian faithfulness.[5] Less obviously, any liberalising trends in Jewish sexual ethics were also rejected. For example, Jesus extended the reach of the Mosaic law to include adulterous *desire* (Matt 5:27–30), and affirmed the one flesh union in marriage of a man and a woman, implicitly condemning polygamy (including its practice in the Old Testament). Both Jesus and Paul narrowed the legitimate grounds for divorce (i.e., not 'any cause', Matt 19:1–9; 1 Cor 7:10–16). That is, contrary to claims often made today, the moral trajectory or movement of the New Testament in both Jewish and Graeco-Roman contexts, was *against* liberalising trends, rather than towards them.

Yet the New Testament does not denigrate sex within marriage!

This was the Corinthians' mistake. They thought that even within marriage 'it [was] good for a man not to touch a woman' (1 Cor 7:1). But they were wrong. It did not matter that their abstinence was sincere and well-intentioned. It did not matter that it concerned what happened (or not) in the privacy of another's bedroom. It was at odds with God's will, and so God's word called upon them to change.

In fact, the source and authority of that word are highlighted

---

4   See a list of possible causes in D. E. Garland, *1 Corinthians*, Baker Exegetical Commentary on the New Testament (Grand Rapids, MI: Baker Academic, 2003) 263–66.

5   For example, in the rise of the so-called 'new woman' in Graeco-Roman society, who rejected cultural conventions of modesty, and dressed provocatively and often had a promiscuous lifestyle. See B. W. Winter, *Roman Wives, Roman Widows: The Appearance of New Women and the Pauline Communities*, (Grand Rapids, MI: Eerdmans, 2003). See other essays in this volume for the rejection of culturally acceptable same-sex sexual activity, particularly 'Family Ties: Marriage, Sex, and Belonging in the New Testament'.

repeatedly in Paul's chapter-long discussion of marriage, sex, engagement and divorce in 1 Corinthians 7, both in an actual command of the Lord (1 Cor 7:10), and in Paul's Spirit-inspired apostolic words (see esp. 1 Cor 7:12, 17, 25, 40, cf. 1:1; 4:14–17; 14:37).[6]

The well-meaning but misguided Corinthians were to learn that, rather than abstinence, husbands and wives could abstain from sexual relations only by mutual agreement, and only then for prayer, and only then for a limited time—in other words, very rarely!

Interestingly, while the clear teaching of Scripture is that children are a blessing from the Lord, and marriage is the proper context in which they are conceived and nurtured, Paul does not make his case for marital sex on the basis of its procreative potential, which was the narrow view of the culture of the day.[7]

Rather, the goal is their own spiritual well-being: their sexual purity and the avoidance of temptation and sin (1 Cor 7:2, 7). This is why, where chastity was possible, the unmarried state was to be preferred, not as a spiritually superior state before God, but because it allowed a man or woman greater freedom to serve God. Either way, the sexual activity of believers mattered because it affected the holiness and mission of the church.

In Paul's later letter, 1 Timothy, the situation has changed from ambivalence about the good of marital sex to public false teaching forbidding marriage altogether, and the church being at risk of embracing this view (1 Tim 4:1–4, cf. 2:15; 5:11–15). It is even

---

[6] Brian S. Rosner, *Paul, Scripture, and Ethics: A Study of 1 Corinthians 5–7*, (Grand Rapids, MI: Baker Books, 1994) 153–76, examines the Scriptural basis of Paul's own understanding of marriage and sexuality.

[7] Cf. Philo, *Spec. Laws* 3.6 §36; 3.20 §113; Josephus, *Jewish Wars*, 2.8.13 §§160–61.

possible the false teaching arose from a misunderstanding of the Old Testament (cf. 1 Tim 1:3, 7–8).[8]

Yet Paul says these Ephesian Christians were without excuse. Not only had they been warned by the Spirit of God that false teachers would come, God's written word also told them that everything God created is good (Gen 1:31). They should have known that marriage was part of God's creation prior to the Fall, and so it is good—a gift from God to be embraced with thanksgiving.

Not surprisingly, as the rest of the letter makes clear, the fruits of marriage—the loving relationship of husband and wife, childbearing and motherhood (implicitly also, marital sex), and family life—are also good, and all proper contexts in which to serve and please God (1 Tim 2:15; 3:2, 4–6; 5:9–15; cf. Eph 5:21–6:4; Col 3:18–19; Tit 2:2–5).

These two windows into the New Testament church show us that from the early decades of the Christian era, the biblical view of marriage, sex and family was being challenged—in believers' lives, in the beliefs of churches, and by false teachers within the church.

They also show that these departures were not met with tolerance of diversity, but with the corrective word of God in the Hebrew Scriptures, Jesus' spoken words, the written apostolic word, and through warnings of the Holy Spirit: different forms of the one word of God, consistently affirming God's original design and intention for marriage, and calling God's people back to it.

These moments from the early church captured in the New Testament are particularly helpful for us, because they highlight a significant difference between the church and Scripture. The church can err, but Scripture does not. The mere fact that something is practised or believed or even taught in the church does not make it right.

---

8   For a recent discussion of the Pauline authorship of 1 Timothy, see R. Yarbrough, *The Letters to Timothy and Titus*, Pillar New Testament Commentary (Grand Rapids, MI: Eerdmans/London, UK: Apollos, 2018) 72–78.

The true and certain measure is Scripture, which does not change, and which, this side of Christ's return, will always be reforming individual believers, and churches, dioceses, and denominations.

What history beyond the New Testament sadly shows is that these corrective calls were not always sufficiently heeded. The trends away from the goodness of marriage and marital sex, and towards asceticism and the (allegedly) spiritually superior state of singleness, and even complete abstinence within marriage, grew in influence, rather than diminished.

So, while Tertullian (AD 160–225) saw God's provision of marriage in creation as 'the union of man and woman ... for the replenishment of the earth and the furnishing of the world' (i.e., procreation) and opposed those who spoke against marriage,[9] he also saw it as merely an accommodation to avoid sin for those whose weakness prevented them from the superior path of remaining unmarried—like Christ.[10]

Likewise, Clement of Alexandria (AD 150–215) thought 'marriage should be accepted and given its proper place', but also wrote that 'marriage is the desire for procreation' and 'to have intercourse without intending children is to violate nature'.[11]

Later, the Spanish Council of Elvira (c. 306) required all clergy to 'abstain completely from their wives and not to have children' under threat of deposition (Canon 33),[12] and later still, Jerome (345–420)

---

9   Tertullian, 'To his Wife' chapters 2–3. https://en.wikisource.org/wiki/Ante-Nicene_Fathers/Volume_IV/Tertullian:_Part_Fourth/To_His_Wife/I/Chapter_2 Accessed 7 November 2018.

10 Tertullian, 'On Monogamy' chapter 5. https://en.wikisource.org/wiki/Ante-Nicene_Fathers/Volume_IV/Tertullian:_Part_Fourth/On_Monogamy/Chapter_5 Accessed 7 November 2018. Christopher C. Roberts, *Creation and Covenant: The Significance of Sexual Difference in the Moral Theology of Marriage*, (New York: T&T Clark, 2007) 16–19.

11 Clement, *Paedogogus*, 95.

12 http://www.awrsipe.com/patrick_wall/selected_documents/309%20council%20of%20elvira.pdf Accessed 2 November 2018.

and Ambrose (378–95) exalted virginity, and believed Adam and Eve only engaged in sexual relations after the Fall, and that the only benefit of marriage was that it produced virgins (i.e., children who might then choose celibacy).[13]

It barely needs saying this is a far cry from the biblical view of marriage, and again shows us that not all change is good, and not everything the church believes or condones accords with God's word.

The church was poised for reformation by the word of God, and it came through the work of Augustine, Bishop of Hippo in North Africa, whose views on marriage are considered among the most influential in Christian history.

The Life and Thought of Augustine

Augustine (AD 354–430) began adult life as an unbeliever, and from his late teens lived with a concubine, which was a legally-recognised and culturally-accepted practice. The relationship lasted fifteen years, and they had a son, who died in his teens. After his first concubine was deported, he took a second concubine, but ended the relationship when he was converted (AD 386).

Augustine was deeply distressed by the lust and desire that dominated his youth, and that drove him to these relationships.[14] After a protracted search, he found peace with God and peace of heart, after reading a few verses of Paul's letter to the Romans (13:13b–14):

> Not in rioting and drunkenness, not in chambering and wantonness, not in strife and envying, but put on the Lord Jesus Christ, and make

---

13 Ambrose, *On Virginity*, Book I.7.35. Jerome, *Ep.* 22.
14 He claims he prayed to God: "grant me chastity and continence, but not yet." For I was afraid lest thou shouldst hear me too soon, and too soon cure me of my disease of lust which I desired to have satisfied rather than extinguished. (*Confessions*, 8.7.17).

no provision for the flesh to fulfill the lusts thereof. (*Confessions*, 8.12.29)

The following year, he was baptised by Ambrose, and from that time onwards reportedly had no desire for 'wife, children of the flesh, wealth, or worldly honors'.[15] His conversion to Christ was also a conversion to 'continence', and he remained unmarried and celibate for the rest of his life.

However, his views of marriage developed over the course of his ministry, as he grew in his knowledge and understanding of Scripture, and responded to different challenges to biblical truth.

In his earliest writings, he regarded marriage and marital intimacy as distractions from the higher pursuit of Christian philosophical thought.[16] Marriage was, at best, a safe place for the expression of lustful sexual desires.[17] At the same time though, he recognised the value of procreation, and opposed those who denigrated marriage, by showing from the New Testament that marriage was instituted by God at the beginning of creation—not after the Fall—and so it continued to be God's will in the Christian era.[18]

Augustine's most sustained treatment of marriage *De bono conjugali* (The Good of Marriage) was written in AD 401. He wrote *De sancta virginitate* (On Holy Virginity) on the celibate life, the same year.

He identified 'three goods of marriage': offspring, fidelity, sacrament. The first two need little explanation (even if they

---

15   Possidius, *Life of Augustine*, 2 http://www.tertullian.org/fathers/possidius_life_of_augustine_02_text.htm#C2 Accessed 21 November 2018

16   D. G. Hunter, 'Marriage', in *Augustine through the Ages: An Encyclopedia*, A. D. Fitzgerald (ed.) (Grand Rapids, MI: Eerdmans, 1999), 535. E.g., *Soliloquies*, 1.10.17

17   Hunter, 'Marriage', 535.

18   Hunter, 'Marriage', 535.

need restating today): marriage had a procreative purpose, and it allowed for the sanctioned expression of sexual urges of those who were not able to practise chastity.

However, we might misconstrue Augustine's meaning of 'sacrament'. He did not mean that marriage was a sacrament in the sense it came to have in the medieval church, and later rejected by the Protestant reformers—that is, as a means of efficient grace—rather he meant that Christian marriages functioned as a sacred sign of the union of Christ and the church, and thereby indicated the indissolubility of the marriage bond.[19]

Significantly, the procreative good of marriage was not an end in itself, but was necessary to create the good of human society and friendship, where the relationship of 'man and wife' was 'the first natural bond of human society'.[20]

This 'natural society' arose from the sexual difference of the husband and wife: a 'true union of friendship between the sexes, with the one governing and the other obeying'.[21] This is why marriages of those past childbearing age are still proper marriages, even if they are without children.[22]

---

19   Hunter, 'Marriage', 536. Cf. *De nuptiis et concupiscentia*, 1.23. John Witte explains the difference between Augustine's view and that of the medieval church: 'Augustine had called marriage a sacrament in order to demonstrate its symbolic stability. Thirteenth-century writers called marriage a sacrament to demonstrate its spiritual efficacy. Augustine had said that marriage as a symbol of Christ's bond to the church *should* not be dissolved. Thirteenth-century writers said that marriage as a permanent channel of sacramental grace *could* not be dissolved. J. Witte, Jr., *From Sacrament to Contract: Marriage, Religion, and Law in the Western Tradition* (Westminster: John Knox Press, 2012 [repr. 1997], 96 (*italics* original).

20   *The Good of Marriage*, 1.

21   *The Good of Marriage*, 3.

22   *The Good of Marriage*, 3. In later works, this companionate benefit was eclipsed by the procreative good, which itself was relativised as he believed the population of heaven was near complete. Roberts, *Creation and Covenant*, 55, 57, on *De Genesi ad litteram*. Cf. *De civitate Dei*, 14.21.

While Augustine's views on marriage continued to develop, the following observations can be made from this brief sketch.

First, Augustine's life and thought show the reforming power of God's word. In particular, he came to believe in and hold to the goodness of marriage as a gift from God,[23] through an increasing grasp of historical and literal exegesis of Scripture as opposed to allegorical approaches commonly used.[24]

Despite this, and second, he still considered celibacy spiritually superior to marriage and to marital sex—so while the direction of change was towards Scripture, his thought (and practice) did not entirely align with it. This again reminds us that Scripture alone is the infallible word of God, and the church and individual believers need constantly to be reformed by it.

Third, the three goods Augustine identified—procreation, fidelity, and the sacred sign of Christ and the church—are helpful summaries of Scriptural teaching and can be seen in Paul's responses to misunderstandings of marriage and sex. Significantly too, Augustine, like Paul, did not rank the 'goods' in order of priority.[25]

Fourth, marriage for Augustine was only between a man and a woman, and the three goods he identified depended on this conviction. This is easily seen with two goods, which are plainly precluded in the absence of sexual difference, since without sexual difference there can be no procreative potential,[26] neither can the union function as a sign of Christ and the church (cf. Eph 5:22–33). It is

---

23　M. Lamberigts, 'Augustine on Marriage: a comparison of *De bono coniugali* and *De nuptiis et concupiscentia*', *Louvain Studies*, 35.1-2 (2011), 32-52.

24　Roberts, *Creation and Covenant*, 54.

25　E.g., Augustine, *Commentary on the Literal Meaning of Genesis*, book 9, chapter 7: 'fidelity, offspring, sacrament'. John Witte, Jr, 'The Goods and Goals of Marriage', *Notre Dame Law Review* 76/3 (2001) 1031, available at https://scholarship.law.nd.edu/cgi/viewcontent.cgi?article=1557&context=ndlr Accessed 20 December 2018.

26　Roberts, *Creation and Covenant*, 49.

also true of the third good, because fidelity lay only in biblically-sanctioned expression of sexual urges, and Scripture condemns all sexual activity outside heterosexual marriage, including same-sex sexual activity.[27] Moreover, Augustine wrote against same-sex sexual activity between women,[28] and most probably men as well.[29] In short, his three goods of marriage do not translate and cannot be applied to same-sex unions.

Fifth, even the companionate good of marriage he identified was a consequence of sexual difference, because the sexual differences of husband and wife were integral to their companionship, and not simply the procreative potential of intercourse.[30] For this reason, Augustine's companionate benefit of marriage cannot be applied to same-sex unions where sexual difference is lacking, even though it is sometimes appealed to in arguments for same-sex marriage.

Sixth, Augustine believed that God's commands governed all people in all times, and had precedence over all customs and laws. This was true even if all nations adopted the same practice, or if God's commands were contrary to common practice, or if it meant certain practices were to be resumed or even established for the first time.[31] What mattered was being on the right side of the word of God, not any other consideration.

As significant and influential as Augustine's thought on marriage was, the next thousand years saw a continued drift away from the

---

27 See discussions elsewhere in this volume, especially 'Family Ties: Marriage, Sex, and Belonging in the New Testament'.
28 Augustine, *Letter* 211.
29 *Confessions*, 3.8.15; 'acts of Sodom'; 'the divine law, which has not made men so that they should ever abuse one another in that way. For the fellowship that should be between God and us is violated whenever that nature of which he is the author is polluted by perverted lust'; *City of God*, 2.328.
30 Roberts, *Creation and Covenant*, 52, 69.
31 *Confessions*, 3.8.17.

biblical ideal.[32] This is perhaps demonstrated nowhere more clearly than in relation to the fate of clerical marriages, which included wives being put away in convents or into lay orders upon their husband's ordination,[33] and the declaration of the Second Lateran Council (AD 1139) that all marriages of clergy were both unlawful and invalid.[34]

The Reformation

This set the stage for the next major reform of marriage, during the Protestant Reformation.

Of course, the Reformation was concerned with much more than just marriage. At its core was the supreme authority of Scripture, and salvation through grace alone, by faith alone, in Christ alone. But the recovery of these foundational Christian truths did not only lead to changes to doctrine and church practice. It also led to the embrace of ordinary family-life and work as a sacred sphere in which to serve God, and to significant reforms of the institution of marriage.

The reformers rejected a range of medieval beliefs and traditions that touched on marriage directly and indirectly because they were contrary to Scripture. Among these were the meritorious ideal of virginity; the perpetual virginity of Mary; the notion that celibacy

---

32 For example, the standard medieval text, Peter Lombard's *Sentences*, spoke of 'the twofold institution of marriage', where marriage before and after the fall are sharply distinguished and qualitatively different, changing from divine mandate to a remedy for sin. He also regards marriage as one of seven sacraments, which both signifies and conveys efficient grace. (e.g., *Sentences*, Book 4, Distinction 26, Chapter 2; Distinction 30, chapter 3, 2; Book 4, Distinction 26, Chapter 6, 420; Distinction 1, Chapter 4, 2, 233). Thomas M Finn, 'The Sacramental World in the Sentences of Peter Lombard', *Theological Studies* 69 (2008) 568, 581.

33 F. L. Cross, E. A. Livingstone, (eds), 'Celibacy of the clergy', in *Oxford Dictionary of the Christian Church* (Oxford: Oxford University Press, 1997) 310.

34 Canon 7. http://www.papalencyclicals.net/councils/ecum10.htm Accessed 28 November 2018.

and singleness were superior to marriage and family life; the validity, necessity and wisdom of vows of celibacy taken by clergy and religious orders, and the associated vows of obedience to religious superiors and the Pope.

Also, two of the five Catholic sacraments rejected by the reformers touched on marriage. They rejected the Sacrament of Holy Matrimony, on the grounds that marriage was not dependent upon faith but was a divinely-ordained human institution, open to believers and unbelievers[35]; and they rejected the Sacrament of Holy Orders, which itself forbade marriage for clergy, which was also rejected.[36]

Alternatively, the reformers taught that the priesthood of all believers meant there were not two classes within the church— a 'religious class' and 'secular class'—but that all were equally members, with freedom of conscience, who merely served God in different ways, as his gifts allowed.[37] They taught that the prohibition against clerical marriage came from the Devil, whereas marriage came from God,[38] and that celibacy was a gift given only to very few, and marriage meant for most.[39]

The medieval view that sexual activity even within marriage was sinful and to be avoided, was replaced by a recognition that joyful and shameless sexual intimacy within marriage was a proper sphere in which to glorify and serve God.[40] The home was viewed as

---

35 *Article* XXV.
36 T. P. Johnston, 'The Protestant Reformation and the Marriage of Clergy', *Midwestern Journal of Theology*, 16/2 (2017) 17. *Article* XXXII.
37 E.g., Luther, *Appeal to the Ruling Class*, 1.i. in J. Dillenberger (ed.), *Martin Luther: Selections from His Writings* (Anchor Books, 1961), 407–8.
38 K. Schütz Zell, *Defending Clerical Marriage* (1524). See http://germanhistorydocs.ghi-dc.org/pdf/eng/Doc.60-ENG-ZellMarriage_eng.pdf Accessed 30 November 2018.
39 H. Oberman, *Luther: Man between God and the Devil* (1982), 272.
40 WATr 5:600 #6317. Cited in W. Lazareth, *Luther on the Christian Home* (Philadelphia: Muhlenberg Press, 1960), 226.

the seminary of the church,[41] and mothers and fathers as 'apostles, bishops and priests to their children'.[42]

However, the Reformers did not merely teach against medieval views, and in support of the biblical view. Their own lives were reformed by God's word, as they renounced monastic vows of chastity, and embraced marriage and family life in the parsonage—often with women who themselves were leaving nunneries. These transformed lives were crucial to the Protestant movement:

> No institutional change brought about by the Reformation was more visible, responsive to late medieval pleas for reform, and conducive to new social attitudes than the marriage of Protestant clergy. Nor was there another point in the Protestant program where theology and practice corresponded more successfully. The reformers argued theologically and attempted to demonstrate by their own lives the superiority of a married over a celibate clergy. In doing so they extolled as had few before them the virtues of marriage and family life.[43]

It is true, there were practical advantages to clerical marriage: it gave clergy a point of contact with their congregations, and answered the notorious inability of unmarried clergy to keep their vows of chastity. But it was not practical concerns that drove the change. It was the reforming power of the word of God. In Luther's words:

> On our side we have Scripture, the church fathers, ancient church laws, and even papal precedent. We will stick with that. On their side [the defenders of clerical celibacy] have the contrary statements of a few church fathers, recent church canons, and their own mischief, without any support from Scripture and the Word of God.[44]

---

41   John Witte, Jr., 'Church, State, and Marriage: Three Reformation Models', *Word and World*, 23/1 (2003) 46.
42   *Luther's Works*, 45:46.
43   S. Ozment, *The Age of Reform*, 381.
44   *Von Priester Ehe*, from Ozment, *Age of Reform*, 383.

That is, the reasons for change were not to fit in with culture, or pragmatically to give the gospel a better hearing, but the consistent application of biblical teaching to real life.[45]

Much more could be said about changes to marriage brought about by the Reformation, but this is enough to observe several parallels with Augustine. Like him, the reformers' personal lives, beliefs, and teachings were changed as a result of more rigorous study of the Scriptures. Like Augustine, they embraced the goodness of marriage and marital sex, children and family life, as part of God's original plan for human flourishing.[46] They likewise considered the complementarity of male and female integral to the one flesh union and relational bond of marriage.[47] The reformers also recognised the three goods of marriage identified by Augustine: fidelity, procreation, and the sign of Christ's love for the church, and the good of mutual society, or companionship.[48] They likewise wrote against same-sex sexual activity.[49]

Yet for all these similarities, there was at least one significant difference: little changed in the church of Augustine's day as a consequence of his views, but a great deal changed as

---

[45] Carter Lindberg, 'Martin Luther on Marriage and the Family', http://www.emanuel.ro/wp-content/uploads/2014/06/P-2.1-2004-Carter-Lindberg-Martin-Luther-on-Marriage-and-the-Family.pdf Accessed 30 November 2018.

[46] *BCP*, Solemnization of Matrimony.

[47] Luther, *The Estate of Marriage (1522)*. Available at https://www.1215.org/lawnotes/misc/marriage/martin-luther-estate-of-marriage.pdf Accessed 21 December 2018. Robert, *Creation and Covenant*, 112.

[48] M. Luther, *Christian in Society II, Luther's Works* [American Edition], eds. Jaroslav Pelikan and Helmut Lehmann (Philadelphia: Mulenberg/Fortress Press, 1955) 45:47: "If then these three remain—fidelity and faith, children and progeny, and the sacrament—it is to be considered to be a wholly divine and blessed estate." *BCP*, Solemnization of Matrimony. Witte, 'Goods and Goals', 1045.

[49] M. Luther, *Luther's Works: Lectures on Genesis*, chapter 15–20, trans. George Schick (St Louis: Concordia, 1961) 255; *Lectures on Romans*, LCC, trans. and ed. Wilhem Pauck (Louisville, KN: Westminster Press, 1961) 32. Calvin, *Calvin's Commentaries*, 3:106–108; 19:79; 20:209.

a consequence of the reformers' views. In fact, the Reformation reluctantly resulted in a fracturing of the Western Church, and gave birth to an alternative Christian tradition, Protestantism, and the Reformation changes around marriage were some of the most visible and tangible expressions of that split, such that,

> one of the indelible markers of a complete break from Rome was when priests and monks were married—thereby irreparably breaking from their vows of celibacy.[50]

The Reformation changes around marriage involved a complete reversal of at least four centuries of church teaching and practice. They show us that significant changes in the doctrine and practice of marriage can and have happened in Christian history, and have been the cause of great controversy and resulted in the fracturing of the church.

However, lest we are tempted to think another such time is upon us with the current push to accept same-sex marriage in the church, we must realise that these changes in the sixteenth century did not introduce anything new. They were a rediscovery and return to the teaching of Scripture on marriage. That is why the reformers staked their lives, their ministries and their reputations on renouncing their vows and embracing the God-ordained institution of marriage. They did it because of what the Bible said, and because the Bible contradicted what they had previously held to be true.

Conclusion

As Australian Anglicans, we too have committed ourselves to the ultimate authority of God's written word, because the canonical Scriptures alone are '[our] ultimate rule and standard of faith

---

50   Johnston, 'Protestant Reformation and the Marriage of Clergy', 17.

given by the inspiration of God'.[51] We believe that God rules his people and his church through his Spirit, by his Word, and that he continues to do so in 21st century Australia.

The reformers recovered the biblical teaching on marriage and changed their belief and practice in order to align with God's word, against the traditions and culture of their day. In our day, we are being asked to change our view of marriage to align with what is being celebrated and embraced by our culture, yet is against the word of God.[52]

God's word should and will continue to bring change—to our personal lives, to the traditions of the church, to how we order our lives together—because we are fallen and broken creatures living in a broken world. Church history is replete with such change, as it should be, given the principle of *semper reformanda*.

But not all change is good change. If it is to please God, honour Christ, and promote human flourishing, the direction of change must always be *towards* the Word of God not away from it.

---

51 *The Constitution of the Anglican Church of Australia*, Part I, Fundamental Declarations, clause 2. Available at https://www.anglican.org.au/data/1._The_Constitution_of_the_Anglican_Church_of_Australia-2016.pdf Accessed 31 October 2018.

52 It is worth noting that same-sex marriage is also against 'tradition', and until very recent history would have been regarded as against 'reason'.

Friendship and Religious Life in the Bible and the Church

Dorothy A Lee[1]

Introduction

It is worth pausing in a study on marriage such as this to give attention to alternative ways of Christian living: friendship and consecrated religious life. Despite friendship being intrinsic to biblical faith, and religious life being integral to the life of the church, neither features in cultural and theological rhetoric and symbolism.[2] In its highest forms, friendship is generally undervalued in contemporary discourse, whether secular or Christian, particularly in comparison with romantic and familial connections. It has been well said of attachments among Christians that 'friendship is the most important and least talked about relationship in the church.'[3] Indeed, in the Western world at large, friendship has suffered an

---

[1] The Rev'd Canon Professor Dorothy A. Lee FAHA is Stewart Research Professor of New Testament at Trinity College, University of Divinity. She is licensed as a priest in the Diocese of Melbourne, and is a Canon of St Paul's Anglican Cathedral, Melbourne, and of Holy Trinity Anglican Cathedral, Wangaratta.

[2] On the theme of friendship in the Gospel of John, see D.A. Lee, *Flesh and Glory: Symbol, Gender and Theology in the Gospel of John* (New York: Crossroad, 2002), 99–104.

[3] Cheryl McGrath, 'The least talked about relationship in the church', https://christiantoday.com.au/news/friendship-the-least-talked-about-relationship-in-the-church.html. Last accessed 27 Jan 2019.

eclipse in recent centuries; friends are dispensable because friendship is no longer valued as it once was. Vowed religious life is even less visible: it is inconceivable to contemporary secularism which sees the explicit expression of sexuality as necessary for human fulfilment.

Friendship

The devaluing of friendship is apparent in our culture in the way that family commitments trump those of friends. Even where family members are not as close as friends, they have the last say over a number of kinds of aspects of ordinary life. Friends are now regarded as optional extras—nice to have but not necessary for well-being. Marriage and family commitments come first and friendships are even lost, as marital and parental responsibilities take over. Weddings, for example, tend to prioritise family members over friends, as do funerals and other rites of passage. Christmas, for example, is celebrated in countries like Australia as a family occasion where contact with close friends may be minimal, despite the different levels of intimacy that may be involved in each. Again and again friendship takes second or third place to marriage and family; sacrifices need to be made to support the latter but not necessarily the former.

This demise of friendship in the West is due to a number of factors. Most prominent is the modern tendency to sexualise all relationships in the wake of Freud, along with the elevation of romantic relationships within the context of the nuclear family. Added to that is the individualism of our culture, with its understanding of freedom as escape from any human bonds that might tie us down.[4] Ben Myers, for example, highlights four 'mythologies'

---

4   Wesley Hill, *Spiritual Friendship: Finding Love in the Church as a Celibate Gay Christian* (Grand Rapids: Brazos Press, 2015), 3–16.

that have undermined friendship and caused its cultural diminishment: that of sex, instinct, family, and work.[5] Some decades earlier, C.S. Lewis argued against the demise of friendship, accounting for it on the grounds that so few of us have actually experienced it, especially with the rise of Romanticism, along with the tendency to interpret all friendship as obliquely sexual.[6]

Yet, counter-cultural as it may seem to many today, friendship is itself a vital form of love. With fewer overt bonds and obligations because of its voluntary nature, it may be seen to lack the fire and excitement of sexual passion or the daily round of kinship and marriage responsibilities. Yet, while friendship may be the least spectacular, it is also sometimes the deepest and most abiding of relationships. Friends can even form a kind of partnership in which, regardless of gender, they share their lives together without overt sexual union, crossing otherwise impassable barriers of race, class and culture.

Friendship in the Ancient World

By contrast to modern Western attitudes, the theme of friendship was popular in the ancient world and widely esteemed, even in a world where the extended family dominated personal relationships. In the Greco-Roman context, alongside its systems of patronage and kinship patterns, personal friendship was deeply valued by philosophers (*philia* in Greek; *amicitia* in Latin). It could flourish across differences in social status based on shared values, virtue and mutual affection, according to Aristotle, who distinguished between different levels of friendship: those based on utility or

---

5 http://www.faith-theology.com/2010/12/disappearance-of-friendship.html. Last accessed 29 Jan 2019.
6 *The Four Loves* (London & Glasgow: Fontana, 1960), 55–60. This is not to buy into Lewis' association of each of the four loves with a specific 'concept-word'.

pleasure, which are temporary and evanescent, and those based on shared love of goodness and virtue, which endure.[7] Friends could even be viewed as part of the household (*oikos*) and virtually members of the family.[8] Indeed, for Aristotle, '[w]ithout friends, no-one would choose to live, even possessing all the other good things of life.'[9] The Roman orator and philosopher, Cicero, likewise saw friendship as immensely valuable, based on kindness, affection and openness, a key source of happiness and an encourager of virtue. For him 'no better thing has been given to man [sic] by the immortal gods'.[10]

Friendship in the Bible

The Bible has its own focus on friendship: not in a single text but across a number of traditions and genres. Biblical friendship shares much in common with the ancient world but also gives it a particular, religious interpretation that goes beyond the values of the Greco-Roman world. For the most part, the core biblical language of relationship revolves around covenant, which defines the relational bond between God and God's people, a solemn bond incorporating friendship as well as kinship, with mutual benefits and obligations on both sides. In particular, the notion of spiritual friendship comes into its own in the writings of the New Testament.

Friendship in the biblical world exists first and foremost in connection to God, the initiative lying entirely on the divine side. If we can speak of grace as prevenient—preceding any response of

---

[7] See Aristotle, *The Nicomachean Ethics* (LCL; Cambridge, MS: Harvard University Press, 1982), Books 8 & 9.
[8] S. van Tilborg, *Imaginative Love in John* (Leiden: Brill, 1993), 149.
[9] *Nicomachean Ethics*, 8.1.
[10] Cicero, *De Senectute, De Amicitia, De Divinatione* (LCL 154; Cambridge, MA: Harvard University Press, 1923), 5,20; also Plutarch, '*De Multitudine Amicorum*' in *Moralia* (LCL; London: Heinemann, 1971), 2.93–97.

ours—then the same may be said of friendship (see 1 John 4:10). God, who is both the giver and source of friendship, takes it so seriously that, in making covenant with Abraham and Sarah, God passes in fire between the parts of the sacrificial animal, as if agreeing to dismemberment if the covenant is broken on the divine side (Gen 15:17–21; cf. Jer 34:18). By contrast, the people of God for their part often fail to keep the covenant and fall back into idolatry and injustice (e.g., Jer 11:10; Ezek 16:59). Despite this, God remains faithful.

Similar ideas of covenant friendship are associated with Wisdom who, as a symbol of divine immanence, gathers around her a community of friends, bound together by mutual friendship (Prov 8:17; Sir 4:12; Wisd 6:12); those whom she loves are loved in turn by God (Sir 4:14; Wisd 7:28). As the image of divine light and goodness, Wisdom descends to earth, renewing and restoring all things, and seeking out friends:

> Being one, she is capable of all things and abiding in herself she renews all things, and down through the generations, crossing over into holy souls, she makes them friends of God [*philous theou*] and prophets. (Wisd 7:27–28)

Indeed, the reward of finding wisdom is the gift of friendship with God (Wisd 7:14), a friendship that is based on covenant values.

The height of biblical friendship is revealed above all in Jesus where it is a major feature of his ministry, defining his relationship with his disciples in a way that transcends the cultural values of his day, particularly in relation to gender. As Alastair Roberts expresses it:

> Jesus' friendships broke boundaries between the sexes, and between social insiders and outsiders. ... Jesus had close friendships with both men and women, including forms of friendship that can be very rarely practiced in certain contexts today, such as profoundly

homoaffective but non-sexual friendships and unsexualized friendships with the other sex.[11]

Theologically, the incarnation and the cross point to God in Christ befriending alienated humanity, drawing them back into covenant friendship through divine self-giving and sacrificial love. Paul speaks of God's reconciling love towards us as enemies, implying that the cross of Christ makes possible the radical renewal of friendship between created human beings and their Creator (Rom 5:6–11). In a similar vein, John's Gospel sees God's desire for friendship revealed in Jesus, the Word incarnate (John 3:16–17). Jesus befriends those who seek him, drawing them into covenant intimacy. In a surprising overturn of the master-slave paradigm, the Johannine Jesus uses the language of friendship to describe the core connection with his disciples: 'No longer do I call you slaves [*douloi*], because the slave does not know what his lord is doing; but you I have called friends [*philoi*], because everything that I have heard from the Father I have made known to you.' (John 15:15)

This saying from the Fourth Gospel reflects a popular aspect of friendship in the writings of the Greco-Roman world: the sharing of knowledge among friends, based on mutual understanding, affection and trust. Yet in the New Testament the concept goes further. At the heart in friendship in the Johannine worldview stands the cross, paradoxical symbol of life and death, light and darkness, hostility and friendship. This cruciform friendship is grounded in the being of God: it manifests itself in the amity between Father, Son and Spirit which is made available to the community of believers through the cross, giving them access to the life of God. Friendship in the biblical world thus has both its origins and its goal in the

---

11   'Friendship', in *Alastair's Adversaria*: https://alastairadversaria.com/2011/10/31/friendship/. Last accessed 15 Jan 2019.

life-giving and relational nature of God. John Chrysostom sums up the love of Christ for his friends in this way:

> Do you not perceive in how many ways He showed His love? By disclosing secrets; by taking the initiative in seeking eagerly for their friendship; by bestowing great benefits upon them; by enduring the sufferings which he then experienced for their sake. And after this He indicated that He would remain always with those who were going to produce fruit.[12]

Friends of God

As well as the community in its covenant relationship, biblical individuals also enter into friendship with God. Abraham, for example, is described as one who shares such divine friendship (2 Chron 20:7; Isa 40:8). Philo speaks of Abraham as 'the friend of God' (*theophilos*),[13] and in line with Wisdom traditions sees friendship as the reward for those who seek God, not for what they can receive, but for God's self alone.[14] Thus God 'no longer talked with [Abraham] as God with man [sic] but as a friend with a familiar person'.[15] Here a significant boundary has been crossed between the divine and the human.

Moses is similarly portrayed as one who converses with God on terms of friendship, particularly in the Tent of Meeting where he meets God and converses, 'face to face, as one speaks to a friend' (Exod 33:11). On Mt Sinai, Moses again speaks with God at the giving of the Law and his face shines so brightly from the encounter that he has to veil it (Exod 34:29–35). The nature of Moses' friendship

---

12 John Chrysostom, *Homilies on John LXX*, PG 59.
13 'On Abraham' in *Philo VI* (LCL; Cambridge, MS; Harvard University Press, 1935), XIX.89. It is hard not to see a connection here to the 'Theophilus' of Luke-Acts to whom the author addresses his writing (Luke 1:3; Acts 1:1).
14 'On Abraham', XXV.129.
15 'On Abraham', XLVI.273.

with God is evident also from the way he can change God's mind, as he intercedes for the people despite their idolatry and lack of trust (Exod 32:7–14). Philo quotes the proverb, 'what belongs to friends is in common', and sees God as bestowing all the divine possessions on the prophet Moses who is 'the friend of God'; hence Moses has power, says Philo, over the natural elements.[16] For Philo, such friendship is grounded in monotheism and deep affinity (*oikeiotês*).

Jesus is friends with Martha and Mary in the Gospels of Luke and John, the latter also including Lazarus, their brother. The language of friendship is clearest in the Johannine version where Jesus describes Lazarus as 'our friend' (*ho philos hêmôn*, John 11:11). Jesus demonstrates his friendship for the Bethany family, not by arriving on time or healing Lazarus at a distance but, more radically, by speaking the authoritative word that will draw Lazarus out of the tomb and free him from his deathly bonds (John 11:38–44). So radical is this friendship that, as the narrative implies, the consequence of Jesus' action in raising Lazarus to life is the laying down of his own life for his friends (John 11:16).

Other Johannine disciples also share friendship with Jesus, notably Mary Magdalene, Mary the mother of Jesus, the beloved disciple, and Simon Peter. Peter, for example, is rehabilitated after his threefold denial of Jesus in the language of love and friendship,[17] with no distinction between the two concepts (John 21:15–19).[18] This is an important point, since older commentaries tended to draw a distinction between the two verbs (*phileô, agapaô*), implying that love was greater than friendship. But such is not the case in the

---

16 Philo, 'On Moses I', XXVIII.156.
17 On the issue of whether John 21 is part of the original Gospel, see F.J. Moloney, *The Gospel of John* (SP; Collegeville: Liturgical Press, 1998), 545–547.
18 See, e.g., Marianne Meye Thompson, *John. A Commentary* (Louisville: Westminster John Knox Press, 2015), 440–443.

Fourth Gospel, where the two word-groups are synonymous and where the archetypal image of friendship is the beloved disciple, who occupies the place of honour on more than one occasion in the Gospel,[19] and at the Last Supper leans on the breast of Jesus (John 13:23, 25). In a similar way, the Johannine Jesus abides 'on the breast of the Father' (John 1:18). The physical pose suggests the comfort, love and trust of true friendship, a friendship that has its origins in God, where anything can be asked and shared between intimates (John 13:24–26).

In this sense, friendship functions as the language and symbolism of discipleship in this Gospel, signifying the divine affiliation with creation in and through Christ. But it does so without diluting divine sovereignty or the summons to obedience. Friendship with God has profound similarities with human friendship, at one level, but there are also significant differences. Moses, the friend of God, approaches God with reverence, prostrating himself in worship (Exod 34:8). The Johannine Jesus paradoxically teaches his disciples that they are his friends 'if you do the things which I command you' (John 15:14).

Human friendships

Within this theological framework—in which friendship has its origins in God—the Bible contains luminous examples of human friendship, sometimes across ethnic, religious and other barriers. Ruth and Naomi's friendship, which overlaps with their kinship-by-marriage, demonstrates a deep and mutual commitment in the connection between the two women. Through this affinity, the younger woman comes to share the older woman's faith and to worship her God, while supporting and comforting her in old age.

---

19 See John 19:25–27, 20:2–10, 21:7, 20, 23–24; also John 1:37, 18:15, and 19:35.

Ruth's words to Naomi when the latter wants to send her home to Moab—back to her own people and her own religion—are often used in contemporary wedding ceremonies, but they belong within the framework of friendship and not of marriage:

> Do not press me to leave you or to turn back from following you! Where you go, I will go; where you lodge, I will lodge; your people shall be my people, and your God my God. Where you die, I will die— there will I be buried. May the Lord do thus and so to me, and more as well, if even death parts me from you! (Ruth 1:16–17)

Another, well-known example is that of David and Jonathan (1 Sam 18:1–4), the close bond of friendship leading Jonathan to risk his own life in order to protect David from his father, King Saul (1 Sam 20). David's lament over the deaths of Saul and Jonathan is deeply evocative, particularly in regard to his friendship with Jonathan: 'I am distressed for you, my brother Jonathan; greatly beloved were you to me; your love to me was wonderful, passing the love of women' (2 Sam 1:26). This is the language of fictive (metaphorical) kinship as well as friendship, and its avowed superiority to sexual love in this context indicates the heights to which friendship can reach, as well as the depths of grief at its loss.[20]

There are examples of friendship also in the New Testament. Paul's relationship with fellow missionaries and workers, in particular, bears many of the signs of enduring friendship. The list of greetings in Romans 16 includes women as well as men: Phoebe, a deacon, who takes the epistle to Rome (Rom 16:1–2); missionaries and teachers, Prisca and Aquila (16:3), with whom Paul also shares a common trade; the apostles, Andronicus and Junia (16:7) as well as others, with whom Paul lives and works on terms of the deepest

---

20 The ancient world, like many moderns, tended to assume that Achilles and Patroclus were lovers in *The Iliad*, but Homer portrays them in terms of the deepest friendship which is nowhere named as explicitly sexual.

friendship.[21] The letter to the Philippians betrays a similar sense of affection, this time between Paul and a Christian community ('my beloved and longed for brothers and sisters', Phil 4:1). In Philemon, Paul speaks warmly of Onesimus in the language of friendship, who is 'no longer a slave, but beyond a slave, a beloved brother, especially to me, but how much more to you, both humanly speaking [lit. 'in the flesh'] and 'in the Lord' (Phlm 16). The Bible has thus outstanding examples of friendship, demonstrating a similar estimation of its worth and status as the ancient world more generally.

Consecrated Religious Life

One of the radical features of the early church was the existence of Christian communities, formed by the gathering together of groups of women and men separately to live a life of prayer and service, bound together by vows of celibacy and poverty. Whereas Roman society made marriage mandatory and Jewish society the normal expectation, the monastic movement gave young people the choice of living in community without marriage and in radical obedience to the gospel. They now had a new sense of autonomy over their own bodies,[22] as well as a new way of expressing their devotion to Christ.

In some cases, individual Christians retreated to the desert by themselves to live as hermits, often with a sense of harmony with the natural world around them. They withdrew from the world, not to escape it, but rather to pray for it and to wrestle against the forces of evil as they encountered them in a harsh and lonely environment. They saw themselves as living with a deeper sense

---

21 For a fictional representation of these relationships, based on recent scholarship, see especially Paula Gooder, *Phoebe: A Story. Pauline Christianity in Narrative Form* (London: Hodder & Stoughton, 2018).
22 Peter Brown, *The Body and Society* (New York: Columbia University Press, 1988).

of spiritual union with the wider church and a profound sense of communion with God.

In both cases, the ultimate example for these early Christians is the New Testament itself. Both Jesus and John the Baptist are associated in the Gospels with the desert: John the Baptist in his missional and ascetic lifestyle—his style of dress and his food—and Jesus in the Temptation narrative. According to the first three Gospels, Jesus retreats to the wilderness to encounter Satan and to find there the heavenly sustenance which enables him to defeat evil (Mark 1:12-13/Matt 4:1-11/Luke 4:1-13). Jesus' subsequent lifestyle also provides an example: unmarried, celibate, without possessions of his own, focussed entirely upon his divine mission, and living in community with his disciples, both women and men, who likewise leave behind their families and possessions to follow him (Matt 8:20; Luke 8:1-3). Jesus' command to the rich ruler to sell his possessions and follow Jesus is also a powerful influence in shaping these early communities (Mark 10:21).

Not only Jesus but Paul also speaks of his own celibate lifestyle in his letters where, in contrast to the Apostle Peter and to other missionary couples (1 Cor 9:5; Rom 16:3, 7), Paul sees the advantages of a celibate lifestyle to free him, and others, from the distractions implicit in marriage and family life (1 Cor 7:7-8, 28b-35). This Pauline commitment to a life lived outside normal the domestic arrangements, based in celibacy, in order to serve God and the church more fully, had a significant influence on the rise of monastic movements in the centuries which followed.

Equally influential is Luke's description of the earliest Christian community, following the events of Pentecost: 'All who believed were together and had all things in common; they would sell their possessions and goods and distribute the proceeds to all, as any had need' (Acts 2:44-45). This common life, with its sharing of possessions and concern for the needy, as well as its commitment to daily prayer and the Eucharist, provided the inspiration for many in the early church to seek to replicate the same lifestyle.[23]

Vowed religious life developed over the ensuing centuries in both East and West, often becoming centres of Christian faith, hospitality, learning and prayer. Within Anglicanism, in the immediate post-Reformation period, the Deacon Nicholas Ferrar moved to Little Gidding in England with his family to begin an informal spiritual community, centred around the *Book of Common Prayer* and service to the local poor. Other Anglican communities, with a more explicit rule of life, grew up around the Benedictine, Franciscan, and other religious traditions, committed to the gospel values of shared possessions, common prayer and service to the poor. This lifestyle remains as a significant alternative to marriage for those who seek an evangelical community, living by the pattern of the earliest Christian communities.[24] They are and remain a living testimony to the gospel, as an alternative to marriage, within the life of the church.

Perhaps the most obvious alternative, however, is that of singleness. Either through choice, or by circumstances, many Christians are content to live a single life. This lifestyle is often ignored by the church, yet it can be immensely valuable in Christian communities, as single people dedicate their time, talents and possessions to the well-being of the church and of those in need. Without explicit consecration, such lives may be chosen and dedicated to God in a less than formal way, and need to be acknowledged within the life of

---

23   Cf. esp. Athanasius' *Life of Antony*. Antony lived in the second century CE as an ascetic and celibate, committed to the principles of the gospel and the lifestyle of the apostles; the book itself had a profound influence on subsequent generations.
24   See esp. Gregory of Nyssa's *On Virginity*.

the church. For such individuals, friendships become of paramount importance in their discipleship.

Vowed Friendships

There is a further aspect to friendship that needs to be mentioned, which provides a more focused alternative to marriage, within the scope of close relationships within the Christian community. In some cases, friendships come close to partnerships, bound by mutual and abiding love. They ought not to be regarded with suspicion or mistrust by either those who condemn same-sex relationships or those who espouse them. Friendship can be an alternative to both marriage and family, as well as existing alongside them, and the church has an important role in supporting such relationships.

This support can involve blessing the commitment of friends to one another, where such is desired. Wesley Hill, for example, suggests the possibility of covenant rituals around the Eucharist to bond friends to one another more formally within the life of the church, both within and outside of consecrated religious life. Drawing particularly on the life and writings of the English saint, Aelred of Rievaulx (c. 1110–1167) and the Russian Orthodox theologian and polymath, Pavel Florensky (1882–1937),[25] Hill outlines the significance vowed friendships have had in the past, where two people have bonded themselves to one another in spiritual friendship, each committed to the other for life.[26] In relation to this kind of friendship in the liturgical practice of the church, both East and West, Hill notes that:

> Where people may have been skeptical of 'spiritual' ties, Christians came to believe that the truest and most durable relationships were friendships that were sealed with the common participation

---

25   Hill, *Spiritual Friendship*, 26–33.
26   *Spiritual Friendship*, 23–44.

in the Eucharistic body and blood of Christ. If blood is thicker than water, then Eucharistic blood is thickest of all.[27]

This was certainly true in some monastic communities, but it also existed beyond the convent or the monastery among Christians. Writing as a gay man who believes himself committed to celibacy, Hill nonetheless sees the vitality and desirability of Christian friendship for the married, unmarried and consecrated alike, regardless of gender. His powerful evocation of spiritual friendship offers a contribution to the church as a whole, despite differences of opinion on same-sex unions.

Conclusion

By definition friendship, along with consecrated religious life, encourage deep attachments between people who are not necessarily connected by blood or marriage: who have no other, obvious human bond. They have the capacity therefore to transcend all kinds of barriers—race, class and gender, even time and space—and are particularly apt, in different ways, for indicating the nature of Christian community. Friendship, in its different forms, including religious life, has its origins in the divine being, self-revealed in creation and redemption, and crossing otherwise insuperable barriers; indeed there is no higher barrier, no wider gulf, than that between Creator and creation.

Friendship is not primarily a human construction but a divine gift bestowed on creation from the beginning, symbolising both the source and goal of creation. God desires an end to alienation and enmity, drawing all things into the divine embrace through the incarnation and the cross, reconciling human beings to God and to each other, as well as to the natural world (Col 1:20; Eph 2:13–14;

---

27   *Spiritual Friendship*, 36.

John 12:32).[28] A theological perspective on friendship thus needs to accord it significant status: on an equal footing with marriage and kinship. It is not an inferior relationship in a theological understanding but one which, though perhaps less formalised because of its voluntary nature, has a similar capacity to reflect the profound amity and communion within, and emanating from, the being of God. In this sense, it too has a 'sacramental' quality: friendship can be as much the reflection of the relationality of God as can marriage. Indeed, unlike the latter, true Christian friendship extends to the earth itself and to earth's creatures.[29]

Friendship lies at the core of Christian community and is central rather than peripheral to it. Once we acknowledge theologically its significance, we can then confirm and support the intimate friendships which exist between Christians, regardless of gender, offering them the possibility of vowed commitments in a liturgical and eucharistic context—much as we often perform the marriage of Christians within the same sacramental context. Similarly, we need to give greater support to religious life within the Anglican Church. These relationships should be accorded equivalent honour to marriage and family within the attitudes, structures and rituals of the church. Indeed, where friendship is given its rightful place, our human relationships can overlap with one another,[30] donating a sense of the breadth and giftedness of our relationality which, in all its diversity, both mirrors and exudes the divine, Trinitarian love.

---

28 Quite apart from the need to befriend the earth in the current context of despoliation and abuse, it is worth noting that the higher mammals are also capable of lasting friendships, both with human beings and with each other.
29 See D. Edwards, *Jesus the Wisdom of God. An Ecological Theology* (Homebush, NSW: St Paul's, 1995), 166–171.
30 Hill, *Spiritual Friendship*, 42.

Friendship and the Trinity

Mark D Thompson[1]

The value of interpersonal relationships is often traced back to the Christian doctrine of the Trinity.
Through the revelation of the Trinity we learn that the living God, the good and true God, is a God who has relationship within Himself and that the values of relationships ultimately belong to reality in its most absolute form. In the light of this doctrine, personal relationships are seen to be the ultimate, are seen to be the most real things that are.[2]

God has created us as social creatures and human life thrives in the web of relationships we call 'community'. The three-in-oneness and one-in-threeness of the divine Trinity seems a natural analogue. 'Social trinitarianism', associated with theologians such as Jürgen Moltmann and John Zizioulas, has even spoken of the intratrinitarian relations in terms of a community of persons.[3] Nicholas Fyodorov once opined, 'Our social program is the dogma

---

[1] The Rev'd Canon Dr Mark D Thompson is Principal of Moore College, Sydney and the head of its Department of Theology, Philosophy and Ethics. His doctorate was awarded by the University of Oxford. He is a Canon of St Andrew's Cathedral, Sydney.

[2] D.B. Knox, *The Everlasting God* (Welwyn, Herts: Evangelical Press, 1982), 51–52.

[3] J. Moltmann, *The Trinity and the Kingdom of God: The Doctrine of God* (trans. M. Kohl; London: SCM, 1981); J. Zizioulas, *Being as Communion: Studies in Personhood and the Church* (Crestwood, NY: St Valdimir's Seminary Press, 1985), 27–49.

of Trinity' and this has been echoed by Miroslav Volf.[4] However, for others this raises the spectre of tritheism,[5] as we apply twentieth and twenty-first century notions of personality to the 'persons' of the Godhead. We are reminded that God is one and the distinction of persons—existing eternally in an equal and yet ordered relation—does not compromise the one substance. As the Athanasian Creed declares 'we worship one God in Trinity and Trinity in Unity'.

Nevertheless, with appropriate qualification it is still possible to speak about an analogue between human fellowship and the eternal fellowship of triune persons. The eternal love the Father has for the Son, which is made manifest for us in the words addressed to human creatures about Jesus of Nazareth, 'This is my beloved Son in whom I am well pleased' (Matt 3:17; 17:5), the unity of purpose and word and action which is reflected in, rather than interrupted by, the incarnation (John 5:36; 8:28; 12:49) impact the whole of creation and provide a model for Christian discipleship ('that they may be one even as we are one'). In the traditional terms of trinitarian theology: the divine missions arise from and reflect the divine processions.[6] It is right and good to celebrate human relationships and to seek to order them according to the other-person-centredness of triune persons.

There is a particular set of correspondences that relate especially to the relationship of marriage between a man and a woman. This much is evident (though its implications are often disputed) from passages such as Ephesians 5 and 1 Corinthians 11. The relation of the incarnate Christ both to the Father (which given the principle

---

4   M. Volf, '"The Trinity is our Social Program": The Doctrine of the Trinity and the Shape of Social Engagement', *Modern Theology* 14/3 (1998): 403–423.
5   B. Leftow, 'Anti Social Trinitarianism', pp. 203–249 in S.T. Davis et. al. (eds), *The Trinity* (Oxford: Oxford University Press, 1999).
6   Thomas Aquinas *Summa Theologiae*, I.q.43.a.2; and F. Sanders, *The Triune God* (Grand Rapids: Zondervan, 2016), 19.

of processions and missions just mentioned must reflect the eternal relation of the Son and the Father) as well as to the Church is pivotal. However, personal relationships more widely, and those we associate with the concept of 'friendship' are also important. *Homo sapiens* ('wise man') may also be described as *homo loquens* ('speaking man'), *homo ludens* ('playing man'), and even *homo adorans* ('worshipping man'), but he or she must also be understood as *homo socius* ('social man') or *homo relationis* ('relational man').[7]

In the Old Testament, a number of Hebrew words are used for friendship. The 'friendship of God' or 'friendship of the LORD' makes use of the word *sôd* (Job 29:4; Ps 25:14). In reference to friendship between human beings, the word for companionship (*re'eh*) or companion (rea', cf. the verb *r'h*), is most often used (Prov 22:24; Gen 38:12; 2 Sam 13:3; 15:37), though sometimes the word for peace (*shalôm*) is used, as in 1 Chr 12:17). Most significantly, when in Exodus Moses is spoken of as one with whom the LORD used to speak 'face to face, as a man speaks to his friend', the word *rea'* is used. Perhaps just as interesting is the way friendship, family and marriage are juxtaposed in Deuteronomy 13:6.

> If your brother, the son of your mother, or your son or your daughter or the wife you embrace or your friend [*rea'*] who is as your own soul [*nephesh*] entices you secretly, saying, 'Let us go and serve other gods', which neither you nor your fathers have known, some of the gods of the peoples who are around you, whether near you or far off from you, from the one end of the earth to the other, you shall not yield to him or listen to him …

Undoubtedly this provides part of the context for one of the most poignant—and one of the most abused—references to friendship,

---

7   P. Tyler, 'Epilogue: Whither Christian Spirituality?', 387–394 in R. Woods & P. Tyler (eds), *The Bloomsbury Guide to Christian Spirituality* (London: Bloomsbury, 2012), 389.

namely that of David and Jonathan. Jonathan 'loved him as his own soul [*nephesh*]'. The suggestion made by some that this implies a homosexual or homoerotic relationship between David and Jonathan is refuted not only by the context of the David narrative but also by the close verbal parallel with Deuteronomy 13.

In the New Testament, often the word *philos* and its cognates is used to speak of friendship (Luke 11:5, 8; 14:10; John 11:11). Jesus famously told his disciples on the night he was betrayed, 'No longer do I call you servants, for the servant does not know what his master is doing; but I have called you friends [*philous*], for all that I have heard from my Father I have made known to you' (John 15:15). James can use the word both positively and negatively: '"Abraham believed God and it was counted to him as righteousness"—and he was called a friend [*philos*] of God' (Jas 2:23); but also, 'Do you not know that friendship [*philia*] with the world is enmity with God?' (Jas 4:4; cf. Matt 11:19). On occasion, however, the word *hetairos* ('companion') is used. One special instance of this is the way Jesus greeted Judas when he arrived at the Garden of Gethsemane (Matt 26:50). He had come as a *hetairos*, not as a *philos*.

These references to friendship are not straightforward analogues of the trinitarian relations. The divine persons are not distinct 'personalities', different at the level of being as well separate centres of consciousness. While I might have an intensely personal relationship with my friend, where we share a common mind, common goals, common experiences and a common perspective on life, I am not one in being with him or her. He or she still has a separate life apart from me and does things in which I am not in the slightest involved. Nevertheless, there is still value and reality to the analogy. The other-centredness of the divine persons does find an echo in the deeply enriching and mutually self-giving instances of human friendship and companionship throughout the Bible.

Human relationships matter, and matter deeply, because the intra-trinitarian relations lie at the very centre of reality and have an important echo here.

One of the tragic entailments of the highly sexualised culture of the late twentieth century is the eclipse of friendship. Companionship has been overshadowed by the expectation that it must routinely have a sexual dimension. Two single friends travelling together, especially when over an extended period and regardless of whether they are of the same sex or of different sexes, are often presumed to be lovers. The insinuation is that this friendship is so close there must be more going on. Companionship is redefined with the suggestion that sexual intimacy is an integral part of it and that to deny the appropriateness of such intimacy, for whatever reason, is punitive, unloving and ultimately a contradiction of the reality of true companionship. Yet this turn in our way of thinking about relationships is itself a tragic loss. Sex is a wonderful gift of God which, when enjoyed in the context in which it was given to be enjoyed—the marriage covenant between a man and a woman—enriches human existence. Yet it is not everything and it does not define our existence. It does not make us human and it does not make us who we are. It is not in itself the remedy for loneliness or being alone. God's gift of friendship or companionship is one way in which our capacity and need for interpersonal relationships can be expressed and enjoyed (cf. Eccl 4:8–12). How 'good and pleasant' a thing it is, David exclaims, 'when brothers and sisters dwell in unity' (Ps 133:1). The writers of proverbs recognise the value of 'a friend who sticks closer than a brother' (Prov 18:24).

Friendship or companionship is a very good thing which needs to be honoured and protected. It is a gift of God that enriches life and matches the way we have been created. It does not rely on sexual activity for its meaning, value or significance. However, for the married just as for the unmarried, for those with many friendships and those with very few, it is our relationship as creatures with our Creator—as sinners redeemed and forgiven by our Redeemer —it is that which secures our identity. We are not defined by our human friendships, our sexual relationships, or even our sexual orientation. We are a new creation because we are 'in Christ' (2 Cor 5:17). Through his perfect life, atoning death, bodily resurrection and ascension, and giving of the Spirit, the eternal relations of Father, Son and Spirit now embrace us, calling us out of darkness and into his marvellous light (1 Pet 2:9). That light is good, holy, true and pure, and in it friendship thrives.

'He Knew He Did Not Belong to Himself': Steps Towards a Theological Understanding of Desire

G. J. Seach[1]

Introduction

As with many of the liturgical riches in the *Book of Common Prayer*, the prelude to the 'Form of Solemnization of Matrimony' is notable for the deep and resonant theological impulses that shape it. Holy Matrimony, worshippers hear, is 'an honourable estate, instituted of God' and which signifies 'unto us the mystical union that is betwixt Christ and his Church'. Given the 'honourable' nature of matrimony, the *Book of Common Prayer* also recognises that such a union is 'not by any to be enterprised, nor taken in hand... lightly, or wantonly, to satisfy men's carnal lusts and appetites, like brute beasts that have no understanding'. In short, we might say, the paragraphs read as an introduction to a wedding ceremony clearly acknowledge both the benefits marriage brings to persons, and the dangers from which, through God's grace, it may protect those same persons.

---

[1] The Rev'd Dr G. J. Seach is the Warden of Wollaston Theological College, Perth, and an affiliate Lecturer at Murdoch University and an Adjunct Fellow in the Schools of Arts and Sciences, and Philosophy and Theology, University of Notre Dame (Fremantle). He gained his doctorate in Theology from the University of Cambridge. He is a licensed priest in Perth diocese.

Though not mentioned explicitly, what lies behind both the promise and the warning is an acknowledgement and recognition of human desire. Included in that is a recognition that desire is, in its origins, a gift from God. Hence, a desire for another that finds its 'consummation' in Holy Matrimony is a clear sign of the desire God feels for all of God's creation, particularly those human beings created in God's image. This is a desire that is revealed, initially, in the overflowing of love that exists between the members of the holy and undivided Trinity into God's loving act of creation. It continues to be seen in God's desire, and consequent calling, of persons, and then a people into covenant relationship with God—frequently described in terms of 'marriage'. Christians believe that God's desire to live in an eternal communion of love with all creation finds its fulfilment in God's self-emptying love, whereby the second person of the Trinity enters fully into creation, assuming full humanity, and initiates and enters into communion with a far wider group of people through a 'mystical union' which finds instantiation in the Church. Indeed, so close is this mystical union, that the Church is also described as the Body of Christ—such that, we might say, the two (God's people and God's Son) indeed become 'one flesh'.

Like all elements of human life, even those gifts we receive from God, however, our desires can be corrupted. This recognition gives rise to the warning about carnal lusts and brute appetites also present in the Form of Solemnization of Holy Matrimony.

As an aid to thinking about the issues raised by same-sex marriage, this essay attempts to outline steps towards a theology of desire. It takes its starting point from a recent helpful volume, in which Sarah Coakley argues that the current 'ecclesiastical furores about "sexuality" [including calls for same-sex marriage]... are the working out of a conundrum about desire and gratification in both the

Christian tradition and the contemporary secular West'.[2] She argues that what is necessary is a clarification of contemporary confusion about 'desire' itself.[3] Importantly, Coakley suggests that 'the notion of desire... requires... prior theological analysis if its full implications for human flourishing are to be understood.'[4] I think Coakley is right. And, in constructing a theology of desire, it is important that 'prior theological analysis' begins, as it were, with God!

Beginning with God

It is axiomatic that any *theo*-logical understanding of desire must begin from reflection on God. But, as Aquinas warns, 'God is not known to us in [God's] nature, but through [God's] operations'.[5] That is, as Karl Rahner reminded us, 'the economic Trinity *is* the immanent Trinity'[6]: God is what God does. As humans, we only know of God as God has been revealed to us in God's actions through the whole salvation history of creation, incarnation of Jesus, redemption through him and election (initially of Abraham and Israel, then, in Christ and by the Spirit, of the Church). This revelation allows the writer of the First Epistle of John to say 'God is love' (I John 4:8)—not *that* God loves (though God certainly does that, as we see and understand from that 'doing'), but that God *is* love.

This means that, from eternity, the eternal love that exists between Father, Son and Holy Spirit and which *is* the Triune God is of such fullness that it overflows, in 'excess', in the act of creation

---

2   Sarah Coakley, *The New Asceticism: Sexuality, Gender and the Quest for God* (London: Bloomsbury, 2015), 2. Coakley's call for a renewed theology of desire was anticipated by both Rowan Williams and Graham Ward — to confine myself to two Anglican theologians — as shall be seen in what follows.
3   Coakley, *The New Asceticism*, 4.
4   Coakley, *The New Asceticism*, 5.
5   *Summa Theologiae*, Ia. Q 13. 8
6   Karl Rahner, *The Trinity*, tr. Joseph Donceel (Tunbridge Wells: Burns and Oates, 1970), 34.

(and creating). Indeed, so 'excessive' is God's love that God creates *ex nihilo*—out of nothing, not requiring anything other than that outpouring of love to bring creation into being. God does not need to create—God's inner-Trinitarian love is complete in itself. But, given the fullness and abundance of that love—its 'excess'— it cannot but overflow. We might say that creation is the first instance of the kenotic love of God towards what is not God—a kenotic love that, as Paul recognised, is most obviously instantiated in the Incarnation of the Divine Son. (Phil 2:5-11). David Bentley Hart characterises this nicely when he writes that 'God's glory and creation's goodness are proclaimed with equal eloquence and equal truthfulness in each moment... in an endless sequence of *excessive* statements of that glory and goodness.'[7]

Perhaps nowhere has this understanding been rendered as precisely as by the enigmatic Pseudo-Dionysius. Writing as early as the fifth or sixth century (though following insights from Origen and Gregory of Nyssa), and for audiences still steeped in neo-Platonism, Pseudo-Dionysius will

> be so bold as to claim that the Cause of all things [i.e., God] loves all things in the superabundance of his goodness, that because of this he makes all things, brings all things to perfection, holds all things together.... That yearning[8] which creates all the goodness of the world *preexisted superabundantly within the Good and did not allow it to remain without issue*. It stirred him to use the abundance of his powers in the production of the world.[9]

---

7 David Bentley Hart, *The Beauty of the Infinite: The Aesthetics of Christian Truth* (Grand Rapids: Eerdmans, 2003), 21. Italics original.

8 The Greek of Ps. Dionysius here is *eros*.

9 Pseudo-Dionysius, 'The Divine Names', IV. 10, in *The Complete Works*, trans. Colm Luibheid (New York: Paulist Press, 1987), 79–80. Emphasis mine. As should be obvious from the title of the work–'The Divine Names'–Ps.-Dionysius is arguing that words such as 'the Good', 'the Cause of all things' are names able to be given to God; along with, *inter alia*, 'the Beautiful' and 'the True'.

In short, God creates out of the love, the yearning, the desire that exists in and *is* God.

A further important point needs to be mentioned. God's kenotic love towards what is not God shows again that what is revealed to us of God in Christ and by the Spirit (i.e., through God's actions) speaks of who God is in Godself. The Father is not the Son, the Son is not the Spirit, the Spirit is neither Father nor Son. Yet the difference in hypostases is a difference-in-relation, a difference-in-communion.[10] Indeed, Christianity is bold to say that this difference-in-communion, given that it proceeds from and is maintained by mutual, indwelling love, is constitutive of the Divine Trinity that is God. Graham Ward rightly grounds this theologically: 'difference, thought theologically, is rooted in the difference of hypostases in the Trinity.'[11] A love which is offered to and drawn from the 'different' or 'other' finds its origin in the love that exists in and is God.

Given creation exists, God desires communion with all creation. Thus, Ward extends 'Rahner's rule' by saying 'There is no immanent Trinity that is not economic—the Godhead holds nothing back in its desire for what it has created.'[12] As the part of creation 'made in the image and likeness of God', it is the place of humanity to be the *creaturely* focus of—more properly, the *response* to ('we love because God first loved us')—that desire for communion. Notwithstanding that human will disrupted and disrupts that communion, God continues to desire such communion, and seeks and acts to re-establish it. Rowan Williams sensibly recalls that the first question God asks humanity in Scripture is, 'Where

---

10   See further on this the essay by M. D. Thompson above, and his reference to Zizioulas and Moltmann.
11   Graham Ward, 'Divinity and Sexual Difference' in *Christ and Culture* (Oxford: Blackwell, 2005), 151.
12   Ward, 'Divinity and Sexual Difference', 150.

are you?'[13] (Gen 3: 9) Even, indeed immediately (in narrative terms), after humans sin, God searches us out, and attempts to re-establish communion and, ultimately, to bring us home.[14] This happens because, Christian tradition has been bold to say, God *desires us*, God wants to make God's home with us (cf. John 1:14; Rev 3:16). Indeed, as the Council of Chalcedon agreed, in Christ, Creator and creature, divine and human, were united to such an extent (in what theologians call the hypostatic union) that they exist without separation, yet without confusion. This is, again, a difference-in-(the closest possible)-communion.

In so viewing God's action towards us, the Church draws upon the same insights that inspired some Jewish thinking: thinking that gave rise to such texts (among others, together with further reflection on them) as Song of Songs. Here, the love songs between lover and beloved have consistently been read analogically as the love song between God and the people of Israel. That is, the relationship between God and Israel, which becomes 'baptized' and expanded in the relationship between Christ and the Church, and will be consummated in the marriage feast of the Lamb (the eternal Bridegroom), is frequently described analogically as marriage. This is, indeed, a 'mystical union' which is found now in the Church. It is a union so close that the baptized, the members of the Church,

---

13 Rowan Williams, 'God in Search: A Sermon' in Williams, *On Augustine* (London: Bloomsbury, 2016), 207.
14 c.f. the words of a post-Communion prayer in *A Prayer Book for Australia* (p. 143): 'Father of all we give you thanks and praise that when we were still far off you met us in your Son and brought us home.' The imagery is, obviously, drawn from the parable of the lost son (Luke 15:18–24). Significantly, however, that parable follows two others, in which it is a shepherd who goes searching for the lost sheep, and a woman who searches for her lost coin. The 'waiting father', who counter-culturally runs to meet his returning son, needs to be read in light of the parallel figures who do the searching.

are described as the Body of Christ. We live, as Paul frequently says, in Christ. Again, Pseudo-Dionysius puts this well:

> This divine yearning [eros] brings ecstasy so that the lover belongs not to self but to the beloved.... This is why the great Paul, swept along by his yearning for God and seized of its ecstatic power, had this inspired word to say: 'It is no longer I who live, but Christ who lives in me.' [Galatians 2:20] Paul was truly a lover and, as he says, he was beside himself for God'. [2 Corinthians 5:13][15]

This divine yearning and ecstasy extends further, through the Spirit, to all God's people, because though we are many, we are one Body.

One last point from a *theo*-logical perspective. We shall witness the fullness of God's desire for God's creation only ultimately, when it is consummated in the marriage feast of the Lamb. Graham Ward is right to say, therefore, that 'true desire is eschatological'.[16] Indeed, this cannot be otherwise, given the source of this desire is the eternal God, and that this God continues to call us into ever deepening relationship. We recognise, as the people of Israel did in the pillar of cloud and the pillar of fire, that God goes ahead of us and calls us into that (eschatological) Promised Land where we will live in communion with God forever. To this end, the Spirit of love (who also comes as fire) continually compels us forward to that communion.

A move to theological anthropology: human desire shaped by God

Having considered desire *in* God, and divine desire for all creation, it is time to consider human desire theologically. As argued above, Christian faith understands that all desire finds its origin in God.

---

15 'The Divine Names', IV. 13, *op. cit.*, p. 82
16 Graham Ward, 'The Erotics of Redemption' in *Cities of God* (Oxford: Routledge, 2000), 187.

Bernard of Clairvaux puts this most starkly: 'The cause of loving God is God'.[17] Human persons respond—positively, negatively, indifferently—to the initial outpouring of love by God, and to the desire God maintains for renewed communion with all creation. Christians respond by turning *to* God in love and desire—hesitatingly, often unwillingly, mostly incompletely; but, in faith, we seek to find the source of our own desire in the One who first loved us. While he was not the first to do so, Augustine makes this especially clear when, at the beginning of *Confessions*, he recognises of God that 'you have made us for yourself, and our heart is restless until it finds rest in you.'[18]

Importantly, however, human desire—even, and especially, desire for God—is, *qua* human, different from divine desire. Nevertheless, while retaining the reality of the difference between created and Uncreated, Rowan Williams rightly affirms:

> The whole story of creation, incarnation and our incorporation into the fellowship of Christ's body tells us that God desires us as if we were God, as if we were that unconditional response to God's giving that God's self makes in the life of the Trinity. We are created so that we may be caught up in this; so that we may

---

[17] Bernard of Clairvoux, 'On Loving God' in *Selected Works*, trans. G. R. Evans (New York: Paulist Press, 1987), 174.

[18] Augustine, *Confessions*, I.1 (trans. and ed. Henry Chadwick, Oxford: OUP, 1990, p. 1). There is not space to explore the full implications of what Augustine meant and said here, and elsewhere in *Confessions*, about desire. Coakley explores this well in another recent volume: *God, Sexuality and the Self: An Essay 'On the Trinity'*, (Cambridge: CUP, 2013). Furthermore, the remarkable work by John Burnaby, *Amor Dei: A Study of St Augustine's teaching on the Love of God as the motive of Christian Life* (London: Hodder & Stoughton, 1938) remains one of the best introductions to Augustine generally, with special significance for this topic. See, too, Rowan Williams, 'Language, Reality and Desire: The Nature of Christian Formation', recently republished in Williams, *On Augustine*, (London: Bloomsbury, 2016), 41–58.

grow into the whole-hearted love of God by learning that God loves us as God loves God.[19]

Combining these insights leads to theological recognition that human desire for God has its origin in God's desire for us. But, just as God's love for us always is, and flows from, the excess of love that *is* God, so our own desire is unable to be fulfilled. That is, there will always exist a yearning in human persons because of the intrinsically unfulfilled nature of our desire for God. Furthermore, given that this desire for God draws a person outside herself or himself, it may be defined as ecstatically excessive. It is from this unfulfilled desire—in its ecstatic excess—that, again theologically (rather than biologically, psychologically or other frameworks we may—and others certainly—use), desire for other persons springs.

A brief review of theological thinking on human desire

A starting point in a move towards a theology of desire is the Song of Songs: those remarkable poems which have exercised reflection throughout Jewish and Christian theological history. At one level, the Song of Songs can be seen as texts (as they possibly were) written in celebration of a royal marriage, delighting in the love shared between man and woman. Theologically, however, the first point to be made, as von Balthasar reminds us, is that 'God is nowhere spoken of'[20] in this text. This creates something of a conundrum for both our Jewish *and* Christian forebears: how are we to make sense of the presence of this highly charged presentation of erotic

---

19 'The Body's Grace', (London: GCM, 1989), 3. Also found in *Theology and Sexuality: Contemporary Readings*, ed. Eugene F. Rogers Jr., (Oxford: Blackwell, 2002), 309–21 at 311–12.

20 Hans Urs von Balthasar, *The Glory of the Lord: A Theological Aesthetics, Vol. VI: Theology: The Old Covenant*, 132. Balthasar also argues that 'nowhere is there talk of marriage, or indeed of children.' 131. Nevertheless, the beloved is referred to as the 'bride'.

desire between two human lovers in Holy Scripture? Especially when, in the poems themselves, as both von Balthasar and, before him, Karl Barth recognise: 'Here reigns only *eros*, for which there is no such thing as shame.'[21] Interestingly, however, at no point is there 'any reference to family or children': this is not *eros* directed to any purpose other than the delight of the lover in the beloved.

One thing we discover in the Song of Songs, in the celebration of love that these poems are, is that ecstasy – being drawn out in joy and desire for the loved one – allows a merging and over-flowing of identity into the identity of the beloved. Precisely because these are *poetic* expressions of love and desire, they are able to rejoice in what might be called 'excessive ecstasy'. Indeed, it may be that the very ecstasy portrayed is what so readily allowed both rabbinic and Christian reflection on these poems to see them as analogies of the love of God for Israel, or of Christ 'the Bridegroom' for his Church 'the Bride', and of Christ for the soul of the believer. Thus, Israel, the Church, and the believer became transformed by the same desire for God. What we discern in these reflections, therefore, is the existence of cultures and ages less fixed upon desire as being solely to do with activities between the gendered, sexual organs of male or female. Such cultures were able to see desire, even *erotic* desire, as a clear figure for the desire of God for God's people, and of a person who gives her or himself to Christ.

Of further note, given that most of the reflections on Song of Songs were written by males—rabbis, in the first instance, and priests and monks later—shows that men, and many celibate men at that, were happy to describe themselves using female terms. They, their souls and all they were, were sought by the bridegroom, the lover who treated them as the beloved. Again, this is

---

21   Balthasar, *The Glory of the Lord*, 135.

an understanding of desire, and (especially in John of the Cross[22]) erotic desire, which is certainly physical but not desire restricted to genital activity, as it usually is in current understanding.

Following Sarah Coakley, I recognise the importance of Gregory of Nyssa in helping contemporary Christians to think more *theologically* about desire. Coakley correctly identifies that for Gregory, in his commentary on Song of Songs, 'desire relates crucially to what might be called the 'glue' of society':

> The 'erotic' desire that originally draws partners together sexually has also to last long enough, and to be so refined in God, as to render back to society what originally gave those partners the possibility of mutual joy: that means...service to the poor and the outcast, attention to the frail and the orphans, a consideration of the fruit of the earth and its limitations, a vision of the whole in which all play their part.... Thus it is the complete intertwinement of physical and *spiritual* in desire that has first to be acknowledged, as well as its moral and 'eschatological' goals, if we are to reverse the modern shrinkage of thought about desire.... [Gregory] tells us that desire (properly understood) needs to be intensified (in God), never constrained or dampened...[23]

It is worth considering one of Gregory's earliest works, his remarkable essay 'On Virginity', which offers considerable help as we think through these issues. 'On Virginity' is an essay written, bizarrely to modern minds, while Gregory was married. In it, he recognises a hierarchy of life, based on an ordering of desire. For Gregory, this hierarchy consisted in two levels: badly ordered celibacy *and* badly ordered marriage, on the lower level. By contrast, *rightly* ordered celibacy and *rightly* ordered marriage exist together on the higher level. In other words, for Gregory,

---

22   Especially in the remarkable 'The Dark Night'.
23   Coakley, *The New Asceticism*, 6–7.

marriage and celibacy are not opposites, but equally opportunities for the right ordering and transformation of desire. What constitutes right ordering is that the outworking of desire, which comes from God and is channelled back to God, is able to overflow into relations with others. Sometimes this will be in marriage. But for Gregory, whether in marriage or the vowed religious (and celibate) life, desire is to be channelled into concern for others: work for the poor and other works of charity. In a particularly fecund image, Gregory compares desire to water: it can either be properly channelled—which means flowing back to God; or improperly dissipated—which sees it leaking everywhere, unable to bring life-giving water to anything.[24] Conversely, rightly ordered desire, which flows from and back towards the over-flowing source that is God, means that the water can draw from God's excess to flow over to nourish all that is around the channel. Thus, it has *social* consequences.

Augustine, like Gregory of Nyssa, sees human desire, once oriented towards God, overflowing into wider social forms. Augustine's *The City of God*, presents that city, as Graham Ward puts it, as 'a specific social form organised according to an orientation of desire towards God.'[25] Mention has already been made of Augustine's recognition in the opening of *Confessions* that our very

---

[24] see 'On Virginity' in *Nicene and Post-Nicene Fathers, Second Series*, Vol 5, ed. Schaff and Wace, (Christian Literature Publishing Company, 1893), ch vii, 352.

[25] Graham Ward, 'The Body of the Church and its Erotic Politics', in *Christ and Culture*, (Oxford: Blackwell, 2005), 99. Indeed, the point for Ward, as well as for Augustine and Gregory, is that no 'desire' for another person can end in the other person. It must always have implications for the relations those persons have with others, and for the shaping of society–the *polis*, from which the 'political' comes–itself, including the society of the Church.

being has its source and end in God's love for the creation, and for us. To put it succinctly, for Augustine, 'God is the end of desire'.[26]

This has especially important consequences for Augustine of how we see and regard others. Relations with other people cannot, for Augustine, be limited to sexual desiring, such as our culture understands it. He is equally keen to warn 'against an attitude towards any finite person... that terminates their meaning in their capacity to satisfy my desire, that treats them as the end of desire...'.[27] The sense that human love, human desire cannot be an end in itself, is crucial for Augustine – not least because to invest any other *creature* with that burden is grossly unfair to the other person. It is, in a way that is as profound and destructive as any other form, abusive of the other – using the other to attempt to satisfy the needs which, from a theological perspective, can only be satisfied by God.

Space is unavailable for further explorations of 'desire' in the Christian tradition. It is significant, however, that throughout Bernard of Clairvaux's remarkable reflections on Song of Songs, issues we have already considered (the excessively ecstatic nature of desire; that desire must lead to love of others in society; the final goal being love of God) predominate. Equally, the writings of those extraordinary Spanish mystics, the Carmelites Teresa of Avila and John of the Cross, consider the same matters, though with a special emphasis on the description of the relationship between believer and Christ as lovers. Throughout the tradition, therefore, explorations of physical and erotic desire have a vital role in exploring and understanding desire for God.

---

26   Rowan Williams, 'Augustinian Love' in Willliams, *On Augustine*, 200.
27   Rowan Williams 'Language, Reality and Desire: The Nature of Christian Formation' in Willliams, *On Augustine*, 44.

A turn to the poetic

As discussed above, Song of Songs is a series of poems, and John of the Cross's most potent representation of his desire for God occurs in the poem 'The Dark Night. In what follows, I invite further thinking on these matters by considering another poetic offering: two passages in D. H. Lawrence's remarkable novel, *The Rainbow*. There, Lawrence 'renders' an instance of desire that is transformative and, ultimately, extends—as Gregory of Nyssa would require—'to render back to society what originally gave those partners the possibility of mutual joy'. Lawrence shows how we might re-imagine Christian desire and thus think more clearly about what desire is. Of special note here is Lawrence's unashamed and continued use of what is obviously and blatantly Christian language.

To set the scene: Tom Brangwen lives and works on the farm his family has farmed for generations. He meets 'a Polish lady', Lydia Lensky. As Lawrence renders this, we are presented with a desire that overtakes Tom as he first encounters this 'strange', 'exotic' woman. When Tom is first conscious that Lydia recognises him: 'A swift change had taken place on the earth for him, as if a new creation were fulfilled, in which he had real existence.'[28] Later, Lawrence will go further in describing Tom's reaction to the 'foreign woman':

> A daze had come over his mind, he had another centre of consciousness. In his breast, or in his bowels, somewhere in his body, there had started another activity. It was as if a strong light were burning there, and he was blind within it, unable to know anything, except that this transfiguration burned between him and her, connecting them, like a secret power... (p.38)

What Lawrence presents here is Brangwen's initial sense of a

---

28   D. H. Lawrence, *The Rainbow*, ed. Mark Kinkead-Weekes (Cambridge: CUP, 1989), 32. All subsequent references are to this edition, and occur in the text.

stirring erotic desire for Lydia – and yet Lawrence is at pains to suggest that, although Brangwen himself can't articulate it, there is something more than is generally understand by erotic desire at work here. Religious language, specifically 'transfiguration', is used to describe it. Tom Brangwen begins to recognize that, beyond his mind, within his body, there is 'another centre of consciousness', another way of thinking, and that it is transfiguring.

Lawrence makes clear also that this desire comes from somewhere unknown. What Lawrence shows being overcome is the self-enclosed ego.[29] There are some echoes here of Augustine, and his warning that we may become 'too easily satisfied and so become... closed in on what *we* understand to be our well-being.'[30]

Later in this remarkable opening chapter, Tom Brangwen makes another significant discovery:

> As he worked alone on the land, or sat up with his ewes at lambing time, the facts and material of his daily life fell away, leaving the kernel of his purpose clean. And then it came upon him that he would marry her and she would be his life....
>
> But during the long February nights with the ewes in labour, looking out from the shelter into the flashing stars, he knew he did not belong to himself. He must admit that he was only fragmentary, something incomplete and subject. There were stars in the dark heaven travelling, the whole host passing by on some eternal voyage. So he sat small and submissive to the greater ordering. (39–40)

Lawrence refers here to a mystery beyond the human self and its inward-facing thought processes – that is, beyond the self-enclosed ego. (Christian readers hardly need reminding of the significance of this scene taking place as a shepherd sits in the fields with his

---

29   Or, in a term current since at least the Reformation, the *cor curvum in se*, the heart turned in on itself.
30   Williams, 'Augustinian Love', *in* Willliams, *On Augustine*, 204.

sheep!) In the midst of the new life being brought to birth by the ewes, and 'aware' of the 'above and beyond him' of the stars 'passing by on [their] eternal voyage', Tom Brangwen knows the 'separate and irreducible otherness' that exists beyond his own life. Tom has no alternative but to sit 'small and submissive' before what Lawrence calls 'the greater ordering.' There is no question that what Tom is feeling here is (or rather, includes) sexual desire: *eros*. But Lawrence deliberately wants to say it is both this *and more*.

Lawrence also renders Nyssa's insistence that what is important is *rightly ordered* desire—ordered so that it serves not only the individual, nor the couple, but overflows to the benefit of others. A passage somewhat later in *The Rainbow* shows Tom and Lydia learning again what rightly ordered desire is. After two years of marriage, and after the birth of their own child, Tom and Lydia reach an impasse, where their love, their desire for one another, has become disjointed or disordered. A moment of crisis is reached and they confront one another. In a remarkable few pages, the full difficulty and complexity of this impasse is explored. Lawrence describes the resolution that occurs in significant language:

> Their coming together now, after two years of married life, was much more wonderful to them than it had been before. It was the entry into another circle of existence, it was the baptism to another life, it was the complete confirmation....
>
> They had passed through the doorway into the further space, where movement was so big, that it contained bonds and constraints and labours, and still was complete liberty. She was the doorway to him, he to her. At last they had thrown open the doors, each to the other, and had stood in the doorways facing each other, whilst the light flooded out from behind on to each of their faces, it was the transfiguration, the glorification, the admission. (90–91)

Here Lawrence shows the rekindling of desire between husband

and wife, and a growth back towards one another. He thus offers a vitally significant reimagining of what is meant by desire, a reimagining using entirely Christian terminology. As one of Lawrence's most perceptive critics has written, what strikes the attentive reader of Lawrence here as religious is:

> the intensity with which his men and women, hearkening to their deepest needs and promptings as they seek to find 'fulfilment' in marriage, know that they 'do not belong to themselves', but are responsible to something that, in transcending the individual, transcends love and sex too.[31]

Lawrence concludes the passage writing of the effect the achievement of the fullness of the relationship between Lydia and Tom has on Lydia's daughter (Tom's step-daughter), Anna:

> What did it matter, that Anna Lensky was born of Lydia and Paul? God was her father and mother. He had passed through the married pair without fully making Himself known to them.
>
> Now He was declared to Brangwen and to Lydia Brangwen, as they stood together. When at last they had joined hands, the house was finished, and the Lord took up His abode. And they were glad....
>
> Anna's soul was put at peace between them. She looked from one to the other, and she saw them established to her safety, and she was free. She played between the pillar of cloud and the pillar of fire in confidence, having the assurance on her right hand and the assurance on her left. She was no more called upon to uphold with her childish might the broken end of the arch. Her father and her mother now met to the span of the heavens, and she, the child, was free to play in the space beneath, between. (91)

Lawrence shows what is possible in and from human desire. He shows, too, what has already been discussed in reflection on

---

31 F. R. Leavis, *D. H. Lawrence: Novelist* (Harmondsworth: Penguin Books, 1985), 132.

Gregory of Nyssa: any rightly ordered desire will move out (ec-statically) beyond the two. This desire, transfigured as it is, has significant implications for the child Anna. And the novel shows it has significant implications for the rural society in which Lydia and Tom live.

But Lawrence also hints—in ways that are surely fruitful for theological reflection and talk—that such desire cannot be understood simply by reference to a human sphere. This is not about 'transcending' the physical, but is recognisably Christian–acknowledges the importance of the created order and of God's taking on creatureliness in the Incarnation of the Divine Second Person. It invites witness to 'transfiguration'—seeing with the eyes of faith both what is physically there, and how this speaks to us of God.

This gives us some rather hard thinking to do. We are brought to realise that, if rightly ordered human life can communicate the meaning of God in the world, then this must mean that human *desire*, too, can be sacramental; *it* can speak of mercy, faithfulness, transfiguration and hope. Humans must not give up on our desires, because they can speak to us of God: indeed, the source of them is God. For all the danger (we might say) and complexity desires carry—not least that they may be disordered—human desire retains the transfiguring and deifying potential given us in Christ.

This brings us back to Gregory of Nyssa and his understanding, in 'On Virginity', of what constitutes the right ordering of desire: the flow of passion, which comes from God and is channelled back to God, is able to overflow into relations with others. If we begin to embrace *this* as a way of understanding, if we let this shape a re-imagining of human desire from a theological sense, we might think more clearly about what 'marriage' truly indicates, and what commitment to the other might mean. From there, in our understanding of desire rightly ordered, we might ask whether such right ordering depends on questions of gender at all. As God is known in and as God's acts in the world, so our acts for the good of our world can also reveal the right ordering of our desires. The purpose of this chapter is to call for reflection on such matters with a more consciously *theological* understanding of desire.

Concluding remarks

The purpose of this chapter has been to argue that the Church's exploration of same-sex marriage requires theological reflection on desire. Until both our understanding of desire, and our desires themselves, are 'transfigured' (to use that word so prevalent in Lawrence), until we recognise our desire as having its source in God, and, therefore, of its being able to speak of God—to ourselves as well as to others, not least *an* other—then it isn't going to have much that we might say is *Christian* about it.

Re-imagining *Christian* desire requires us to explore again what it means to live *embodied* lives. We can see eruptions of desire—including sexual, erotic desire, with a consequent loss of egoistic ability to control—as signs of the in-breaking of God's Spirit, which transfigures human lives. Further, just as Tom and Lydia Brangwen's desire is imaginatively presented by Lawrence as spilling over its banks to assist the child Anna, so we need to imagine our desires as being able, by their very energy, to overflow and assist others. We are called to imagine how lives transfigured by a desire for God can continue to overflow to be of service, and inspiration, to others and to the greater glory of the God who is the source of all desire.

Nevertheless, like all elements of this fallen world, our desires can be corrupted, can become abusive and destructive: not least when they are trapped in egotistical self-satisfaction.[32] Desire for another

---

32   Indeed, as we read in God's warning to Cain, sin can 'lurk at the door', and it can desire us. But Cain is invited to 'master' sin (see Gen 4:7b).

person can become focussed exclusively on genital sexual expression—such that it can be described as a satisfaction of 'carnal lusts and appetites'. More distressingly, corrupted desire can be yoked with an unhealthy and all-too often unrecognised need for power over another—such that the expression of that desire occurs in abuses of power over women, younger and/or other vulnerable persons, and, as we have shockingly discovered all too frequently, children.

Marriage has been one attempt by the Church to assist humans in a right ordering of desire. So also has been the vowed religious life and, sadly, there is no space in this essay (or this collection) to consider how that element of our tradition may need to be re-imagined, and certainly revalued. In each and every age, the Church needs to think deeply to discern how such right ordering can take place, and how marriage and our transfigured understanding of it may, or may not, assist in this. Alongside that must go consideration of whether the right ordering of desire that marriage promises, certainly in *BCP's* introduction to the solemnisation of marriage, is available to persons of the same gender. Close attention to the issues raised here does not permit simplistic answers and solutions—not least because the Scriptures and tradition of the Church entail honest, because complex, presentations of the remarkable complexities of human life.

It is our responsibility to continue to ask such difficult questions, and not to foreclose on answers too quickly. Our continuing and deepening desire for God, our desire to come into closer relationship and understanding with the God who is love, must lead us ever deeper into these questions. From there, we can allow an overflowing of banks, to relationships which reflect to the world that love of God—not least in our dealings with one another, as Church, while we continue to consider hard questions.

To What End? The Blessing of Same-Sex Marriage

Rhys Bezzant[1]

While Christian scholars are debating the contours of same-sex attraction and same-sex marriage from biblical and ethical perspectives, and clergy are negotiating concrete pastoral concerns emerging from the recent Australian postal vote, bishops and deans of the Anglican Church in our country have begun to suggest in public media that the time has come to offer our blessing to same-sex couples who have been married in civil ceremonies. These statements of course have pastoral care as the intention, but, laying aside for a moment the scriptural warrant for such a position, the ramifications of such doctrinal and liturgical innovations are significant in terms of the bonds of fellowship, constitutional integrity, and theological convergence of the national Church.[2]

The goal of this paper is not to rehearse these concerns generally or to focus on particular biblical texts concerning homosexuality—these

---

[1] The Rev'd Dr Rhys Bezzant serves in Melbourne, where he teaches Church History, Theology, and Christian Worship at Ridley College, and is a Canon of St Paul's Cathedral, Melbourne.

[2] We note that in Australia changes to principles of doctrine and worship must be justified on the following constitutional grounds: 'Provided, and it is hereby further declared, that the above-named *Book of Common Prayer*, together with the Thirty-nine Articles, be regarded as the authorised standard of worship and doctrine in this Church, and no alteration in or permitted variations from the services or Articles therein contained shall contravene any principle of doctrine or worship laid down in such standard' (Constitution, s.4).

emerge in other chapters of this volume—but instead to raise theological questions concerning the language and liturgical nature of 'blessing' as a strategy for pastoral care, which are elided in much private conversation and public communication. Concerns about the blessing of same-sex marriage are matters of high principle, not just the pragmatics of pastoral care.[3] While recognising that the Liturgy Commission has produced a draft rite for the blessing of a civil marriage, I argue on biblical and liturgical grounds that the blessing of same-sex union is different from blessing Holy Matrimony and ought not to be regarded as morally equivalent activities. Rather we should conduct an alternative conversation regarding the nature of prayer and pastoral care for individuals who seek same-sex blessing.

Adopting the language of blessing in same-sex marriage debates

In common usage, the language of blessing means something like approval or encouragement, for example, parents may stand to offer their blessing or support to a daughter or son during a wedding service, but this is not the way the word 'blessing' is best understood theologically.[4] In the scriptural story-line, a blessing is

---

3   Such a pragmatic approach was taken in the report of the Anglican Church of New Zealand, Aotearoa and Polynesia concerning blessing same-sex marriage: 'Our mandate was not to consider the differing theological positions or to interpret scripture on this point.' See http://www.anglicantaonga.org.nz/features/extra/wg_interim.

4   There is of course another way of using the language of blessing, which is not here my chief concern. Human beings, in the Psalter, as elsewhere (for example, James 3:9), can bless the Lord, which is a synonym for praise, affirming God's purposes for the created order, of which our worship is a constituent part. In 1 Cor 10:16, the cup is blessed but commentators also see this as a synonym for giving thanks, the language of which appears in the synoptic accounts: 'Early Jews and Christians understood that they did not need to bless food or drink. They did not bless the cup itself, but blessed God (gave thanks to God) for providing them with the good gifts of food and drink.' See Roy E. Ciampa and Brian S. Rosner, *The First Letter to the Corinthians* (The Pillar New Testament Commentary; Grand Rapids: Eerdmans, 2010), 472.

chiefly concerned with the commendation and promotion of God's purposes for the creation and for humankind within it. Such a blessing can be offered by God or by someone with representative authority. In the first four days of creation described as 'good' in Genesis 1, God brought order out of chaos by separating elements of the creation, for example making a distinction between day and night, but they are not blessed even though they are good. Distinction is preparatory to blessing.

However, on the fifth day, God blessed the fish and birds by virtue of their procreative power (1:22), and on the sixth day God blessed men and women as his image-bearers capable of both dominion and procreative power (1:28), which now calls for the acclamation 'very good' (1:31). The nature of God's blessing in these instances is not merely to fashion the creation but to promote divine purposes within the creation, which focus on human flourishing and the exercise of dominion.[5] The seventh day, the climax of the creation, is also blessed (2:3) because on that day God not only outlines but celebrates his purposes for creation, at the heart of which is intimate communion with human beings. The creation too flourishes in this vision for interdependent life. Blessing is chiefly defined around well-being which is set within eschatological parameters. The language of blessing must promote not individual validation but a corporate vision for the created order. It is a theological recommendation, not a therapeutic affirmation.

Further, in Genesis 3, after men and women sin, the language of blessing becomes something more akin to a 'public declaration of a favoured status,'[6] given that it is now possible not to receive

---

[5] I note that the language of dominion does not equate to the language of domination.

[6] William E. Brown, 'Blessing,' in *Evangelical Dictionary of Biblical Theology* (ed. Walter A. Elwell; Grand Rapids: Baker, 1996), 70.

the divine blessing, but to experience the curse. As an elect people, Abraham and Sarah's progeny will be blessed in order to bless others (12:1–3). As Link notes, the account of blessing here is distinctive because it is not based in magic but is circumscribed by historical, promissory and covenantal categories.[7] It is defined in relation to the divine purpose. Ancient Near Eastern assumptions concerning automatic access to divine power are thereby rejected. At the end of Deuteronomy, the Israelites on the brink of entry into the Promised Land are encouraged by the prospect of blessing and warned of the possibility of curse: blessing is located within the covenantal purposes of the Lord. Indeed, the Aaronic blessing in Numbers 6 is not an offer to all of humankind but to the covenant people, for it is commanded to Moses, then mediated to Aaron, and uses the name of YHWH throughout. Blessing is not even for all of those descended from Abraham: in Genesis 49, not all the sons of Jacob are blessed, but Joseph alone. The prospect of seeing God's face depends on appeal to and obedience within the covenant as the precondition of blessing.[8] Being favoured by God in this way is not an indiscriminate or incidental offer.

In the New Testament, the language of blessing implies an experience of communion within the covenant renewed and defined by

---

[7] H.G. Link, 'Blessing, Blessed, Happy,' in *The New International Dictionary of New Testament Theology*, Volume I: A-F (Exeter: Paternoster Press, 1975), 208-209.

[8] In some minds, the case of Job highlights the possible disconnect between obedience and blessing, for Job asserts that his suffering is not the result of unfaithfulness. However his complaints to God appeal to the link between obedience and blessing. The fear of the Lord normally results in blessing (Proverbs 9:10-11), and Job ultimately learns to trust God's sovereign will for the world, after which his fortunes restored (Job 42:10-17). Wilson argues that the book of Job 'no more denies the idea of retribution than it rejects the notion of God's justice.' See Lindsay Wilson, *Job* (Grand Rapids: Eerdmans, 2015), 230. Böstrom has argued that wisdom does more than connect obedience with reward but goes deeper to connect character with blessing. See *The God of the Sages: The Portrayal of God in the Book of Proverbs* (Stockholm: Alqvist & Wiksell, 1990), 138.

Christ, perfected by the Spirit. In Matthew 2–4, with Jesus recapitulating the story of Israel in Egypt, at the Jordan and in the wilderness, the nation is being redefined around the person of Christ, so the blessings spoken in Matthew 5 in the Sermon on the Mount are not generic to humankind but are to be understood as distinctive to the people of God. Preaching the Beatitudes frequently highlights virtues to be encouraged in individuals, but thereby misses the eschatology of the Beatitudes and their relation to the Kingdom. The call to wise and virtuous living here is intensified with reference to the apocalyptic intervention of God, for these beatific characteristics belong to the eschatological people of God who are prepared to be different from the world around them: the Kingdom of Heaven belongs to those who are persecuted for righteousness' sake, for our reward in heaven awaits (Matt 5:3, 10, 12). In Luke's account of the Beatitudes, Jesus directed his blessing to those around him when he said 'you' (Luke 6:20–23) and went on to pronounce a woe on some who were standing there too (Luke 6:24–26). Blessing is not a right but a fruit of our elect status (Eph 1:3–4) and is a result of steadfastness in suffering (Jas 5:11). In Revelation, not all will be blessed and welcomed to the marriage supper of the Lamb (19:9), nor is blessing an automatic right for all those who die (20:6, 22:14). The language of blessing cannot serve the generic purpose of encouragement, but has a distinct shape within the biblical narrative, to which we must pay attention. If blessing affirms and promotes the divine order, but homosexual practice is sinful, then it is not possible to bless a homosexual union in the name of a holy God.

Just as the ancient Hebrews discovered that being a nation in possession of the Temple did not secure their inviolate status as God's people nor did it automatically secure divine blessing (Ezekiel 10), so we must recognise that the language of blessing must be used sparingly and consistent with God's words, so that we do not give false assurance or mislead those who might be recipients of the blessing that their status within the covenant people of God is assured.

Providing a liturgy of blessing for couples in same-sex union

If blessing is a theological recommendation, and the publication of liturgical rites reinforces the normative value of the recommendation, then investigating theological assumptions in our practice is a pressing concern. Yet in spite of all the talk about blessing, we note that the practice of blessing is infrequent in the published liturgies of the Anglican Church of Australia. Priestly blessing does not appear in the Daily Offices, nor in services of the Word. In *APBA*, it is used in services of Baptism, and Communion, and is an option in the Second Order of Marriage and in Ministry with the Dying. Its function is to pray for God's power, but only because those receiving the blessing have been absolved of their sins in the service and are being reassured of their status as members of the covenant as they depart to take their place in pursuing God's purposes in the world. After experiencing the special grace of God in the sacraments of Baptism or Holy Communion, the priestly blessing at the conclusion of the service assures those in Christ of the constancy of grace beyond the liturgical celebration of the sacraments. Such a concluding blessing affirms the rule of God over the world which the parishioner is about to re-enter, and therefore each person is encouraged to depart not in fear but with knowledge of God's favour. It is striking that the First Order of Marriage does not contain a priestly blessing—it is not essential to the rite—though its inclusion in the service of Ministry with the Dying is the counterpart to the confession and absolution earlier in that liturgy. The practice of a blessing upon departure is assumed to grow out of earlier household rites, in which the family member leaving the security of the home is prayed for and commended to divine keeping. It is taken up in Leviticus 9 as a priestly blessing at the conclusion of worship.

The language we deploy in liturgical settings is not incidental to the definition of marriage but substantially shapes it. The attempt in other Anglican jurisdictions to justify same-sex marriage has introduced the thick vocabulary of covenant joined with the language of blessing to provide such a theological rationale, even though these are largely innovations in usage. Note the parallel here: the liturgy created in 2003 by the Diocese of New Westminster is named 'A Rite for the Celebration of Gay and Lesbian Covenants,' or elsewhere 'A Rite of Blessing.'[9] Contrast this with the traditional Anglican service of marriage in *BCP*, which assumes a heterosexual relationship, but where the language of covenant nonetheless appears in only one place (a prayer), and is absent entirely in *APBA* and *AAPB*. Anglicans have been reserved in their use of the language of covenant—most surprisingly in baptism—so there appears to be no theological warrant for its use in these revised marriage rites.

Further, in this service of the 'Celebration of a Covenant,' traditional theological terminology is studiously avoided, and thereby shows itself to be at odds with the notion that same-sex marriage is consistent with traditional views or Anglican formularies. The selection of readings provided does not include any texts which affirm the creational good of marriage. The expectation that children might be received into the life of the family is absent, though children born of previous relationships should be appropriately supported and cared for. The call to receive marriage as an opportunity for sanctification is absent, unlike the prayer in *APBA*: 'God the Son make you holy in his love.' Indeed, the rubrics in the New Westminster text explicitly commend the opposite: 'Regardless

---

9   See http://www.vancouver.anglican.ca/worship/sacramental-rites/pages/blessing.

of the specific characteristics of the relationship, the act of blessing does not make the relationship more holy but rather, in giving thanks to God and invoking God's holy name, releases the relationship to realize its full potential as an expression of God's love and peace.' This language of blessing is therapeutic at the expense of being theological.

Rather than build upon the creation narrative, this liturgy appeals instead to the narrative of redemption in the Scriptural witness. Though traditional views regard marriage as a creation good reflecting common grace, the New Westminster order of service works very hard to appeal to the language and categories of special grace, seeing for instance same-sex unions solemnized in church as a kind of 'exodus' or 'liberation,' which enables them to value 'their unique and sacred gift.' The category of 'covenant' is applied to family and friends indiscriminately. The blessing of such same-sex unions appeals to the congruence of inner spirit, rather than bodily structure. Standing back from the presenting issue, it is worth remembering that as Anglicans we pray our doctrine, and good liturgy rehearses the story of the people of God and our place within it. We must make use of the creation narrative from Genesis 1 and 2 in marriage liturgies. Further, according to speech act theory, there is a performative aspect to any declaration of blessing, which intensifies the objective dimension of the prayer, highlighting the seriousness of blessing in any rite. If as some argue same-sex marriage is morally equivalent to heterosexual marriage, there would be no reason for using categories different from those that constitute the traditional marriage service as the Diocese of New Westminster has done; in fact it feels like special pleading to apply the language of redemption as a means of validation.

In summary, applying the language of blessing to same-sex unions in liturgical contexts is at odds with our own liturgical heritage, modest application of priestly practices, and the place of marriage in an economy of grace. The foreshadowing in our baptismal rites of the judgement of God, for which passing through the waters is a biblical trope, frames the eschatological drama of all human relationships and is the larger context of our debates concerning the definition of marriage. We cannot bless all human relationships regardless of their shape, given our understanding that God will discriminate between us 'according to our works' (Rom 2:6).

Pursuing pastoral care for those with same-sex desires

Behind these reflections lies the rightful insistence that we pursue thoughtful pastoral care strategies for those who come to us for pastoral support in dealing with matters of same-sex attraction or union. Much of the energy for establishing the equivalence of same-sex marriage with traditional conceptions of marriage, even when the language and categories for expressing it are contested, comes from a good desire to provide pastoral care for those who have faced significant social or ecclesiastical ostracism. This is an urgent need for those who are same-sex attracted members of our congregations, or for parishioners' family members who identify in this way but are not members of the congregation. Just as God pours out the rain on all humankind, it is right that we love in practical ways, which maintain the integrity both of our theological commitments and of our compassionate outreach even when this is in the context of moral disagreement.

However, I note that the Lambeth Resolution 1.10.5 (1998) equates the 'blessing of same sex unions' with 'legitimising' same-sex unions. Consequently, turning to the blessing of same-sex marriages as a form of pastoral care under present conditions is not a pastoral category that we are at liberty to adopt without declaring our church to be in breach of its constitution and out of step with this resolution accepted by the worldwide college of bishops. Our chief task as Christians is to love, not hurt, and we seek ways to do this by rejoicing with those who rejoice and weeping with those who weep. But the apostle reminds us that, at least in so far as it depends on us, we should live peaceably with our neighbours where at all possible (Rom 12:18). We have responsibilities for peace-making with individuals in same-sex marriages, but this is not something we do without recognition of prior theological commitments or reasonable pastoral constraints.

In terms of parish events, we must start with the welcome we offer to any who enter our doors. The background or lifestyle of any guests to our services is irrelevant to our care. We should treat all generously and be careful in our speech to avoid insensitive comments and be quick to offer an apology for misspeaking. We recognise nonetheless that there is an ethical difference between giving offence and taking offence. We also want to affirm that our desire to do good may include the use of lectionary readings which ultimately prove uncomfortable for listeners, but this should not mean that we avoid preaching the whole counsel of God. Attending small groups or parish functions can be powerfully pastoral for those who choose to participate in this way. Training members of the congregation as mentors, and building a culture of honesty and accountability, thus enabling deep friendship, are strategies for healthy types of inclusion, not just in matters of sexuality.[10] Nurturing not just individuals but the church is a chief responsibility: 'The church as a whole needs help in reassessing its attitudes. Counselling on this scale becomes in effect a task or re-education, so that the church may be recalled to its vocation as a healing

---

10   See the papers in this volume by Thompson and Lee on friendship.

community. It is important for Christians (and society in general) to face up to their responsibility for the irrational manifestations of homophobia.'[11]

In terms of personal interactions, conversations with the clergy or pastoral staff of the parish are a significant opportunity for providing care. This will no doubt provide the context for the growth of trust in an environment where suspicion might linger. The agenda for such meetings should be established by the person(s) seeking the counsel of the leaders of the parish, and where appropriate advice can be given to empower those with pastoral issues to seek out other support mechanisms. Those who are single may be yearning for new levels of support and friendship. Those who are already in a committed same-sex relationship, whether married or not, may be seeking greater clarity concerning their commitments, spiritual journey, or social support. Gentle integration is paramount. Of course, these opportunities for care may be available outside of the church as well, or even preferred. Our task is to be ready, not to be insistent.

In terms of the national Church, it is incumbent upon us to provide resources for training church members in the complex psychological and social realities that meet us in our communities, workplaces, and churches. This begins with nuanced definitions of the various presenting sex and gender identities for those who are uninformed, thereby establishing nuanced kinds of care, then moves toward the upskilling of clergy in their own pastoral competencies. Pastoral care involves liturgical rites but goes far beyond them. Rather, it is an ongoing and theologically shaped aspiration, which recognises the ultimate care of the Good Shepherd whose voice through the Scriptures guides and nurtures those who listen.

---

[11] E. R. Moberly, 'First Aid in Pastoral Care XV. Counselling the Homosexual,' *Expository Times* 96 (1985): 264.

We should also respect those who have acknowledged their same-sex orientation, whether married or not, but who have sought and found some measure of healing or transformation by virtue of their Christian discipleship, whereby their longings for sexual intimacy are addressed in non-erotic ways. (Similar respect and support of course should be given to individuals with opposite-sex orientation who seek pastoral guidance to deal with inappropriate erotic longings.) This might not be the majority of those identifying as same-sex attracted, but it is nonetheless a variety of pastoral care which presents itself as an option. Testimonies concerning the pastoral resources available in the body of Christ are powerful and real, which can be another strategy of pastoral ministry available to the clergy. Indeed, Paul recognised that amongst the Corinthians there were at least some whose story included dramatic reorientation towards the possibilities of the Kingdom of God: 'such were some of you ... you were washed, you were sanctified, you were justified.' The importance of pastoral care transcends assumptions concerning the blessing of same-sex marriage at the front of conversation in contemporary Australia.

Recognising the larger ecclesiological context of our debates

It has been my aim in this paper to outline some of the tracks that conversations concerning the blessing of same-sex marriage follow, and to provide some points of biblical, liturgical and pastoral reflection to earth our debates. Though conversations concerning the blessing of same-sex marriage have been rehearsed in several locations internationally among Anglican Christians, the issues in Australia have been no less painful, though we have the benefit of their earlier decisions, mistakes and insights. This volume of essays is designed to promote understanding between Christians with differing approaches as a means of reaching some measure of national doctrinal consensus, even if in the meantime we continue our conversation on the limits of disagreement. We trust that our written labours will be of assistance beyond the Doctrine Commission and beyond debates on same-sex marriage in personal, parish, and synodical settings in all types of human relationships. Confessing that the church is both one and holy has been an ongoing project since the earliest days of the Christian movement, and contemporary theological, ethical and liturgical challenges give us cause to investigate our unity and holiness once again.

Disagreement and Christian Unity: Re-evaluating the Situation

Stephen Pickard[1]

In this chapter I offer a number of theses for consideration regarding disagreements in the Church; and make some proposals regarding Christian unity and their implications with respect to disputation in the Church in relation to same-sex relationships, blessings of same-sex union and same-sex marriage.

1. Separation and division does not settle the current contentious nature concerning matters of human sexuality

Disagreements in the Church are to be expected and the history of the church stretching back into its earliest days is proof enough of this. The reasons for disagreements are many and various. Moreover, the consequences range from minor irritants, settled recognition of different perspectives, strained relations, fierce dispute, impaired relationships, and conflict that leads to fractured relations.

The question for this chapter can be simply put: Does the Church's

---

[1] The Rt Rev'd Professor Stephen Pickard is an Assistant Bishop in the Diocese of Canberra and Goulburn; the Director of the Public and Contextual Theology Research Centre and Executive Director, Australian Centre for Christianity and Culture, Charles Sturt University.

public endorsement of same-sex relationships and marriage, and the authorization of liturgical rites of blessings for same-sex unions and/or marriages constitute grounds for division and separation?[2]

In relation to this question I note the following. First, separation and division are decisive actions arising out of a judgment regarding significance and seriousness of impaired relations. When a question is posed about the limits to unity the issue is more often about the *degree* of impairment that obtains within the ecclesial body.

Second, in the context of the Anglican Church of Australia and given its particular Constitution the question of a change of the marriage rite to permit same-sex marriage is not the subject directly considered in this chapter. Indeed, it is difficult to imagine how such a constitutional change might be achieved even if significant sections of the Church considered this was justified. However, the logic of my argument offers an approach to such an unlikely eventuality with respect to questions of division and separation. In this respect, I note the valuable and important work by the Christian ethicist, Robert Song of Durham University, UK. His book, *Covenant and Calling: towards a theology of same-sex relationships* moves beyond the sharp binaries of much of the present debate (i.e., traditional marriage and same-sex marriage).[3] Song strikes out on a different course offering a cogent argument for a Christian theology of marriage between a man and a woman, and goes on to develop a theology of covenant partnerships that traverses a variety of sexual orientations and different kinds of relationship. It seems to me that in the Australian Anglican context we need to give renewed attention to such covenantal partnerships

---

2   For example, through synodical and diocesan decisions, and public statements by such bodies and/or bishops.
3   Robert Song, *Covenant and Calling: Towards a Theology of Same-Sex Relationships* (London: SCM Press, 2014).

alongside a contemporary Christian theology of what used to be quaintly called, Holy Matrimony.

Third, the question of whether marriage, according to the Constitution of the Anglican Church of Australia, is a matter of faith is more complex than at first appears. While some might argue that it is a matter of order others argue that it is a matter of faith. If the former, then it appears to leave more scope for future change; if the latter, it is argued that being a matter of faith implies no change ought or even can in principle be countenanced. However, both approaches require more careful consideration. Recognising belief and/or practices that are of the faith of the Church requires some careful discrimination and nuance, and legal interpretation. The reason is clear, not all matters of faith are of the same kind or weight. For example, some matters of faith embodied in the ecumenical creeds (Tertullian's Rule of Faith; Hooker's 'few fundamental words') circumscribe that public faith is requisite for the being of a church as such and belong to the profession of faith in Christ. On the other hand, those beliefs that appertain to the salvation of any particular person are far more fluid. What is of the faith for individuals is ultimately a matter that lies within the gift and grace of God. In fact, the distinction between those articles of belief and faith for the being of a church and those things necessary for a person's salvation is a critical, highly contested and controversial matter; if the evidence of the history of the English Reformation and henceforth is anything to go by. So 'of the faith' has a double reference (a) those matters for the being of a church and those beliefs necessary for the salvation of any individual and (b) deciding the relative weight to be given to a matter of faith in relation to the heart or substance of the gospel of Jesus Christ. For example, the confession of Christ as Saviour and Lord is not of the same order as belief in the church or, in the present context, the doctrine of marriage.

Anglicans usually discuss this kind of thing in terms of fundamentals and non-fundamentals of faith and also invoke the reformation concept of *adiaphora*—things neither commanded nor forbidden.[4] The Roman Catholic Church these days refers to the concept of a hierarchy of truths. It is a recognition that not all matters of belief are of the same order in relation to the substance of faith.

The burden of my argument is that separation does not settle the contentious nature of the issues before us at this time with respect to matters of human sexuality. In fact, division only exacerbates an already fractious situation and maintains the cycle of fragmentation in relation to the truth of the gospel. This is not to diminish the importance of the matters before us in terms of the faith and order of the Church of God. They are real and serious but they cannot be successfully negotiated according to the usual dialectic that pits truth and unity as separate elements that vie for precedence. This default strategy in ecclesiology bedevils our life in Christ and institutionalises fracture and fragmentation. Something more is required of the Church at this time in its history; something more is required of the Anglican Church of Australia.

2. The nature of the Body of Christ in which disagreements occur generates an ethical imperative about the manner in which disagreements are conducted

Disagreements do not occur in a vacuum; nor can they be sealed off from the context in which they occur. Disagreements in the Church are often conducted as if the Body of Christ was a distant observer

---

[4] *Adiaphora* properly describes those areas where Scripture is either silent or gives freedom—e.g, you may be circumcised or not; it does not matter. However, a matter of *adiaphora* can become a matter of significance when it is insisted upon by one party or the other—e.g, you can eat meat offered to idols; it doesn't matter, unless your brother notices and is disturbed and then it becomes a matter of substance.

of the quest and contest for truth. When, in the course of disagreements, disputants ignore or simply fail to recognise that they are members of the Body of Christ (members one of another—Romans 12:5), they effectively deny their own ecclesial identity as Christians. In this process, the reality of the Church is bracketed out from the conduct of the disagreement. The effect of this is to drive a wedge between two things (i.e., the body of Christ and the disputed matter) that cannot be divided without harm to either.

When Christians disagree with one another they disagree as members of the one body; not as isolated individuals or groups, but as people yoked together by Christ. This makes the Church more than a mere context for disagreements. The Body of Christ, like the water in which the fish swims, is the life and soul of those whose lives it nourishes through word, sacrament and witness in the world. The Church is not simply the passive recipient of outcomes of disagreements. Disagreements have to take stock of the very ecclesial nature of faith. In other words, it is the Body of Christ that is the natural home in which disagreements occur. This reality gives shape and form to the character of disagreement. Disagreement, if it is to be what is referred to as 'godly' has to assume a pattern and tone congruent with the risen Christ in the midst of the Church. This of course has an ethical and moral dimension but prior to this it is a matter of the being of the Church. The organic relationship that inheres among the members of the Body of Christ is established, enriched and sustained according to the pattern of Jesus Christ. As such the Church is not configured to its own image, nor is it the product of its own determinations and presumptive claims. Rather the configuring of the Church to its Lord is shaped by Holy Scripture under the discipline and energetics of the Holy Spirit.

3. **Often the fact of the Church as locus for disagreements is**

simply ignored when handling disagreement over controversial matters such as same-sex relationships and marriage

There is a paucity—indeed, neglect is not too strong a word—of discussion of an ecclesiological nature on matters to do with human sexual diversity in general;[5] specific issues concerning homosexuality in the Church; and more recent issues concerning same-sex unions, gay marriage and ordination. It is worth pointing out that we only have controversy and disagreement about these issues now because the Church is trying to be honest about the reality of its own life; its internal struggles and the challenges of engaging with the world for the sake of the gospel.

Understandably there is quite a deal of scholarly work of a biblical and pastoral kind on such matters. And this draws significantly on modern understandings of human sexuality from the social sciences and anthropology. There are also significant issues regarding the relationship between a host culture and the life of the Church in a particular place. The influence can be a two-way affair however, where the Church is not a major voice or in decline within the dominant culture the latter is more likely to exert an influence towards the ecclesial world and can have important consequences for attitudes towards homosexuality and same-sex marriage. This ought not be surprising in so far as the gospel is always embedded in a particular context.

But what is the ecclesial status of such interdisciplinary inquiry? And how are we to assess the impress of host cultures? What are we to make of continuing disagreement, controversy and conflict among the people of God in such a complex, fraught and contested

---

5   The works of James Alison are an exception to this e.g., *Faith Beyond Resentment: Fragments Catholic and Gay* (London: DLT, 2001 & New York: Crossroad, 2001); *On Being Liked* (London: DLT, 2003 & New York: Crossroad, 2004). For further see, Graham Ward, *Christ and Culture* (Oxford: Blackwell, 2005), chap. 3, 'The Body of the Church and its Erotic Politics'.

area as human sexuality? There is of course no general consensus on such matters in the Church considered as a whole. Indeed, it seems that diversity of opinion and practice has become the new normal. Negotiating a new consensus seems out of the question. This is particularly difficult because today we are more aware than ever that our global society is drawing us out of our enclaves towards a more connected and globally aware society. At the same time, we also see counter trends of a more insular, protective and tribal kind. Consensus, even toleration, seems harder to achieve within national denominational structures. In any case such consensus has proven in the history of the Church to be highly unstable and temporary.

It is not as though fracture and division are particularly new phenomena for the Church! The ancient Donatist controversy is an early example that reappears in different guises in the Church. There is a host of matters of a doctrinal, moral and ecclesial nature that have proved divisive within churches and between churches that go back almost two millennia. Might it not be the case that the drive for unity in the body of Christ is premised on the reality of division; that the stubborn insistence on being united feeds off deeper fractures that afflict the people of God. Further, might these institutionally and culturally embedded fractures so dominate ecclesial behaviour and attitudes that they mask or suppress the fundamental reality of the way of God configured in Christ and unfolded in the Scriptural narrative? And might not such fundamental realities prove decisive for our future as the one body of Christ?

Given the predilection for rivalry and division how might the people of God live together with contentious issues? How might Christians listen to and behave towards one another in a Christian manner? We have to reckon with the Body of Christ as the fundamental reality in which, through which and often about which disagreement occurs. And this changes everything about how disagreements are conducted.

4. Oneness in Christ is the precondition for dwelling and growing in the truth as it is in Jesus

The question of truth is co-related to the question of the unity of the Church. This is captured in the Johannine parable in chapter 15 of John's Gospel of the vine, the vine-grower the branches. In this discourse abiding in Christ (the true vine) is the precondition for (a) bearing fruit for the kingdom of God (b) abiding in the words of Jesus (c) finding resonance between human desire and God's will. This organic image is a rich vein for ecclesial life in Christ. Oneness in Christ is signalled by abiding in Christ as the branches remain in the vine. Unity and truth are co-related as becomes even more clearly articulated in chapter 17. The relationship between a passion for the truth of the gospel and the desire for Christian unity has been a perennial one in the Church of God. For example, it surfaces in the 16th century and finds echoes in the differing approaches to controversy and conflict in the Church between the Reformer Martin Luther and Desiderius Erasmus. Luther's rediscovery of the power of the gospel and the truth that issued forth from the gospel provided a sharp critique of Church teaching and practices. Erasmus too was aware of the need for reform but was convinced that it was only as the Body of Christ remained in unity that the truth of the gospel could be found.

The quest for truth and unity are co-related. In this sense, they condition and influence each other. But how are these two ordered? One approach is to assign priority to the question of truth. The logic of this is that the truth of the gospel generates a fellowship in Christ and the latter enables the truth of Christ to flourish. A tendency in this kind of ordering is to resolve matters of belief into propositional terms.

In this context unity can easily become that which is established among those who share a set of commonly held statements of faith. The focus then becomes right believing and/or believing in a particular way in order to remain in unity. The danger of this approach is that fracture and division over conflicting opinions/interpretations becomes the default way of functioning as the Body of Christ.

Another approach gives priority to unity. The logic of this is that finding and dwelling in the truth is related to the degree of unity existing. As identified above in the case of Erasmus, the assumption is that it is only as the body of Christ lives as one that that the truth of faith can be discerned in its fullness. The greater the degree of fracture in the body the more partial is the grasp of the truth. This approach regards diversity and disagreement within the body of Christ as the pre-condition for finding and dwelling in the truth. The danger in this approach is that the quest for unity can be pursued without reference to truth concerns. This is captured in the well-known phrase: unity at any price.

Neither of the above two approaches are satisfactory. Both highlight a fundamental problem that arises when truth and unity concerns are disaggregated and treated as separate elements. As argued throughout this chapter, truth and unity are fundamentally given in and with each other, i.e., they mutually inhere. This approach arises from an understanding of Christ who embodies both the truth and unity of God. This requires more teasing out than can be done at this point. This means that truth and unity are symbiotically related to each other and together are constitutive of the being and life of the body of Christ. Whatever disrupts and/or deforms that relationship is in danger of undermining or overturning the gospel faith.

The prevailing problem in the history of the Church has been one of fracture as the truth is divided up through multiple divisions and separations. The history of Protestantism and, for example, the Roman Catholic Church in the medieval period, has been a history of fragmentation and division. In particular, post-Reformation Protestantism has struggled with difference, diversity and conflict and has tended to fracture under stress. Anglicanism, as a Reformed Catholic tradition, has consistently placed high value on an organic understanding of the Church as the natural environment for the contest for truth and disagreements to be conducted. As such it has always regarded schism as a dangerous act in extremis; and divisions always at risk of fracturing the gospel of Christ.

There are of course different kinds of unity that fall short of the gospel ideal. For example, there is a kind of unity so heavily focussed on the maintenance of aspects of the Church's institutional life and power that the Church is danger of losing reference to its deepest reality in Christ. And there is the ever-present danger of an ecclesial unity more in tune with popular sentiment and less attentive to the prophetic call of the gospel. And unity ought never be absolutized—i.e., unity at any price. Unity ought to be organically related to concern for truth and both are to be referred to the Lord of the Church as witnessed to in Holy Scripture and experienced in the power of the Holy Spirit. It is only as the quest for unity and the passion for the truth of the gospel are constantly referred to Christ and not reified apart from Christ that the true light of God can shine for the world to see and respond.

It is also important to recognise that a breach of unity, no matter how stretched and frail it may be, can only ever be a serious matter and should never be taken lightly. Thus, the apostle Paul speaks of believers 'bearing with one another in love, eager to maintain the unity of the Spirit in the bond of peace' (Eph 4:2-3). There is a reason why this will require 'humility and gentleness' (Eph 4:2). If in extreme situations separation is considered necessary—and some would point to a situation as described in 1 Corinthians 5:11 as a case in point—then this is of utmost seriousness, a matter for mourning not triumphalism.[6]

The difficulty the Church faces today regarding questions of truth and unity is that these two are often pitted against each other. Underlying this is a commonly held belief that unity and truth are two elements that exist in some kind of tension. When this obtains there can be no resolution, only continued tension and trade-offs. In this process both unity and truth are diminished; the reason being that they are no longer located in the life of Jesus Christ; rather their reality is bounded by institutional, political and doctrinal constraints. The latter in particular is more often driven by notions of truth and error which lacks the resources and/or will to recognise difference and/or handle the contested nature of doctrinal conflict.

Historically the outcome of this approach to unity and truth has been to consign unity to the realm of invisibility and prioritise truth concerns in the concrete life of the Church.[7] There are various theo-

---

[6] The question of division, separation and schism is difficult. For example, in the Reformation, Luther insisted that he had never intended to leave the Roman Church, but that in effect the Roman Church had abandoned him. The contentious events over the past two decades in the Anglican Communion have witnessed the formation of the ACNA, Gafcon and its ecclesial networks and the emergence of alternative episcopal oversight in various parts of the Communion and significant litigation. The matter is fraught and complex. It makes the discussion (let alone determination) of division, separation, and schism exceedingly difficult. Thus, some claim that for the sake of truth and the gospel they have chosen to separate from a church that is regarded as having departed from the faith of the church. Others claim that leaving is an unjustified schismatic act. Claim and counterclaim are features of the ecclesial landscape.

[7] Ephraim Radner, refers to an 'age-old Protestant reliance on unity as something existent within a spiritual and invisible realm, ... outside the visible boundaries of the church.... At the same time, the realm of truth was maintained according to fragmented lives and claims in a way that has now been mirrored by postmodern culture'. See, *A Brutal Unity: The Spiritual Politics of the Christian Church* (Waco, Texas: Baylor University Press, 2017), 109. This does not imply indifference to truth concerns but it does mean insisting on not relegating concern for unity to a secondary matter.

logical strategies to relocate unity matters beyond the concrete life of the Church. In the first instance unity is regarded as a spiritual interior reality and signalled in the public domain through adherence to a common set of beliefs held in particular way. When 'right believing' becomes the critical criterion for unity (and evidence of a rightly orientated spirit) the result is that institutional boundaries and polities are marginalised or effectively set aside. Second, this ecclesiology of the like-minded is allied to a dualist ecclesiology that subsists at the local level (the local congregation) and the heavenly realm. Organisational arrangements that obtain beyond the local structure are not considered to carry ecclesiological significance. This means that while an organic theology of the body of Christ is formally affirmed the organic union between Christ and believers is spiritualised in such a way that detours around, or operates under the radar of the concrete visible Church in its variety, diversity and division. In short, the spiritual and organic unity of the body of Christ subsists among the correct believing Christians. The result of this approach to unity is a constant fracturing and fragmentation of the Body of Christ. A Church of the like-minded is inherently unstable since every new matter that requires decision regarding its truth or error generates continued fracturing in pursuance of the fantasy of the pure ecclesial body.

The irony of this spiritualised theology of unity is that division for the sake of truth does not leave division behind in the newly created ecclesial structure and polity. The broken body of Christ carries within its bosom the fractures, frailties and follies of its life. The ideal of, and aspiration for, a purer ecclesial body is self-defeating. Truth and unity only find their proper reference in relation to Christ whose oneness with God is the truth for all reality. Unity and truth are co-present and active in a singular manner. They can't be played off over against one another; nor can one have priority over the other, at least not if they are constitutive of the infinite identity of Christ. The Church gets itself into an impossible tangle and cycle of fracturing, in so far as unity and truth are atomised and separated. The extent to which this occurs is a sign of the failure of the Church to be configured to its life in Christ under the form of Scripture.[8]

5. We advance towards the truth via disagreement and this process involves trust, testing, negotiation and consensus

The idea that the history of disagreement, dispute and conflict in the Church is a smooth lineal progress from mistaken understandings towards clearer perceptions of truth is naïve in the extreme. The history of the Church shows that the move from disagreement to a more settled acceptance in relation to a controversial matter could be a long and arduous process of reception in the Church. In this respect John Henry Newman drew attention to the importance of the wider faith community as an essential criterion for assessment and judgments regarding disputed matters such as innovations in belief and practice. The *consensus fidelium* becomes fundamental in the process.[9] Here the critical factor is the existence of communities of interpretation in which change occurs, is assessed and in turn transforms the *ecclesia*.

Where such communities of interpretation lack coherence and adequate interconnectedness the notion of *consensus fidelium*

---

8   See the powerful argument for a Christological focus for truth and unity discussion in Ephraim Radner, *Hope Among the Fragments: The Broken Church and Its Engagement of Scripture* (Grand Rapids, Michigan: Brazos Press, 2004), chapter 6, 'The Figure of Truth and Unity', 111–120.

9   Paul Avis has commented that '*Consensus fidelium* has now established itself as one of the key concepts of contemporary ecclesiology'. See Avis, *Ecumenical Theology and the Elusiveness of Doctrine* (London: SPCK, 1986), 60.

retracts into ecclesiastical enclaves.[10] This is a feature of the contemporary context of the Church. It belongs to an adversarial culture that in many ways mimics rivalrous host cultures. The Church is more often blind to its enmeshment with the values and aspirations of its host culture. One consequence is that we are constantly in danger of forgetting who we are and whose we are. The danger is that the Church simply apes culture rather than transforms it. This is why word and sacrament are so critical for our remembering and re-appropriating of our identity in Christ and the Spirit. The impact on the Church of a competitive rivalry can be observed with respect to dialogue, discussion and debate about controversial issues to do with human sexuality; and in particular at this time about homosexuality, same-gender unions, gay marriage etc. Responses to such matters tend to define an enclave. In the short term this default may appear attractive for both advocates and opponents but in the longer term it only ensures loss of capacity to exercise a sympathetic ecclesial imagination for one another's position/perspective.

This suggests that disagreement has a very positive function of facilitating deepening understanding and clarity about the implications of the gospel. And the very disagreements point to the fact that the Body of Christ is not monolithic but diverse and admits of very differing views on many matters of practice and belief. Of course, not everything is up for grabs so to speak. The ancient creeds map out the contours of the heart of Christian faith concerning the triune God and Christ as Lord and saviour. But even at this

---

[10] Sociologist Bryan Turner refers to the evolution towards 'the enclave society' as a feature of society and organised religion. He states, that 'With the emergence of enclaves, ghettoes, diasporas and walled communities, society as a whole is divided and fragmented'. See Bryan Turner, *Religion and Modern Society: Citizenship, Secularisation and the State* (Cambridge: Cambridge University Press, 2011), preface ix.

most central focus for faith there will always continue to be discussion, testing, probing and new insights as the Church in every age reconnects the faith proclaimed with the eternal gospel.

6. Disagreements can be assessed in terms of their intensity, extensity and substance

Clearly not all disagreements are of equal significance. Some matters are deemed to threaten the well-being of the Church, some matters may be considered close to the very heart of faith while other things may be simply differences over which Christians will hold different views but ought not lead to rifts and fractures. In the Anglican tradition, there is a long-established appeal to the fundamentals of the faith in contradistinction from what is deemed to be non-fundamental. However there has been a long history of disagreement over precisely where to draw the line! A more nuanced approach to weighing the significance of disagreements makes a threefold distinction concerning a dispute being (a) *intense*—i.e., generates high degree of sustained and unresolved debate that threatens the unity of the Anglican Communion; or that requires urgent attention, (b) *extensive*—i.e., not confined to one section or region of the Church; has significant implications for mission and ecumenical relations; has a wider social impact and (c) *substantial*—i.e., concerning an actual issue, and not for example, simply being generated by the media. When this criterion was considered by the Inter-Anglican Theological and Doctrinal Commission in 2003 it concluded that if a disputed matter was deemed of such significance with reference to its intensity, extent and substance that it makes for the disunity of the Church, then the matter needed to be addressed at the higher levels of the Communion, i.e., beyond the local diocese.[11] The Commission's approach was an attempt to focus on the nature of ecclesial communion, authority and decision-making in the context of tensions and conflict.

With respect to the presenting issue of human sexuality and specifically same-sex relations and marriage, it is worth pondering why it is so intense and should it be so?

In part the intensity stems from the fact that whether one is for or against same-sex marriage, the matter is viewed as going to the integrity of the gospel. For some this is an issue of salvation. This intensity is compounded by the fact that matters of sexuality bring to the fore our essential vulnerability, weakness and incompleteness as human beings; our fundamental interdependence; our remarkable creative capacities; our deepest fears about identity and our shared hopes for human flourishing. From this point of view the criterion of *intensity* is not so difficult to grasp. Perhaps what makes it even more difficult to transact has to do with the ecclesial body in which such matters are attended to. Anglican polity is not by nature conflictual but it is possible to skew it in a direction that is generative of controversy; indeed, almost requires it for the energetics of the ecclesial system.

What might be required of the Church in order that it might more appropriately and humbly harness the intensities of its life that can hinder its witness to the gospel of Christ? In this respect, the Anglican theologian Daniel Hardy offered an insightful comment based on aphorism of S.T. Coleridge: 'He, who begins by loving Christianity better than Truth, will proceed by loving his own Sect

---

11 See letter to the Primates of the Anglican Communion on the Anglican Communion website. http://www.anglicancommunion.org/media/107645/IATDC-Inter-Anglican-Theological-and-Doctrinal-Commission.pdf

or Church better than Christianity, and end in loving himself better than all'.[12] Hardy comments:

> The greatest threat to Anglicanism today is that the personal will (what each person wants), and the will of sectional interests in the Church are displacing love for the truth. By the logic of Coleridge's aphorism, the result can only be a downward spiral to self-love. What is needed is to move radically in the opposite direction: attentiveness to the truth, to the infinite identity of God in acting (in Christ through the Holy Spirit) in the world to bring it to its final end: attentiveness to God for God-self. All will depend on whether we can 'place' everything in relation to the truth of God's own life, as that is found through the right kind of attentiveness to the richness of God's presence and blessing as they are found in worship and corporate life when they respond to God's purposes for the world.[13]

The point about Hardy's reflection is that it orientates the people of the Church beyond their own desires towards the grace and mercy of God in Christ. Here above everything else is the true locus for our intensity of life and the measure by which the Church is equipped to discern the nature and weight to be given to the disagreements that too often assail us.

7. In disagreements, the ends determine the means; the ends do not justify the means

Let us for a moment presume that the purpose of disagreement within the Body of Christ is to find a way for the grace and truth of Jesus Christ to shine forth with glory. This being the case it is

---

12 S. T. Coleridge, *Aids to Reflection*, ed. John Beer (London: Princeton University Press, 1993), 107.
13 Daniel Hardy, 'Anglicanism in the Twenty-First Century: Scriptural, Local and Global', unpublished paper, American Academy of Religion, 2004.

axiomatic that the means deployed by which this might be achieved in disputation ought to be consonant with the end hoped for. In this sense, the ends determine the means, by which we mean the ends shape the manner and character of the means employed. This can be easily short-circuited by resort to means that exert undue power and or coercion over those with whom disagreement occurs. Such behaviour neither honours the Lord of Glory nor does it give due respect and honour to those with whom one disagrees. This points to the fact that the manner of engagement in disagreements bears witness to the manifestation of the fruits of the Spirit in our personal lives and the character of the Church. A certain humility is incumbent upon all of the Body of Christ who contest for the truth of the gospel. Such humility is not simply a matter of our behaviour towards others and evidence of awareness of one's own limited understanding. It is also a sign of trust and openness to others and ultimately to the voice of the living God and the self-discipline of the Holy Spirit. Humility is the critical virtue for growing into the truth of the gospel.

8. Our unity and truth in Christ is a dynamic and expanding reality

Oneness in Christ, who is the way, the truth and the life, has an organic and inter-related character. This is the framework within which we inquire about the nature of Christian faith and what makes for the flourishing of the unity of the Church and what threatens and fractures it. This organic ecclesial framework is at odds with the prevailing social contractual ways of engagement of Western society. In this latter mode, it is more usual to emphasise assents and conformity for social togetherness of a quasi-legal nature.

Disagreements that lead to ruptures and fractures in the Body seriously impair the Church's witness to the gospel. Living as the Body of Christ is not a simple state of affairs but a dynamic and restless reality wherein the Lord of the Church is always drawing the Body deeper into the life of the Spirit and in ever widening circles of reach into the world. The *koinonia* of the Church is fostered and nurtured by constant innovation—new responses in new contexts that seek faithfulness to the tradition and relevance in the modern world. In other words, innovation belongs to the gospel of God. Yet *koinonia* is also constantly threatened by innovation as many of our current controversies about human sexuality indicate. Innovation is thus inherently conflictual and unavoidable. For these reasons innovations appear in the life of the Church as undecidable yet at the same time they require determination (albeit provisional) for the sake of our discipleship in the world. This suggests that a key question for Anglicanism might be: How do Anglicans cultivate a Christian ethos that can respect and engage with difference, controversy and disagreement?

Perhaps there is a moral vision of the kind of ecclesial life we are called to be which provides the framework and substance of our shared life. It cannot be one that seeks simple default solutions through authoritarian top-down or democratic majority bottom-up approaches. Rather it will be one that recognises the organic nature of the Body of Christ and does not see freedom and faithfulness as necessarily opposed.

9. The organic relationship between truth and unity makes it difficult to draw a line regarding the limits to unity

There are it seems some matters (e.g., doctrinal, moral or polity) that prove so divisive and are regarded by some as so contrary to the gospel such that they warrant separation and division. Not surprisingly this was regarded as a serious matter from the earliest days of the emerging Church as local Christian communities tried to deal with difficult matters of belief and practice (e.g., 1 Cor 5:11;

2 Thess 3:6, 14-15; 2 John 8-11). Such matters ought never be treated lightly especially insofar as they are judged to have implications for the integrity of the gospel. For example, some would argue that while the Church may be able to find a way of coping with individual dissent and even doctrinal novelty, even heresy, they would regard it as an entirely different matter when there are attempts to change what is the public, official doctrine of the church. Others argue that the Church has to respond to what they perceive is the prophetic call of the gospel in a new situation and that this necessitates such change. Both positions deserve careful attention as the matter remains contested.

However, my argument at this point is slightly different. My concern is to tease out more clearly the close relationship between unity and truth. My concern is that these two concerns are not treated as different elements in the Church that can be separated from one another. When this does occur, it is too easy to give priority to either truth or unity in the concrete reality of the Church (see discussion in 4 above). When this situation obtains the matter resolves into identifying the error that requires expunging and if it is deemed sufficiently serious the result is division. On this basis, there are very real limits to unity. There are it seems some matters pertaining to the truth of the gospel which do not admit of compromise for the sake of remaining together. And of course where the substance of the gospel is directly and wilfully overturned then the foundation of faith is imperilled. And it is appropriate to ask in those situations: what price unity? What are its limits?

However, the problem is that the determination of those limits (e.g, who has authority to decide?) has been over the history of the Church a highly contested matter. In trying to find a resolution in controversial matters of faith and practice it is not uncommon for pre-existing internal fractures along 'party lines' or different church factions to become the basis for ongoing and more radical divisions. The actual history of the Church on such matters is clear evidence that resultant divisions on the basis of separating truth from error, thereby expunging heresy and/or separating ideas of true religion from false, do not create a more holy and truthful ecclesia.[14] When unity is relocated to an invisible realm and truth concerns are located in the concrete present Church fracturing is institutionalised. The irony is that schisms (small and great) violate the truth of the gospel.

Unity and truth do not in fact represent an either/or for the life of the Church. The binary approach can only deliver continued fracturing of the body of Christ; can only deliver a divided Christ. When this is the case the Church remains locked in its own suffering and is unable to genuinely enter into the suffering of Christ for the world.

10. Nurturing unity in Christ involves referring everything to the Lord of the Church

I began this chapter with a question: Does the Church's public endorsement of same-sex relationships and marriage, and the authorisation of liturgical rites of blessings for same-sex unions and/or marriages, constitute grounds for division and separation? In other words, are such eventualities sufficient justification for

---

[14] Radner, *A Brutal Unity*, discusses the tendency from the Reformation period to label any threat as heresy. Christian deviant or apostate, Muslim or Jew were all de facto functional equivalents because they all embodied in some way a notion of religious deviance and guilty of fundamental error that consigned them all to another realm 'outside the "real"' (p. 86); i.e., the realm of false religion that has to be opposed by true religion (p. 84). Non-Christian religion and heresy converge. Radner's comment is telling if worrying: 'intra-Christian discord becomes completely coincident with apostasy and/or denial of Christ, and Christian division is read in terms of religious antagonism in a strong modern sense'.

division and separation? Clearly the actual recent history of these matters in the wider Anglican Communion indicates an unfolding fracture of significant proportions. And given the way this matter, like most contentious matters in the Church, has been cast continued fracture and fragmentation is the likely scenario. Given the way in which unity and truth has been handled in the history of the Church the conclusion for some seems clear: unity has its limits and on this matter division, as much as it is not desired, is nonetheless an imperative of the gospel for the sake of the gospel. Unity through exclusion of divisive elements is a well-worn path in the history of the Church. Some passages of Scripture (e.g, see above in thesis 9) have been appealed to as warrants for such actions. I do not wish to make light of this. However, the brutal reality of two millennia of division, fracture and schism ought to strike a note of caution in the use of such texts to justify attempts to purify the Body of Christ.[15]

The burden of the argument presented here is that unity through exclusion cannot cleanse itself of division. But it does ensure the continued fracturing of truth. The reason being that reaching agreement across differences—or even more so among the likeminded—has limits and is never as stable as it might seem. It is *this* learning that we shy away from that we refuse to receive, but it is precisely at this point that the Church has something to learn that is quite fundamental to its being and the character of true Christian unity. The Church has to learn again and again the reality of the fundamental instability of its life as the body of Christ. In this recognition and confession of its own brokenness and instability, it

---

15 Compare scriptural injunctions against division (e.g., Rom 16:17; Titus 3:10). Appealing to a particular scripture text relevant to a local church community in the New Testament as warrant for an ecclesial division on a major scale (or for that matter remaining in communion when something more decisive is required) is inherently dangerous and problematic. It may be warranted (only time will tell).

is poised to learn 'the character of divine love, whose form is given in Christ and ordered for the final purpose of human creation-the only truly stable incongruence in agreement that could possibly exist'.[16] Herein lies the secret of divine unity. It is located in the self-giving of God in Christ to a broken and fractious people. God gives freely to that which 'is utterly and irretrievably "other", paradigmatically as the opponent, the "enemy"' (459). This being the case the Church's unity is the face or appearance of God's divine condescension and union with a broken and fractious world and church. 'It is the giving over of and standing beside of God's self within a "community of enemies", such that its communal reality is established by the One whose life is love that bears the enemy himself or herself' (460).

Radner's language is arresting and challenging to say the least! 'Community of enemies' has to be first understood as those for whom Christ died and rose again (Romans 5:8-10; 'while we were still sinners ....'). Those who formerly were at enmity with God have been drawn into the orbit of God's reconciling love in Christ. They are no longer enemies of God but the community of the reconciled. We are on familiar territory here. However, Radner's provocative challenge is for us to remember that as frail human beings (Luther's 'always sinner, penitent, and justified') we are forever in danger of behaving as enemies; of engaging in rivalrous behaviour. The gospel of Christ calls us to relinquish this spirit of enmity and take on the mind of Christ (Phil 2:5-11).\ What might this look like from a practical point of view? Minimally I believe it means that Christians who are highly conflicted with respect to the matter before us i.e. same sex relationships and marriage, will need to gather beyond their own silos of certainty and clarity. The

---

16   Radner, *A Brutal Unity*, 459. Hereafter page numbers in text.

gospel invites us to gather at the place in ancient times called 'the commons'. This is that place/space that none can lay claim to but is open to all to find sustenance.[17] It is sometimes suggested that we must first be clear about the common ground upon which we all stand prior to arguing our points of difference and disagreement. But the idea of the commons goes beyond that. This latter notion reminds us that none in fact can lay claim to a justified place of standing notwithstanding our rhetoric to the contrary. To find our common ground we need to travel metaphorically and spiritually to the commons. This will require that 'patient acquiescence' that Radner deploys so tellingly. It is only at the commons that the people of God, so conflicted and proud, enter the domain of the Holy Spirit who alone can discipline the hearts and minds of unruly people and open new horizons of faith and discipleship for the sake of the world. Moreover, at the commons we can't second guess the outcome; we are simply called to walk by faith and not by sight.

I am suggesting that staying with the suffering Church—the visible and concrete Church that suffers its own internal enmities—may be the only way in which the Church is able to genuinely bear witness to the character of God's suffering love for the world. This will require sacrifice; a giving up without claim; a new way of engaging with those with whom we profoundly disagree; a kind of non-rivalrous disagreement; even one might say a truly 'godly disagreement'. The logic of the gospel is that only self-giving can make oneness truly one. This represents a particular kind of unity that goes beyond a procedural unity that attends to process and decisions but often avoids the substantive theological matter at hand. The kind of unity we need is perhaps beyond the capacity

---

17 For a recent discussion of the idea of the commons see Diana Butler Bass, *Grounded: Finding God in the World. A Spiritual Revolution* (HarperCollins, 2017), chapter 7, Commons.

of a fractious and proud Church. It has to do with the 'practice of acquiescence' (409). This is fundamentally moral and spiritual in form and content. This kind of 'unity in truth' and 'truth in unity' only makes sense because it is grounded in Christ who, though he was rich, for our sake became poor. What this means is that the character of true unity is fundamentally kenotic in form and substance as it is configured to Jesus Christ in the power of the Spirit. Such a unity remains a deed in progress—unlimited in possibilities—that lies beyond our own powers to determine but remains forever close at hand.

THE CASE FOR
AND AGAINST

The Case for Same-Sex Marriage

Matthew Anstey[1]

Introduction

What precisely is the issue before us? On this we need to be clear in order to focus our deliberations on the primary issue, from which many other secondary issues—such as the question of the blessing of same-sex marriages—take their bearings. I wish to pose it as clearly as possible: does God approve, bless, and delight in same-sex marriage, or does God condemn, reject, and judge it sinful? For if God judges it sinful, there is no Christian blessing nor Anglican liturgical consideration possible. But if the heart of God rejoices in same-sex marriage wholeheartedly, then blessing and liturgical recognition of such will follow as night follows day.

Putting the question in such a manner reinforces why the stakes are high in this debate, for we are considering a moral-doctrinal issue which has—not to put the matter too mildly—diametrically opposed views. Hence grave implications follow for Anglican unity, missional integrity, and pastoral practice. Whether both sides can

---

[1] The Rev'd Associate Professor Matthew Anstey is a Research Fellow of the Public and Contextual Theology Strategic Research Centre of Charles Sturt University, an Honorary Visiting Fellow at The University of Adelaide, and a priest in the Anglican Diocese of Adelaide.

co-exist with 'two integrities',[2] as we do for instance with women's ordination, is uncertain.

Furthermore, it is my view, influenced by many years both studying and teaching theology, that the consideration of all matters doctrinal and moral in the life of the church requires a particular disposition, a stance. To my mind, no one articulates this more evocatively than James Alison:

> I would like to create with you something like a space in which a heart might find permission to come close to cracking. It is a space which I am discovering to be necessary for participation in theological discourse. This close-to-cracking comes upon us at a moment when we do not know how to speak well, when we find ourselves threatened by confusion. It is where two principal temptations are either to bluster our way out of the moment, by speaking with too much security and arrogance so as to give the impression that the confusion is not mine, but belongs somewhere else. Or on the other hand to plunge into the shamed silence of one who knows himself uncovered, and for that reason, deprived of legitimate speech. This space of the heart-close-to-cracking, poorly as it seems to promise, and difficult though it be to remain in it once it is found and occupied, seems to me the most appropriate space from which to begin a sketch of ways forward towards the stutter of a theology for the third millennium.[3]

It is in this spirit that I invite the reader to consider my argument for the case for same-sex marriage, to which I will turn after first

---

2   Susannah Cornwall, personal communication. Susannah is a prominent UK lay Anglican theologian writing in the area of human sexuality. See futherSusannah Cornwall, *Un/familiar Theology: Reconceiving Sex, Reproduction and Generativity* (London: Bloomsbury, T&T Clark, 2017).

3   James Alison, *Faith Beyond Resentment: Fragments Catholic and Gay* (New York: Crossroads, 2001), 27.

reflecting on some significant ways in which this particular debate takes place.

On taboo and testimony

Many of us who have participated in debates on this topic in church synods, social media platforms, or among friends and family, have encountered a number of recurring themes, and reflecting on these is important before moving to the main arguments for and against.[4] Three themes, which I label *unnaturalness*, *calamity*, and *encounter*, are in my view significant:

Unnaturalness—People in the LGBT+ community (and many others) struggle with the frequent allusions in this debate to notions such as disgust, unnaturalness, contamination, and, perhaps worst of all, 'abomination'? Any anthropologist will recognise this cluster of concepts as pertaining to *taboo*.[5] And this explains in part why debates on this topic are often so fraught, because 'taboo language is rooted deeply in human neural anatomy.... Taboo is identified with emotional release, aggression, lack of control, intemperance and intolerance'.[6] Acknowledgment of the way highly emotive language can interfere with our emotional regulation and rational

---

[4] The important book by Mark Vasey-Saunders, *The Scandal of Evangelicals and Homosexuality: English Evangelical Texts, 1960–2010* (Aldershot: Ashgate, 2015), demonstrates the significance of the *the manner in which* this debate is undertaken: 'This book examines the history of evangelical responses to the issue of homosexuality, setting them in a wider historical and cultural context and drawing on the work of René Girard to argue that the issue of homosexuality has come to symbolise deeply-held convictions within evangelicalism. The conflict over the issue that is now becoming apparent within evangelicalism reveals deep divisions within the evangelical community that will have great significance for the future' [backcover].

[5] For our purposes, the linguistic dimensions of taboo are most prominent. See Keith Allen and Kate Burridge, *Forbidden Words: Taboo and the Censoring of Language*, (Cambridge: Cambridge University Press, 2006).

[6] Ibid, 249.

thought is thus very important (and especially so for church leaders overseeing debates).

Calamity—Given then the seriousness of this issue, it is not surprising that dire warnings of spiritual calamity are oftentimes proffered to those who support same-sex marriage.[7] In my experience, such fears are indeed often a reality for those contemplating a change of mind on this issue. So let me speak candidly: most of my friends, and I too, nowadays support same-sex marriage and previously did not. So together we have travelled the journey of the consideration of this issue over the last decades. And yes, we have considered seriously whether the affirmation of same-sex marriage entails rejection of other core Christian beliefs. In my view, it absolutely does not, and the people I know who have changed their mind on this issue continue to identify as orthodox Christians, be it evangelical, Reformed, Wesleyan, Pentecostal, Catholic, or so forth. It is vitally important to recognise this in order to mitigate such fears: the imagined calamity is a just that, imagined.[8]

Encounter—The third theme common in the debate on this issue is stories of encounter with gay Christians and the impact this has upon one's thinking, especially if it is a family member.[9]

My wife and I were in our mid-twenties and recently married when we joined a Bible study at our local Anglican church. We met together for two to three years and the fellowship was wonderful, Spirit-filled, and centred on Christ and the Scriptures. But it was

---

[7] Which is further evidence in fact that this is a taboo topic, because the violation of taboos in all cultures are most serious when pertaining 'to things thought to be ominous, evil or offensive to supernatural powers,' ibid, 237.

[8] And given this issue is so emotive and touches on taboo, in fact we should expect calamitous thinking to be present (given the processing of taboo language belongs to the limbic system).

[9] Such stories are found throughout the literature on same-sex marriage, and are heard regularly at Synods.

not until about the end of the second year that Liz and I discovered that two of the men lived together as a committed Christian gay couple. Needless to say, this surprised us greatly, as we had both grown up in churches opposed to same-sex marriage and had believed it was wrong. But we could not deny the depth and authenticity of these two brothers in Christ.[10]

This type of encounter and testimony is very common and I believe it must be taken into account.[11] Kelly *et alia* demonstrate the significance of such encounters in forming beliefs: 'our findings suggest that high levels of contact with sexual minorities have the potential to modify moral judgments about sinfulness, personal choice, and God's design for sexuality.'[12]

In raising these three themes, I hope to bring to the surface some of the dynamics of the way this debate too frequently occurs in churches and elsewhere, and to suggest that attending to such is vital.

I now turn to the issue at hand.

Scripture and Moral Reasoning[13]

Imagine the Bible contained not a handful of passages about homosexuality, but rather hundreds and hundreds, and that these

---

10 The couple have given permission for me to tell this story. They were recently married and remain actively involved in the Anglican Church.

11 Mark Achtemeier, *The Bible's Yes to Same-Sex Marriage: An Evangelical's Change of Heart* (Westminster John Knox, 2014), 2, reflects on a similar encounter: '[Kristi's] testimony was disturbing because none of it matched up with the Bible's teaching about how faith and discipleship are supposed to work.' I recommend in this regard, Roberta S. Kreider, *Together In Love: Faith Stories of Gay, Lesbian, Bisexual, and Transgender Couples* (Kulpsville, PA: Strategic Press, 2002).

12 H.L. Kelly, G. W. Sutton, L. Hicks, A. Godfrey, G. Cassidy, 'Factors Influencing Christians' Moral Appraisals of Nontraditional Sexuality', *Journal of Psychology and Christianity* 37(2) (2018), 162–177.

13 See also my chapter in this collection, 'Scripture and Moral Reasoning'.

passages were unequivocal in their condemnation of homosexual desire and practice. Would those who support homosexuality then change their mind, given that the majority of Christians would want to take Scripture seriously? Or would some perhaps hesitate, and then stay the course, because for a variety of reasons they have made a moral judgment that homosexual practice is not sinful?

Imagine, then, the inverse, that the Bible contained hundreds and hundreds of passages that celebrated, promoted and delighted in homosexuality, without exception. Would those who oppose homosexuality then change their mind, given that they too want to take Scripture seriously? Or would some perhaps hesitate, and remain opposed, because they too for a variety of reasons have made a moral judgment that homosexual practice is sinful?

What interests me in these two thought experiments is this *hesitation*, which we can reasonably imagine people to have if faced with such a situation. The hesitation occurs because two dominant factors are at play in the moral judgments we make, namely, the interpretation of Scripture and moral reasoning.

Let me illustrate this with an example.

[16]The LORD spoke to Moses, saying: [17]Speak to Aaron and say: No one of your offspring throughout their generations who has a blemish may approach to offer the food of his God. [18]For no one who has a blemish shall draw near, one who is blind or lame, or one who has a mutilated face or a limb too long, [19]or one who has a broken foot or a broken hand, [20]or a hunchback, or a dwarf, or a man with a blemish in his eyes or an itching disease or scabs or crushed testicles. (Lev 21:16–20)

The difficult theological issue here is not so much the prohibitions on cultic participation, which actually are revoked in later texts (see Isa 56:1-7; Acts 8:26-39), but that the problematic theological rationale for such prohibition is widespread in Scriptures, namely, of 'identifying disability with sin' as Shane Clifton puts it.[14] Clifton, himself a quadriplegic and a theologian, explores how embedded this view is in the Scriptures[15] and the necessity of providing a theological critique of it (which includes conversation with those Scriptures that offer a countervailing view).

So even though the Scripture here commences with, 'The LORD spoke to Moses, saying...', a Christological exposition of what it means to be made in the image of God, I would argue, entails the rejection of the theological rationale that identifies disability with sin. This is not a rejection of Scripture; it is quite the opposite, it is treating all of Scripture and its witness with utmost seriousness, reading the whole in conversation with tradition and experience to discern the mind of Christ.

In other words, the formulation of doctrine based, so the argument goes, *solely* by the so-called 'plain reading' of Scripture never actually occurs, and claims of such are simply denying the moral logic everywhere present in one's arguments.[16] It never occurs because moral-doctrinal judgments are made through rational argument *in conversation with* Scripture *and* analytical reasoning,

---

14   S. Clifton, *Crippled Grace: Disability, Virtue Ethics, and the Good Life* (Waco, Texas: Baylor University Press, 2018), 33. See especially Shane's personal reaction to, and theological reflection upon, this text and the biblical witness (pp. 58ff).

15   Such as how disability is a metaphor of false idols 'who cannot speak,... cannot feel, ... cannot walk' (Ps 115:5-7) and is associated often with vulnerability, ineffectuality, and dependence, and how healing from disability is frequently construed as a sign of God's blessing and presence.

16   Moreover, it fails even on completely non-controversial matters, for why is it the case that no one ever puts forth a Christian argument in favour of adultery? It cannot be because we think it's wrong solely because 'God says it is wrong' in the Scriptures; rather, it is because the moral-doctrinal reasoning that undergirds this position is cogent and coheres with a fulsome Christian theology.

scientific evidence, lived experience,[17] ecclesial synods and dialogue, and so forth. Thus claims to be following 'Scripture only' on this or any issue are in my view untrue, eliding the interpreting community of God's people to whom God is present by the Spirit.

Throughout its history, the church has had the courage to formulate moral-doctrinal views that are at odds with, or in tension with, particular texts within Scripture, where it is judged that the theological rationale for the position is compelling (leaving aside debate on what counts as 'compelling'). The modern church for instance has no qualms in viewing Paul's injunction to forbid women from speaking in church (1 Cor 14:34), or to 'greet one another with a holy kiss' (given five times: Rom 16:16; 1 Cor 16:20; 2 Cor 13:12; 1 Thess 5:26; 1 Pet 5:14), as not applicable to us. Many other examples can be adduced.

This is how the church operates—denominations through their synods and councils and forums will prepare books and reports, conduct conversations, hold vigorous debates, and then eventually (no matter how many years it sometimes takes) make a decision to change (or retain) its doctrinal position, be it on polygamy, the status and ordination of women, slavery, interracial marriage, capital punishment, contraception, divorce, or in this case, same-sex marriage.[18]

And this is no less precisely what is happening in this debate, in the Anglican Church of Australia. Are we not all participating in the exercise in the formulation of Christian doctrine, taking into account all these perspectives? Are not all contributors to

---

17   And hence my appeal above to take seriously the stories of encounter with and testimony of gay Christians.
18   As of June 2019, according to https://www.bbc.com/news/uk-35278124 eight Anglican provinces have affirmed the same-sex marriage and/or ordination of gay clergy (Brazil, South Africa, South India, Scotland, New Zealand, ECUSA, Canada, Wales).

this volume for instance drawing their arguments together from a range of sources and endeavouring to articulate the strongest possible case for their view? Are we not participating in the ongoing 'dialectic between [the Church] and scripture'?[19]

Towards an Argument for Same-Sex Marriage

Let us take stock—I have argued that all forms of arguments about same-sex marriage involve scriptural interpretation and moral reasoning, including serious engagement with scientific evidence, human experience, church history and tradition, and so forth, and that such arguments must be credible.[20]

What I am not going to do now, however, is offer a detailed examination of the Scriptural materials—this is done elsewhere in this volume, and even more so in a large number of books and journal articles.[21] As a biblical scholar, moreover, I am altogether

---

19 R. A. Greer, *Anglican Approaches to Scripture: From the Reformation to the Present*. (New York: Crossroad, 2006).

20 Pailin, ibid, 234: 'A theology must be so formulated that its statements are "credible to human existence as judged by common experience and reason"', citing Shubert M. Ogden, *The Point of Christology*, (London: SCM Press, 1982), 4.

21 For further reading, see Mark Achtemeier, *The Bible's Yes to Same-Sex Marriage: An Evangelical's Change of Heart* (Louisville, KY: Westminster John Knox, 2014); Bernadette J. Brooten, *Love Between Women: Early Christian Responses to Homoeroticism* (Chicago: Chicago University Press, 1996); William Brownson, *Bible, Gender, Sexuality: Reframing the Church's Debate on Same-Sex Relationships* (Grand Rapids, MI.: Eerdmans, 2013); Alan H. Cadwallader (ed.), *Kaleidoscope of Pieces: Anglican Studies on Sexuality* (Adelaide: ATF Press, 2016); Susannah Cornwall,. *Un/familiar Theology: Reconceiving Sex, Reproduction and Generativity* (London: Bloomsbury, T&T Clark, 2017); John Bradbury & Susannah Cornwall (eds.), *Thinking Again About Marriage: Key Theological Questions* (London: SCM Press, 2016); Tobias S. Haller, *Reasonable and Holy: Engaging Same-Sexuality* (New York: Seabury, 2009); Loader, ibid; Robert Song, *Covenant and Calling: Towards a Theology of Same-Sex Relationships* (London: SCM Press, 2014); Matthew Vines, *God and the Gay Christian: The Biblical Case in Support of Same-Sex Relationships* (New York: Convergent Books, 2014); Brian Walsh, 'Sex, Scripture and Improvisation', In *One God, One People, One Future: Essays in Honour of N. T. Wright*, Edited by John Anthony Dunne & Eric Lewellen (London: SPCK, 2018), 287–315.

reticent to articulate here what would need to be dramatically abbreviated interpretation of complex texts.

What this growing body of scholarly literature demonstrates is that the interpretation of the seven texts on homosexual practice is deeply contested and requires in depth consideration of a large number of interrelated hermeneutical issues such as questions of gender, orientation, procreation, creation, nature and so forth.

And so, the church is faced with a situation akin to the debates on other major moral-doctrinal matters, such as slavery. Consider for example this confident statement in favour of slavery:

> The Bible's defence of slavery is very plain. St. Paul was inspired and knew the will of the Lord Jesus Christ, and was only intent on obeying it. And who are we, that in our modern wisdom presume to set aside the Word of God ... and invent for ourselves a 'higher law: than those holy Scriptures which given to us as "a light to our feet and a lamp to our paths," in the darkness of a sinful and polluted world?'[22]

Thus wrote the Episcopalian Bishop of Vermont, Dr John Henry Hopkins, in 1864. Three years later he was invited to the First Lambeth Conference and preached the opening sermon, and received at the same time an honorary doctorate from the University of Oxford. That such a view was argued by an Anglican Bishop is hard for modern readers to comprehend, yet at the time his view was widely held. Thankfully, the abolitionist proponents won the

---

22   John Henry Hopkins, *A Scriptural, Ecclesiastical and Historical View of Slavery, from the Days of the Patriarch Abraham to the Nineteenth Century: Addressed to The Rt. Rev. Alonzo Potter, D.D., Bishop of the Protestant Episcopal Church, in the Diocese of Pennsylvania* (New York: W. I. Polley & Co., 1864), 16–17, cited in W. Swartley, *Slavery, Sabbath, War, and Women: Case Issues in Biblical Interpretation* (Scottdale, Pennsylvania: Herald Press, 1983), 31.

day with their arguments, and in his study of *how* this debate transpired, Willard Swartley makes the following observation:

> Abolitionist writers gave priority to theological principles and basic moral imperatives, which in turn put slavery under moral judgment. The point we should learn from this is that theological principles and basic moral imperatives should be primary biblical resources for addressing social issues today. These should carry greater weight than a specific statement on a given topic even though the statements speak expressly to the topic under discussion.

This is the view I take, namely, that the debate needs to centre on 'theological principles and basic moral imperatives' rather than individual texts.[23]

Now it might surprise the reader, but I believe that the seven main Scriptural texts on this matter (Genesis 9:20–27; 19:1–11, Leviticus 18:22, 20:13; 1 Corinthians 6:9–10; 1 Timothy 1:10, Romans 1:26–27) are all opposed to homosexual practices. And though I also agree with the many scholars who argue that 'what the New Testament writers have in mind when they refer to homosexual practice could not have been the loving and stable same-sex unions of the sort that exist today, of which they knew nothing',[24] let's assume for the sake of argument that they do so apply. I would still nevertheless argue that the theological principles and moral

---

23 It is important however to note that Swartley, *Homosexuality,* argues that the debate on homosexuality in some respects is unlike the debates on slavery, Sabbath, war, and women, because he argues that Scripture is opposed in all cases. In my view, Swartley fails to follow his own reasoning around the formulation of doctrine to its logical conclusion, namely, that theological principles and basic moral imperatives, in their totality, must remain primary, even where Scripture is one-sided. See Bruce Hiebert, http://www.cascadiapublishinghouse.com/dsm/summer05/hiebbr.htm for a critique of Swartley (2003).

24 Steven Chalke, *A Matter of Integrity: The Church, Sexuality, Inclusion and an Open Conversation,* https://www.openchurch.network/sites/default/files/A%20MATTER%20OF%20INTEGRITY.compressed.pdf.

logic (as argued below) still 'carry greater weight than a specific statement on a given topic.'

In other words, I am putting forward three interrelated claims, namely that

1. the theological rationale for affirming same-sex marriage counters those texts that oppose homosexual practice;
2. appealing to a theological rationale is precisely that which the Church has in practice followed in all its deliberations of moral-doctrinal matters it has considered through the ages; and, accordingly,
3. claims that any particular moral-doctrinal argument is only following the plain teaching of Scripture are false.

So, finally, let us now consider the theological principles and moral arguments regarding same-sex marriage, in three arguments: the gender complementarity argument, the 'missing sin' of homosexuality, and the nature of same-sex desire.[25]

The Gender Complementarity Argument

First, I wish to counter the most common theological argument used against same-sex marriage, the gender complementarity argument.[26]

This relatively new argument against homosexuality is that our

---

25 It needs to be acknowledged that there are some who argue for same-sex covenantal unions as an alternative to same-sex marriage. In their view, this retains marriage as a heterosexual covenant and allows same-sex couples to have their own distinctive form of covenanted public life. See R. Song, *ibid*, for exposition of this approach.

26 Though the Anglican theologian Ephraim Radner has recently made a more Catholic-like argument against same-sex marriage on the basis of the procreative imperative of human sexuality. See E. Radner, *A Time to Keep: Theology, Mortality, and the Shape of a Human Life* (Waco, TX: Baylor University Press, 2016) and E. Radner, http://www.anglicancommunioninstitute.com/2013/07/same-sex-marriage-is-still-wrong-and-its-getting-wronger-every-day/ for a summary article.

gender complementarity reflects the *imago dei* in some necessary or essential way; that is, heterosexual marriage only is justified because the relational nature of the Trinity is refracted in the complementary nature of male vis-à-vis female. This argument is supported by appeal primarily to the two creation accounts, in which humankind is made in the image of God male and female (Gen 1; Gen 2) and thus requires maleness and femaleness in order so to represent this image.

Moreover, human marriage, given its procreative potential and its (for some, sacramental) symbolism of the relationship of Christ and the church, sanctions male-female relations,—and here the argument hinges— and in so doing negates the possibility of same-sex marriage. Given Jesus makes no reference to homosexuality, his citation of Genesis 2 in his discussion of divorce is interpreted as Christ's endorsement of heterosexual marriage only (i.e. heteronormativity).

If the reader is baffled by this argument, that is I suggest because the argument is indeed baffling. There are I submit theological (Christological and eschatological) problems with both its basic assertions, and the inference from these assertions to the doctrine of heteronormativity is unwarranted.

Christ is the full and complete *imago dei*, telling the human story in the way we have all failed to tell it. Hence the *imago dei* is refracted in our humanness, and not in any gendered or marital form thereof. This is the Christological rebuttal in succinct form. Eschatologically, gender and marital vs single differences are irrelevant, and what's more, this future reality is to inform our current doctrine and practice ('in Christ there is neither male nor female' Gal 3:28). Hence any underlying assertions of gender complementarity as representative of the *imago dei* are to be rejected. Moreover, even if they were to accepted, the inference that same-sex relationships are therefore sinful does not follow. That male-female marriage is a symbol of the Church does not rule out same-sex relationships any more than it rules out celibacy (or parent-child relations, sibling relations, etc.), nor any more than procreative heterosexual marriages rule out childless ones.[27]

To put it simply, the affirmation of the goodness of heterosexual marriage does not entail the wrongness of homosexual marriage.[28]

The 'missing sin' of same-sex marriage

The most common statement one hears when talking with those outside the church is, 'But I just don't see what's wrong with it'. I believe there is wisdom in this. I submit that the secular public, unhindered nowadays by taboo around homosexuality and so able to discuss the matter freely, and unhindered by a religious tradition that tells them homosexuality is wrong, has been able to grasp with clarity that there is no coherent moral objection to homosexuality. (And just because society works something out before the church does not mean society is wrong, as history shows us repeatedly.)

So, I invite the reader: ask yourself, *what specifically is wrong about homosexual marriage?* We all know gay couples—what sin is committed arising from their union as gay people? When two people of the same gender give their lives to one another in covenantal fidelity and love, what sin is being enacted? What harm is being done? What evil is being propagated? Of course, I am not talking about all the regular shortcomings of human relations; that misses the point

---

27   See M. DeFranza, *Sex Difference in Christian Theology: Male, Female and Intersex in the Image of God* (Grand Rapids, MI: Eerdmans, 2015) for excellent discussion of this issue, and A. Thatcher, *Redeeming Gender* (Oxford: Oxford University Press, 2017).

28   See further Cornwall, 2016 'Faithfulness to our Sexuate Bodies: The Vocations of Generativity and Sex' in S. Cornwall & J. Bradbury (eds), *Thinking Again About Marriage: Key Theological Questions* (London: SCM Press, 2016).

entirely. I am talking about the fact that there is no sin committed specifically as a result of the couples' identical gender. And more to the point, the loving, fruitful, positive same-sex relationships of countless people is a compelling witness to its goodness.

What I find most telling in this regard is the marked absence in literature opposing same-sex marriage of an articulation of the precise nature of the specific sin being committed. If we take other types of sexual practice, such as adultery, incest, paedophilia, bestiality, sexual abuse, and so forth, the articulation of the harm and wrongness of the specific sexual activity is straightforward to articulate (and the rationales for such are broadly agreed to in modern secular society), and again, more to the point, the harm and wreckage of such forms of sexual expression is self-evident.

But for homosexuality, opponents typically provide no comment on this; rather, its wrongness is simply assumed. The one 'argument'—I use the term reservedly—present in such literature is one of *divine fiat*—homosexuality is wrong because God (it is claimed) declares it wrong. But that is not an argument, that's simply a brute assertion. If it is indeed wrong, there needs to be a thoughtful, compelling, coherent account for its wrongness. But I know of no such argument, neither in scholarship nor, in all seriousness, at the local pub.

The heart of the matter

> Thoughtful conformity to Christ—not unthinking conformity to either contemporary culture or textual prohibitions—should be our unchanging reference point.[29]

Desires matter. So much so that Jesus, and subsequently the

---

29 S. Chalke, *A Matter of Integrity: The Church, Sexuality, Inclusion and an Open Conversation*, 2013, https://www.openchurch.network/sites/default/files/A%20MATTER%20OF%20INTEGRITY.compressed.pdf.

church, has taught that if one has lustful desires, one has committed the sin, even when it is not enacted (see Mat 5:28). What determines the sinfulness is the desire. One could not commit an act of lust without the lustful desire, because what makes the act lustful is the lustful intentionality contained within the lustful desire.

Now let me clarify two matters. One can of course experience arousal without it leading to lust, so for the sake of argument, I am talking of lust in its negative sense throughout. Moreover, all of us experience life as a jumble of entangled good and bad desires, so again, for the sake of argument, I am considering good desires and bad desires as if disentangled.

On both sides of the debate about homosexuality, there is agreement that same-sex attraction desires are not sinful. Given that all our desires and intentions and actions fall under the purview of God's judgment, these desires therefore must be good desires. There are no neutral desires when the desire pertains to the wellbeing of another person and the body politic no less.

Or, to put it positively, same-sex love is like all other good love (when it is good and not something distorted): it selflessly seeks the well-being of (*agape*) and union with (*eros*) the other, as Aquinas so argued.[30] It is directed toward the other and yearns for that which is good and true and beautiful for them, and given its reciprocity, it yearns to be loved in equal measure, freely and completely, and to be united bodily with the other. Such love is Christ-like and Christ's love for us is in fact the measure and standard of all love.

Therefore, given the bond between good desire, good intention, and good action, the expression of this love must be good, Christ-like, godly. And thus there is no rationale for saying—as the case against does—that the expression of such love sexually is wrong (and fatally

---

30   *Summa Theologiae*, I–II. Q28.

so according to some), but that any non-sexual expression is fine. This is because sexual attraction and expression of love is part and parcel of what constitutes reciprocal, exclusive love (i.e., marital-type love) between couples. More to the point, that is in fact one of its defining characteristics, because it is only within that form of relationship (marriage) that the church sanctions the expression of sexual love. The fact that some couples for various reasons do not engage in such sexual activity does not negate the argument.

The case against, I submit then, actually posits a genuine absurdity, best illustrated thus: same-sex attracted couples could live together, plan their lives together, share their bank accounts, holidays, hobbies, even share the bed together—I assume even hold hands (non-sexually!)—provided there is no genital sexual activity. This is a most plausible illustration, and not a hypothetical red herring: it brings into focus the juxtaposition of faithful, reciprocal, all-encompassing love with an arbitrary prohibition on sexual activity. The unravelling of the argument against same-sex marriage I believe lies in such bifurcation of desire from enactment, and the absurdity that flows from that disjunction.

In my view, it would be more tenable, then, for the case against to argue that all same-sex desire and attraction is *intrinsically* sinful, disordered, wrong before God, that any form whatsoever of the desire to give one's heart and life utterly and entirely over to another person of the same gender, in lifelong, monogamous, faithful relationship, is sinful all the way down and wrong without remainder.

Such an argument, in which desire and its enactment are properly tethered, would be in my view morally (and doctrinally no less) coherent, but at a terrible price—all those who experience persistent self-identifying same-sex attraction are in a permanent state of sinfulness, and not by choice (given that those opposed to same-sex marriage in this volume argue it is not a choice). Homosexuals, so the argument goes, unlike heterosexuals, are filled with desires that inherently and intrinsically sinful; they are not able to change and are condemned by God (in the view of some, for all eternity). That this price is too high goes without saying—our illustrative couple are doomed.

So to return to the argument in favour of same-sex marriage, I put it thus: when one ponders seriously and deeply the nature of the love same-sex couples have for one another, and when one sets aside all those counter arguments which appeal to fallen human nature (given that such counter arguments count equally against heterosexual marriage), the faithful enactment of such same-sex love must necessarily be deemed to be good, wholesome, and, indeed, Christ-like.

To put it simply, God revealed in Christ through the Spirit affirms same-sex marriage.

The Case Against Same-Sex Marriage

Michael R Stead[1]

The previous essay poses the issue before us sharply—does God approve, bless, and delight in same-sex marriage, or does God condemn, reject, and judge it as sinful?

I argue that God does not approve, bless, and delight in same-sex marriage, both because of what the Scriptures *affirm* about marriage (especially that marriage necessarily involves the pairing of a man and a woman) and because of what the Scriptures *prohibit* in relation to other expressions of human sexuality (especially the prohibition of same-sex sexual intimacy). That is, I am making the claim that the Scriptures are sufficiently clear on this issue as to resolve the matter for us.

However, since the argument in favour of same-sex marriage involves tradition, reason and experience in addition to the Scriptures, this essay will address these matters too. It will consider the arguments based on scripture, tradition (especially our Anglican interpretative tradition), reason and experience, bearing in mind that these are not four coordinate authorities. Scripture stands as arbiter and authority over all arguments from tradition,

---

[1] The Rt Rev'd Dr Michael Stead is the Bishop of South Sydney. He gained his doctorate in Biblical Studies from the University of Gloucestershire, and is a Visiting Lecturer in Old Testament at Moore Theological College, Sydney.

reason and experience. It only is the written word of God that carries the authority of God.

A. The Anglican Interpretative Tradition

The question of how we should interpret and apply the Scriptures—technically known as hermeneutics—is central to this debate. Hermeneutics helps us navigate from ancient text to modern reader.

There is a vast array of approaches to Scripture. Some are grounded in unbelief—that the Scriptures are not in any sense the word of God. Some are grounded in an assumed tension—that the Old Testament is about anger and law, which is contradicted by the New Testament message of love and grace. Some are grounded in suspicion—that we must not take the Bible at face value, and instead must find (and undo) the power, privilege and bias of the authors of the Bible.

There are, however, certain principles which are foundational for our approach—as Anglicans—to the Scriptures. For example, Article 20 of the 39 Articles describes the Scriptures as 'God's Word written', and mandates that the Church must not 'expound one place of Scripture that it be repugnant to another'. Article 7 tells us that 'Holy Scripture containeth all things necessary for salvation', and Article 8 declares that the Old Testament is not contrary to the New, as both Testaments ultimately point to salvation through Jesus Christ. Article 7 recognises that not all of the Old Testament continues to apply to the New Covenant believer—the 'Ceremonies and Rites' and 'Civil precepts' of the Law of Moses are no longer binding, but the 'Moral Commandments' remain binding. Of course, this doesn't entirely answer every question, because it is not always clear what distinguishes a moral commandment from a civil precept, for example.

Nevertheless, Anglicans across the centuries have successfully used these principles to navigate from ancient text to modern reader. We do not practise the animal sacrifices of the Old Testament because of the New Testament declaration that Christ came as the fulfilment of the whole sacrificial system. We all recognise that the Old Testament precepts that separated Israel from the other nations are transformed now that the invitation to salvation has gone out to all nations. We understand that the Old Testament is not in conflict with the New, and that points of difference are often because of a movement from promise to fulfilment between the two—for example, the Old Testament promises the inclusion of the Gentiles, and this is fulfilled in the New Testament.

We all recognise that there are some commands and prohibitions in the Old Testament that do not apply to the New Covenant believer, and some that do. The key question is, which is the appropriate category for the Old Testament teaching on marriage and same-sex sexual intimacy?

Some arguments for same-sex marriage seek to bypass or ignore this question, using a variation on the *Letter to Dr Laura*. Dr Laura Schlessinger, an American radio personality of Jewish faith, told her listeners that homosexuality is wrong because the Bible says so. The *Letter to Dr Laura* satirised her position.[2] The letter begins as follows.

---

2   The 'Letter to Dr Laura' went viral on the internet in the year 2000, and received a wide exposure when a version of the argument was included in the 'Midterms' episode of *The West Wing* in Oct 2000.

Dear Dr. Laura,

Thank you for doing so much to educate people regarding God's Law. I have learned a great deal from your show, and I try to share that knowledge with as many people as I can. When someone tries to defend the homosexual lifestyle, for example, I simply remind him that Leviticus 18:22 clearly states it to be an abomination. End of debate.

I do need some advice from you, however, regarding some of the specific laws and how to best follow them.

a) When I burn a bull on the altar as a sacrifice, I know it creates a pleasing odor for the Lord (Lev 1:9). The problem is my neighbors. They claim the odor is not pleasing to them. Should I smite them?

b) I would like to sell my daughter into slavery, as sanctioned in Exodus 21:7. In this day and age, what do you think would be a fair price for her?

c) I know that I am allowed no contact with a woman while she is in her period of menstrual uncleanliness (Lev 15:19-24). The problem is, how do I tell? I have tried asking, but most women take offense.

d) Lev. 25:44 states that I may indeed possess slaves, both male and female, provided they are purchased from neighboring nations. A friend of mine claims that this applies to Mexicans, but not Canadians. Can you clarify? Why can't I own Canadians? [3]

The rhetoric of the *Letter to Dr Laura* suggests that since these Old Testament rules are not (and should not be) followed in the modern world, the prohibition of same-sex sexual intimacy likewise must

---

3   The full version of the Letter to Dr Laura is at https://www.snopes.com/fact-check/letter-to-dr-laura/.

not apply today. That is, since some of the Old Testament no longer applies, none of it applies. This hermeneutic is inconsistent with *Anglican* approaches to Scripture.

The *Letter to Dr Laura* presupposes a 'flat reading' of the Old Testament—a reading which ignores the wider context of the Scriptures and ignores the Bible's progression towards salvation in Christ. This kind of 'flat reading' is not—and has never been—an Anglican way of reading Scripture. The principles reflected in the 39 Articles mean that we must consider any particular text in the context of the Scriptures as a whole (so as not to read one part as repugnant to another), and must always consider how a particular text points to salvation through Jesus Christ. This is how we work out how the ancient text applies to the modern reader.

That is not to suggest that the answer to the hermeneutical question is always obvious or uncontested. But this is no reason to fail to ask the essential question—what parts (if any) of the Old Testament teaching on marriage and same-sex sexual intimacy have relevance for us?

To foreshadow the argument that I will develop below, the fact that Jesus reiterates the teaching about marriage in Genesis 1–2, and that Paul reiterates both the principle and the language of Leviticus 18 and 20 in relation to same-sex sexual intimacy demonstrates that what the Old Testament *affirms* in relation to marriage and what the Old Testament *prohibits* in relation to other expressions of human sexuality continue to apply to the New Covenant believer.

The abandonment of our Anglican interpretative tradition is the fatal flaw in a number of arguments sometimes made in support of same-sex marriage. These arguments, and the reasons why they fail, are summarised below.

- **The Analogy with Slavery**

   It is sometimes argued that our current debates on same-sex marriage are like the nineteenth century debates on slavery, which used the Bible in support of slavery. This argument is based on the claim that the two are analogous. Any argument from analogy must establish that the analogy (X is like Y) holds. In this case, the analogy does not hold. In the slavery debate, what ultimately won the day was that there were compelling arguments *from Scripture* for abolition. The New Testament does not *affirm* slavery. It addressed how to endure the social reality of slavery when powerless to change it (e.g., 'Were you a slave when you were called? Don't let it trouble you—although if you can gain your freedom, do so'—1 Cor 7:21), and also how the Christian should change it when able to do so (e.g., Paul's appeal to Philemon to receive back the runaway slave Onesimus 'no longer as a slave, but better than a slave, as a dear brother'—Phm 16). Historically, it was the NT teaching *against* slavery that sowed the seeds which led to the widespread abolition of slavery in the 19th century in the western world. By contrast, in the same-sex marriage debate, there are NO scriptural arguments in support of same-sex sexual intimacy. Those scholars who have analysed the arguments in the slavery debates and compared them with the modern debates about same-sex marriage conclude that the analogy does not hold – that X is **not** like Y. See, for example, Willard Swartley[4] and William Webb.[5]

---

[4] *Homosexuality: Biblical Interpretation and Moral Discernment* (Scottdale, Pennsylvania: Herald Press, 2003).

[5] W. J. Webb, *Slaves, Women & Homosexuals: Exploring the Hermeneutics of Cultural Analysis* (Downers Grove, IL: InterVarsity Press, 2001).

On a related analogy argument in relation to the church's recognition of the equality of women, Kevin Giles concludes 'The issue of homosexuality and women's liberation cannot be equated... The two matters are to be contrasted rather than compared... To affirm the substantive equality of women is to prioritise the primary and foundational view of women given in the Bible. It is not a capitulation to modern secular culture. In contrast, to affirm homosexual relations is to reject the primary and foundation understanding of sex given in the Bible. It is to capitulate to modern secular culture.'[6]

- **The Bible does not give us God's 'definition' of marriage**

  It is sometimes argued that the Old Testament does not provide a prescriptive pattern of marriage that God has established for all people, because of the variety of forms of marriage recorded in the Old Testament. Instead, the Old Testament merely describes how Israel had adopted and adapted the practices of marriage from the culture around them.

  Is there a definition of marriage in the Bible? It is important to distinguish between a MUST definition and a SHOULD definition. The Bible's definition of marriage is a SHOULD definition—'this is how things SHOULD be'—which can recognise departures from the norm as still being marriage (albeit less than perfect ones). To take the example of polygamy, multiple wives is clearly a

---

[6] K. Giles, 'Paul's Condemnation of Porneia: Sexual Immorality in 1 Corinthians 6:9-10', published online at http://www.ethos.org.au/online-resources/Blog/Paul-s-Condemnation-of-Porneia--Sexual-Immorality-in-1-Corin.

departure from the Genesis 1–2 pattern of one man and one woman, but a polygamous marriage is still a marriage. As the storyline of the Old Testament unfolds, it is clear that polygamy is a poor version of marriage precisely because it departs from the pattern—it is not how things SHOULD be. Another way of putting this is to say that the Bible establishes God's **normative pattern** for marriage.

The aberrant forms of marriage in the Old Testament do not invalidate the God-given pattern of marriage, any more that the proliferation of idolatrous worship in the Old Testament invalidates God's commandment against idolatry. The only thing that aberrant practice demonstrates is that God's people are not very good at obeying God's commands.

The argument that Genesis 1-2 is merely **descriptive** and not **normative** is inconsistent with what Jesus says in Matthew 19. In Matthew 19, Jesus interprets Gen 1:27 and Gen 2:24 as establishing a normative pattern of marriage. In Matthew 19, Jesus answers a question about divorce by pointing to God's purpose for marriage:

> He answered, 'Have you not read that the one who made them at the beginning **'made them male and female'** [*quoting Gen 1:27*] and said, **'For this reason a man shall leave his father and mother and be joined to his wife, and the two shall become one flesh'**? [*quoting Gen 2:24*]. So they are no longer two, but one flesh. Therefore what God has joined together, let no one separate.' (19:4–6)

Jesus' quotation of Genesis 1–2 with reference to a then-current debate about divorce demonstrates that he understood these verses to be more than merely *descriptive* of Adam and Eve's marriage. Rather, he treats Genesis 1–2 as normative for the pattern of marriage established by the Creator for his creatures, in which God joins a man and a woman in a 'one flesh' relationship. Marriage is more than a social custom which ancient Israel adopted from the surrounding culture. Marriage is 'instituted by God' (BCP).

- **The analogy with the inclusion of the Gentiles—God is doing something new**

    Some who support same-sex marriage argue for a parallel between the inclusion of Gentiles in the first century, and the inclusion of LGBT+ people today. Prior to Acts 10, it is claimed a 'plain reading' of the Scriptures said that Gentiles had to become Jews to share the kingdom of God. But a work of the Holy Spirit—evidently manifest in the lives of the Gentiles—overturned this understanding. Likewise in our day, we should discern the work of the Spirit manifest in same-sex unions that show marriage-like commitment and love.[7]

    However, the inclusion of the Gentiles is promised in the Old Testament—Isaiah 56, Zechariah 2, Zechariah 8 etc. While there is something genuinely and radically new occurring in the New Covenant, this is consistent with, and foreshadowed by, the Old Testament. In contrast, there is nothing in the Old Testament (or indeed the New) that hints about a possible reversal of the condemnation of same-sex sexual intimacy.

---

7   See, e.g., D. Gushee, *Changing Our Mind* (Canton, MI: David Crumm Media, 2014), chapter 17.

B. Scripture

In my view, the key Scriptural texts in this debate are Genesis 1–2 and Matthew 19 (affirming a normative pattern of marriage) and Romans 1 and 1 Corinthians 6 (prohibiting same-sex sexual intimacy). I have already commented on Genesis 1–2 and Matthew 19 above, and won't repeat that argument here, except to restate the conclusion that Jesus' words in Matthew 19 make it clear that the Genesis 1–2 pattern of marriage—those created male and female (Gen 1:27) being united by God into one flesh (Gen 2:24)—is God's normative pattern for all marriage. We should resist any argument that seeks to divorce Genesis 1 from Genesis 2—what Jesus has joined together, we must not put asunder.

However, if we suppose (contrary to my conclusions above) that there was no clear normative pattern of marriage in the Bible, there still remains the issue of the condemnation of same-sex sexual intimacy in Romans 1 and 1 Corinthians 6.

For those who wish to argue for same-sex marriage and consider themselves bound by what Scripture allows and prohibits, it is essential to demonstrate that Romans 1 and 1 Corinthians 6 do not apply to consensual and committed same-sex sexual intimacy. For example, Steve Chalke argues that 'what the New Testament writers have in mind when they refer to homosexual practice could not have been the loving and stable same-sex unions of the sort that exist today, of which they knew nothing.'[8]

In relation to Romans 1, this argument is based on three interrelated claims.

1. It is **not** addressed to those who are, by nature, attracted to those of the same-sex, but to heterosexual persons who

---

[8] S. Chalke, 'A Matter of Integrity: The Church, Sexuality, Inclusion and an Open Conversation', https://www.openchurch.network/sites/default/files/A%20MATTER%20OF%20INTEGRITY.compressed.pdf.

'reject their natural orientation'. As the Ven. Rod Bower put it on ABC Q&A, 'what the Bible is really saying, if anything, is that heterosexual people shouldn't have gay sex'.[9]

2. It is **not** addressed to consensual gay sex, but to those who engage in abusive and predatory gay sex.
3. It is **not** addressed to committed (i.e., monogamous) gay sexual relationships, but only to uncontrolled promiscuity and licentiousness.

These three claims are essential to the argument that Romans 1 does not apply to consensual apand monogamous same-sex relationships. Each of these three claims is contradicted by Romans 1.

Claim 1: Claim 1 takes the phrase 'contrary to nature' (*para physin*) in Rom 1:26 to mean 'contrary to their own nature'. This is an unnatural reading, proposed by Boswell in 1980,[10] which has, to my mind, been repeatedly shown to be untenable.[11] The argument is untenable because Rom 1:26–27 itself defines what Paul means by 'natural', by contrasting 'natural relations' with those 'against nature'.[12] In verse 27 Paul explains that 'natural relations' for men

---

9   Q&A, 28 May 2018, https://www.abc.net.au/tv/qanda/txt/s4837221.htm.
10 Argued in J. Boswell, *Christianity, Social Tolerance, and Homosexuality* (Chicago: University of Chicago, 1980), 109—'the persons Paul condemns are manifestly not homosexual: what he derogates are homosexual acts committed by apparently heterosexual persons.'
11 See, for example, R. B. Hays, 'Relations Natural and Unnatural: A Response to John Boswell's Exegesis of Romans 1' *Journal of Religious Ethics* 14 (1986), 184–215; J. B. De Yong, 'The Meaning of 'Nature' in Romans 1 and Its Implications for Biblical Proscriptions of Homosexual Behavior' JETS 31 (1988), 429–441; M. Davies, 'New Testament Ethics and Ours: Homosexuality and Sexuality in Romans 1:26–27 *Biblical Interpretation* 3 (1995), 319–20; R. A. J. Gagnon, *The Bible and Homosexual Practice: Texts and Hermeneutics* (Nashville, TN: Abingdon, 2001), 380–92. J. Dallas & N. Heche, *The Complete Christian Guide to Understanding Homosexuality* (Eugene: Harvest House, 2010), 131–33.
12 This verse does not say that they 'abandoned natural **desires**', but that they 'abandoned natural **relations**' (*chresis*).

are relations 'with women', whereas those who forsake natural relations become 'inflamed with lust [for men]' (NIV). That is, in the internal logic of Rom 1:27, it is 'against nature' for a man to be 'inflamed with lust for men'. 'Against nature' is thus an objective standard, rather than a reference to the subjective desires of the individual.[13] This is also true in the wider Greco-Roman usage of the phrase 'against nature'.[14]

The description of the behaviour in verses 26–27 is not of heterosexual men dabbling in a bit of homosexual sex on the side—these men 'abandoned natural relations with women and were inflamed with lust for one another'.

Furthermore, if this interpretation was correct, it has the implication that being 'inflamed with lust for men' is only 'wicked' if it doesn't come naturally. But this would have the bizarre implication that all the other sins listed in Romans 1—envy, covetousness, pride, etc.—would also not be sinful if they came naturally. The rhetorical goal of Paul's argument in Romans 1–2 is to establish that all people are 'without excuse'. The interpretation of those like Chalke leads to

---

13 Paul uses the same phrase in Romans 11:24 to refer to God's 'unnatural' grafting of wild branches onto olive tree as a metaphor for the inclusion of Gentile. Paul writes 'you were cut out of an olive tree that is wild by nature (*kata physin*), and contrary to nature (*para physin*) were grafted into a cultivated olive tree.' Here, 'contrary to nature' means 'contrary to the natural order of things', not 'contrary to the nature of the wild branch'.

14 Plato's *Laws*, (636C), 'When male unites with female for procreation, the pleasure experienced is held to be due to nature (*kata physin*), but contrary to nature (*para physin*) when male mates with male or female with female.' http://www.perseus.tufts.edu/hopper/text?doc=plat.+laws+1.636c, Josephus, *Against Apion* 2.273, 'And why do not the Eleans and Thebans abolish that unnatural (*para physin*) and impudent lust, which makes them lie with males', http://www.perseus.tufts.edu/hopper/text?doc=Perseus%3Atext%3A1999.01.0216%3Abook%3D2%3Asection%3D262, Philo, *Spec. Laws* 3.39, 'let the man who is devoted to the love of boys submit to the same punishment, since he pursues that pleasure which is contrary to nature (*para physin*)', http://www.earlychristianwritings.com/yonge/book29.html.
See further R. B. Ward, 'Why Unnatural? The Tradition behind Romans 1:26-27' HTR 90.3 (1997) 263–84.

the opposite conclusion—that some people have an excuse, because their homosexual desires come naturally.

Furthermore, the claim made by Matthew Vines (and others) that 'the concept of same-sex orientation didn't exist in the ancient world'[15] is deeply misleading. After an extensive review of ancient Greco-Roman sources, Preston Sprinkle concludes

> ... there were many men who preferred to have sex with the same gender and were even believed to have been biologically oriented this way. Some may have been considered masculine by ancient standards; others may have been viewed as feminine. But such men, who preferred sex with men over women (sometimes exclusively) would have been considered (and considered themselves) at the very least bisexual or even gay today.[16]

Similarly, Branson Parler concludes

> Though the NT thought world did not use our modern terminology of sexual orientation, the time frame from Plato to Ptolemy shows that thinkers of antiquity were well aware that sexual inclination was often fixed and not a matter of mere volition.[17]

Thus, those who argue a version of claim 1 are caught on the horns of a dilemma. On the one hand (or horn), if (against the evidence) they assert that Paul had no understanding of homosexual orientation, their argument nonetheless depends on the concept of 'orientation' to interpret the passage—'contrary to nature' in essence means 'contrary to one's personal sexual orientation'. But if Paul didn't know about homosexual orientation, then it is not logical to assert that his words are addressed only to those with a

---

15 M. Vines, *God and the Gay Christian: The Biblical Case in Support of Same-Sex Relationships* (New York: Convergent Books, 2015), 102.

16 P. Sprinkle, 'Romans 1 and Homosexuality: A Critical Review of James Brownson's Bible, Gender, Sexuality' *BBR* 24.4 (2014) 515–28, at 525.

17 B. Parler, 'Worlds Apart?: James Brownson and the Sexual Diversity of the Greco-Roman World' *TrinJ*. 38NS (2017) 183–200, at 200.

heterosexual orientation (i.e., non-homosexual) acting contrary to their nature in Rom 1. As Richard Hays comments,

> to suggest that Paul intends to condemn homosexual acts only when they are committed by persons who are constitutionally heterosexual is to introduce a distinction entirely foreign to Paul's thoughtworld and then to insist that the distinction is fundamental to Paul's position.[18]

But on the other hand (or horn), if they accept that Paul *was* aware of men whose sexual inclination was for men (and likewise women, for women), then it is clear that Paul is also speaking against those sexual practices, because there is no 'bracketing out' of those with innate desires in Romans 1.

Claim 2—That Romans 1 only addresses abusive/predatory same-sex sexual intimacy.[19]

There is nothing in the language of Romans 1 that would suggest that it is limited to abusive or predatory same-sex sexual intimacy. Romans 1:26–27 refers to 'degrading passions', men who are 'consumed with passion' for one another, and who committed 'shameless acts' with other men. This passage does not use any of the Greek words for pederastic relationships.[20] It explicitly refers to man-to-man,[21] not man-to-boy sexual intimacy. There are no words that suggest prostitution, and the fact that both parties to the sex act are equally culpable undercuts the argument that this is only

---

18 Hays, 'Relations Natural and Unnatural', 200.
19 This argument is developed in full in J. Brownson, *Bible Gender Sexuality: Reframing the Church's Debate on Same- Sex Relationships* (Grand Rapids: Eerdmans, 2013) and Robin Scroggs, *The New Testament and Homosexuality* (Philadelphia: Fortress, 1983).
20 In the Greco-Roman world, pederasty (*paiderastês*) involved a romantic and sexual relationship between an adult male (*erastes*) and a (teenage) boy (*eromenos*).
21 Or, to be precise, 'men-in-men' (*arsenes en arsesin*).

addressed to slaves used for sexual purposes, since the slave who had no choice in the matter should not be culpable.

Some versions of claim 2 recognise that there is nothing in the language of Romans 1 that limits its application to abusive or predatory same-sex sexual intimacy, but instead argue that the **only** forms of same-sex sexual intimacy of which Paul was aware were those which involved 'domination, control, lack of consent, and lack of mutuality'[22] such as pederasty, slavery or prostitution—or to say the same thing another way, that Paul knew nothing of 'the loving and stable same-sex unions of the sort that exist today' (Chalke).

Claim 2 puts those advocating for same-sex marriage in an awkward position. On the one hand, they argue that same-sex orientation is a 'natural' and immutable variation of human biology. This presumably means that the proportion of same-sex attracted men and women relative to the general population would be more or less the same in antiquity as it is today. On the other hand, they are also arguing that the modern same-sex relationship was unknown in antiquity, and the only relationships were pederastic or otherwise abusive.

The evidence of antiquity attests the existence of consensual and loving same-sex unions. While this supports the argument that there is something innate about same-sex attraction, it fatally undercuts the argument that Paul could not have known about loving and stable same-sex unions.

Parler provides a string of examples of 'mutual, consensual same-sex relationships from Greece and Rome', and concludes

> Even in the Greek culture that often exalted pederasty, there are numerous examples of consenting adults engaging in same-sex relationships, up to and including life-long commitments. In the Roman culture, which at first was more resistant to Greece but

---

22 Brownson, *Bible, Gender, Sexuality*, 247.

was gradually Hellenized, there are also numerous examples of consenting adults engaging in same-sex relationships, up to and including life-long commitments.[23]

Sprinkle conducts a similar analysis, and concludes 'There was a broad spectrum of same-sex relations available to Paul. We cannot assume that Paul only had nonconsensual and unhealthy homosexual relations in view and therefore condemned (only) these types of relations. Paul most probably was aware of at least some consensual, even marital, unions among both men and women to the same gender.'[24]

This evidence means that Chalke's argument—that 'what the New Testament writers have in mind when they refer to homosexual practice could not have been the loving and stable same-sex unions of the sort that exist today, of which they knew nothing'—is unsustainable.

Claim 3—that Romans 1 only addresses uncontrolled promiscuity and licentiousness

This claim is similar to claim 2, and vulnerable to the same refutation—that the evidence of antiquity demonstrates that some same-sex relationships were loving and consensual. There is nothing in the language of Romans 1 to suggest that it only refers to uncontrolled promiscuity and licentiousness same-sex sexual intimacy—it refers to men who are 'consumed with passion', using similar imagery to that which Paul applies to heterosexual relationships ('it is better to marry than to be aflame with passion'—1 Cor 7:9).[25]

---

23 Parler, 'Worlds Apart?',198.
24 Sprinkle, 'Romans 1', 527.
25 Cf. the conclusion of Loader, 'Reading Romans 1', 134—'What for Paul makes these strong passions a manifestation of sin is not so much their intensity or excess but their misdirection.'

In summary, then, these three claims, which are essential to the argument that Paul couldn't possibly be referring to consensual and committed same-sex relationships in Romans 1, cannot be sustained.

First Corinthians 6:9

The similar argument in relation to the meanings of *malakoi* and *arsenokoitai* in 1 Cor 6:9 is likewise flawed. It is special pleading to say that these words refer only to pederastic or exploitative relationships, and cannot apply to loving, consensual homosexual sex. If Paul had intended to refer to a limited set of homosexual acts, ancient Greek had a well-established vocabulary for this (see footnote 18).

Instead, Paul coins a new word—*arsenokoitês*. The word *arsenokoitês* is a compound word made from the components *arsenos* (male) and *koitos/koitê* (literally 'bed', but often with sexual connotations). If the meaning of this new word derives from its two components, then an *arsenokoitês* is a 'male-bedder' (i.e., a man who sleeps with a man).

Some claim that it is totally illegitimate to derive the meaning of the word in this way, labelling this as an etymological fallacy. However, while it is true to say that the components and origins of a word do not necessarily determine its meaning for all time, in this particular case there are two reasons why the components are very relevant to the meaning in 1 Corinthians 6.

Firstly, this is a 'neologism' (a new word). Paul's usage of the word *arsenokoitês* in 1 Corinthians 6 is the first recorded instance in extant Greek literature. Neologisms do not have a wide semantic range, because there is (at that initial point) no other uses to broaden the range of possible meanings. When an author coins a new word, it has a single meaning. To the extent that an author wants readers to understand a neologism, he or she relies on etymology (the meaning derived from the component words) and literary context to guide readers to the meaning of this new word. The constituent elements of other New Testament neologisms provide a reliable guide to the meaning of the new word. The etymology of a neologism, therefore, cannot be dismissed as irrelevant to meaning.

Secondly, this particular neologism (*arsenokoitês*) joins together two words used in close proximity in the Old Testament (OT) in Leviticus 18:22 and 20:13.

> Lev 18:22   You shall not lie with a male as with a woman
> (LXX: *meta **arsenos** ou koimêthêsê **koitên** gynaikos*)
>
> Lev 20:13   if a man lies with a man as with a woman
> (LXX: *meta **arsenos koitên** gynaikos*)

Given the patterns of Paul's other neologisms elsewhere in the NT, it is beyond doubt that the OT context of Leviticus 18:22 and/or 20:13 provides the background source for *arsenokoitês* in 1 Corinthians 6:9. There are no other clues from the context of 1 Corinthians 6 that suggest a meaning other than that provided by the etymology and OT context of the word *arsenokoitês*, and the pairing with *malakos* (which in the context of this vice list probably refers to the passive partner in homosexual sex) supports the meaning derived from etymology and the OT—an *arsenokoitês* is a man who has sex with a man. Those who do this, together with 'fornicators, idolaters, and adulterers' are 'wrongdoers'.

'Extraordinary manoeuvres'

I finish this section with a comment from Professor William Loader. Loader is a world-recognised expert on homosexuality in the NT and ancient world. Loader is convinced that Paul condemns homosexual practice, but notwithstanding this, he believes that the modern church should now embrace homosexual practice, because Paul simply got it wrong at this point. His understanding of scriptural authority allows him to do this, but he acknowledges the difficult situation of those who wish to affirm same-sex sexual intimacy and at the same time hold to an understanding of scriptural authority that means Paul and the other human authors of Scripture do not get it wrong. He comments

> For those of us whose understanding of scriptural authority does not entail such belief we can only stand and wonder at the extraordinary manoeuvres which have been undertaken to re-read Paul as not condemning homosexual relations at all.[26]

D. Reason and Experience

There is no argument from our Anglican interpretive tradition in support of same-sex marriage. There is no argument from Scripture in support of same-sex marriage. The only arguments for same-sex marriage are, in the final analysis, arguments from a reasoned reflection on human experience

- **Argument from the 'fact' of same-sex desires**

    One of the arguments put in favour of same-sex marriage is that, since God made people with same-sex desires, he must intend them to act on those desires.

    This argument misconstrues what the Bible says about 'desire'. It is helpful to distinguish between three nuances of the word 'desire' (which pertain to both modern English and to the biblical languages). 'Desire' can refer to:

Innate desire	e.g., orientation, longing
Activated desire	e.g., lust
Enacted desire	e.g., sex

---

26 W. Loader, 'Reading Romans 1 on Homosexuality in the Light of Biblical/Jewish and Greco-Roman Perspectives of its Time' *Zeitschrift für die Neutestamentliche Wissenschaft* 108 (2017) 119-149 at 120.

The Bible does not attach moral culpability to our 'desires' in the first sense (i.e., longings). There is no condemnation in the Bible for someone who is attracted to someone of the same sex. That is, the experience of same-sex sexual temptation is not itself sin. The Bible's condemnation of 'degrading passions' is directed at activated desires ('consumed with passion for one another') or enacted desires ('committed shameless acts'), not at innate desires.

Most people who are same-sex attracted do not experience their orientation as a choice. They would say that they were 'made that way'. But this this does not mean they are free to 'act that way'. The mere fact we experience unfulfilled desires does not validate acting on these desires.

All Christians experience unmet longings to some degree, and are all afflicted by disordered desires. Obedience to Christ entails the (often difficult) choice not to activate or act on these desires. The single heterosexual person and the single homosexual person are in the same situation. God has given them sexual desires that cannot be appropriately expressed, because they are not married. For many, this is a struggle and a frustration and, as such, it is one of the many painful consequences of living in a broken and fallen world. Because same-sex sexual activity is contrary to God's plan for humanity (just as is opposite-sex sexual activity outside of marriage), same-sex sexual desires must not be inflamed or acted upon.

- **Argument from the 'fruit' of LGBT+ relationships**

    Another argument made in support of same-sex marriage

is that the fruit of the Spirit seen can be seen in the relationship of a gay or lesbian couple, which testifies to the fact that God blesses that relationship.

This argument claims too much for experience, in that it also would validate the spiritual authenticity of (say) the Buddhist or the Muslim who lives a life of love, justice and mercy. Most people (Christian or otherwise) display some of the virtues that could be mistaken for the fruit of the Spirit—we all know non-Christians who (apparently) live lives of love, joy, peace, patience and so on—but this does not prove that they are Christians. And even for a Christian, the fruit of the Spirit is not proof of God's validation of every part of our behaviour. The hypothetical fruit of the Spirit in the homosexual partners posited by the argument may genuinely be the gracious work of God in each of their lives, without necessarily being God's validation of their relationship.

- **Argument from the 'frustration' of being alone**

    Another argument made in support of same-sex marriage is that it cannot be God's will for people to have to live alone, without an appropriate way to express their sexual desires, and with the 'mutual society, help, and comfort' (*BCP*) of marriage.'

    This argument would apply equally to a heterosexual person as to a homosexual person. There are many single heterosexual people in churches who wish to be married, who doubt that they have the gift of celibacy, but have no prospects of marriage (and indeed are of an age where this is now very unlikely). They, like their homosexual brothers and sisters, have to make the difficult choice to obey Christ rather than to indulge in sexual activity that God has forbidden.

This argument also undervalues what the Bible says about singleness. Marriage is not the only or ultimate way to live a fulfilled Christian life. The fact that Jesus Christ lived a single life highlights the goodness of singleness. A fulfilling sex-life is not the only answer to the frustration of 'being alone'. God has provided friendship, family and the Christian community.

- **Appeal to reason — the wrongness of sin must be established by rational argument**

This argument is premised on the assertion that, whereas other sins such as adultery, incest, paedophilia, bestiality, and sexual abuse are morally wrong because of their evident harm, this is not the case with same-sex sexual intimacy. Same-sex sexual intimacy is not sin (so the argument goes) unless compelling and coherent arguments for its moral wrongness (in terms of the harm it causes) can be established.

This argument makes human reason the final arbiter in the definition of sin—if thoughtful, compelling and coherent reasons why something is harmful cannot be established, then it is not sin.

On that argument, it is hard to see why the sin of Genesis 3 was a sin. God made all the trees of the garden, and it appears to be an arbitrary distinction made by God between those trees from which Adam and Eve are allowed to eat, and those which they are prohibited from eating.

Moreover, if this principle was more broadly true for all of our knowledge of God, it would undercut the foundations of Christian theology. We would NEVER have worked out the mystery of the cross through unaided human reason—it would have forever appeared as 'foolishness' to us. On our own, we would never have discovered that God is trinity. Without God's revelation, we would never have discovered the character of God, and so on.

Suppose with any matter including same-sex sexual intimacy, that 'all' that we have is a divine command that defines an act as sin. If we say that this 'divine fiat' is arbitrary and not relevant to us, have we not fallen into the sin of Genesis 3—being led astray by the deceptive question 'Did God really say?', and acting in disobedience to what God has said.

Ultimately we are thrown back on the person and character of our Creator God, his innate goodness and his thoroughgoing commitment to the welfare of the creatures he has made. Where he chooses to give us the reasons for his commands, these confirm that goodness and compassion. Where he does not choose to give us reasons, then his person and character are still grounds for affirming that the command is good or the prohibition is gracious and compassionate.

Where to from here?

'Expanding' marriage to include same-sex couple is not in fact an expansion at all. The only way to include same-sex coupling within the definition of marriage is deny that the Bible defines marriage, and to read down the purposes of marriage. The amount of collateral damage that must be done to our doctrine of marriage can be seen by what this would do to the preface to the *BCP* marriage service.

DEARLY beloved, we are gathered together here in the sight of God, and in the face of this Congregation, to join together ~~this man and this woman~~ in holy Matrimony; ~~which is an honourable estate, instituted of God in the time of man's innocency, signifying unto us the mystical union that is betwixt Christ and his Church~~; which ~~holy estate~~ Christ adorned and beautified with his presence, and first miracle that he wrought, in Cana of Galilee; and is commended of Saint Paul to be honourable among all men: and therefore is not by any to be enterprised, nor taken in hand, unadvisedly, lightly, or wantonly, ~~to satisfy men's carnal lusts and appetites, like brute beasts that have no understanding~~; but reverently, discreetly, advisedly, soberly, and in the fear of God; ~~duly considering the causes for which Matrimony was ordained~~.

~~First, It was ordained for the procreation of children, to be brought up in the fear and nurture of the Lord, and to the praise of his holy Name.~~

~~Secondly, It was ordained for a remedy against sin, and to avoid fornication; that such persons as have not the gift of continency might marry, and keep themselves undefiled members of Christ's body.~~

~~Thirdly,~~ It was ordained for the mutual society, help, and comfort, that the one ought to have of the other, both in prosperity and adversity. Into which holy estate these two persons present come now to be joined.

If we change our Church's doctrine of marriage, the upheavals that have occurred internationally in the Anglican Communion over the past twenty years would suggest that there will be a similar outcome in our Church. Blessing a same-sex relationship, blessing a civil same-sex marriage and solemnizing a same-sex marriage have been deeply problematic for conservative Anglicans elsewhere, because all three liturgical acts purport to declare God's blessing on a marriage-like relationship which conservatives believe is explicitly prohibited by Scripture. This has been the point of no return, at which conservatives feel conscience-bound to withdraw canonical obedience to a bishop who has permitted such acts. The percentage of clergy and congregations who have been compelled to leave has varied from diocese to diocese, but in some places has been up to 25% of the church.

The argument of this essay is that we must not change our doctrine of marriage, because

- It is *sufficiently clear* from the Scriptures that God's pattern for marriage involves the union of one man and one woman toward a threefold *telos* ('goal') involving companionship, sexual union and procreation. A marriage is still a marriage, even if it falls short of this threefold *telos*.
- It is *sufficiently clear* from the Scriptures that God prohibits same-sex lust and same-sex sexual intimacy as contrary to God's purposes for human sexuality.

I have deliberately used the expression 'sufficiently clear', to acknowledge that sometimes there are debatable matters over which Christians will interpret the Scriptures differently, but at the same time to make the point that this is NOT one of those debates. This is not a case where there are scriptural arguments for and against. Rather, the Scriptures on this issue are clear, and can only be bypassed by 'extraordinary manoeuvres', which I find to be completely unsustainable.

In our Anglican interpretative tradition, Scripture has the highest, though not the sole, authority. Richard Hooker, who is often appealed to as giving equal balance to the 'three-legged-stool' of Scripture, Reason and Tradition, in fact gives Scripture the primacy.

> What Scripture doth plainly deliver, to that first place both of credit and obedience is due; the next whereunto is whatsoever any man can necessarily conclude by force of reason; after these the voice of the Church succeedeth. That which the Church by her ecclesiastical authority shall probably think and define to be true or good, must incongruity of reason over-rule all other inferior judgments whatsoever.[27]

Reason and tradition necessarily come into play in the process of interpretation, and it would be naïve to think otherwise. But these should be the servant of the Scriptures, not the master. This understanding is expressed and embedded in the Fundamental Declarations of The Constitution of the Anglican Church of Australia, which holds the Scriptures to be 'the ultimate rule and standard of faith given by inspiration of God and containing all things necessary for salvation'.

Both the biblical text and the history of Christian interpretation tell us that we *can* and *do* get things wrong when it comes to interpreting the Scriptures. Especially for those in the Protestant tradition, we affirm that it is possible both for the church to misinterpret the Scriptures, and for the church to be led astray by the false values of the world. The text of Scripture, therefore, needs to be given its own voice, heard on its own terms and received as the word of God, even if its message clashes with contemporary values. Indeed, if we believe that it is possible that our own heart might be devious and perverse and beyond understanding (Jer 17:9), and if we believe that it is possible that, in the process of interpretation, we might in fact be seeking to hear only what our itching ears want

---

27 Hooker, *Laws*, Book V, 8:2; Folger Edition 2:39,8-14.

to hear (1 Tim 4:3), then our hermeneutical approach ought not to presume that, where the clear meaning of the text clashes with what we and the world around us want the text to say, that it can't mean what it says. Otherwise, our hermeneutic will preclude us from hearing God's word say anything that doesn't sit comfortably with the prevailing cultural context.

Instead of a **hermeneutic of resistance**—which says we can 'resist the Bible's "plain sense"'[28]—we should adopt a **hermeneutic of humility**. This means a humility that is willing to submit to the authority of the Scriptures and a humility toward our interpretations (both ancient and modern). Humility means viewing our traditional interpretations as provisional and open to correction in light of greater understanding. There *is* a hermeneutical gap between ancient text and modern world, and we must 'mind the gap' in our interpretation. The same principle also works in reverse. That is, humility also means that we must view with suspicion our modern interpretations that happen to conform to the prevailing culture and so naturally appeal to us, lest we interpret away the gap between the ancient text and the modern world to suit our modern tastes or preconceptions. Any way of reading Scripture that empowers the individual reader or the voice of modern culture to declare that the Bible cannot mean what it says is not an Anglican way of reading Scripture.

In the current debate, there is no argument from Scripture in support of same-sex marriage. There is no argument from our Anglican interpretive tradition in support of same-sex marriage.

---

28 Richard Trelor, 'On "not putting new wine into old wineskins", or "taking the Bible fully seriously": An Anglican Reading of Leviticus 18:22 and 20:13.' Pages 13-30 in *Five Uneasy Pieces: Essays on Scripture and Sexuality*. Adelaide: ATF Press, 2011. 26-27.

The arguments from reason and experience do not (and cannot) overturn what the Scriptures say.

So then, how should we respond pastorally to the same-sex attracted couples who are present in our world and in our churches? If redefining the doctrine of marriage is not the answer, and if purporting to bless what God does not bless is not that way forward, then what is? The way forward may well be what was suggested by the then Primate, Peter Carnley, in his Presidential Address to the General Synod in 2004.

> The category of 'marriage' is best reserved for monogamous heterosexual unions which we understand to include, as one intended purpose of such unions amongst others, the procreation of children. The concept of marriage therefore necessarily implies sexual activity. By contrast same sex relationships are best spoken of by using the category of **friendship**, which does not so much as raise an implication, let alone the logical necessity and thus the expectation, of sexual activity. Also, as Christians we should not allow ourselves to be browbeaten by the permissive society into the view that chastity and abstinence from sexual activity is an entirely unrealistic impossibility amongst adults.

www.ingramcontent.com/pod-product-compliance
Lightning Source LLC
Chambersburg PA
CBHW051935290426
44110CB00015B/1991